ABOUT THE AUTHOR

Peter Camejo began his study of the Reconstruction period while an activist in the civil rights struggles of the early sixties. A prominent speaker and organizer in the student movement against the Vietnam War, he is today a leader of the Socialist Workers Party. As its 1976 presidential candidate, he was the first person of Latin American descent to be nominated for that office.

NEW ORLEANS, 1874
White League forces attack the Radical state government

Racism, Revolution, Reaction, 1861-1877

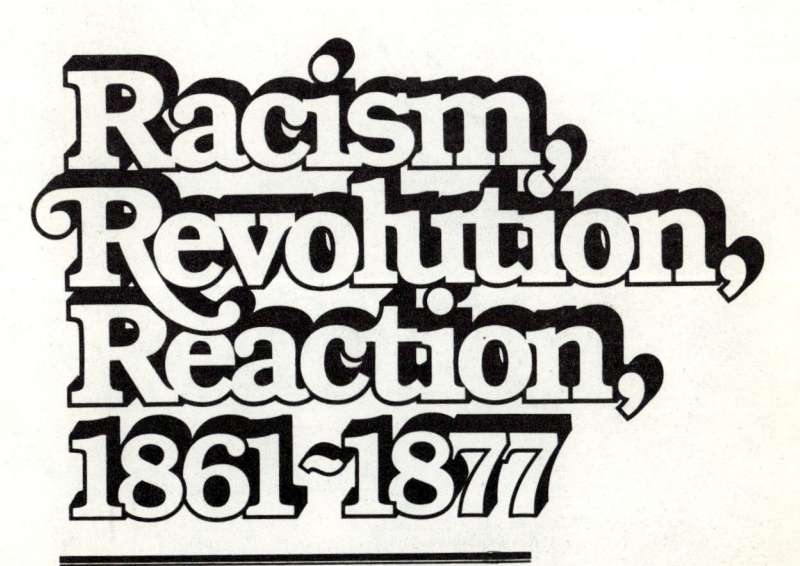

The Rise and Fall of Radical Reconstruction

PETER CAMEJO

MONAD PRESS, NEW YORK

*Copyright © 1976 by the Anchor Foundation
All rights reserved*

*Printed in the United States of America
Library of Congress Catalog Card Number 76-24184
ISBN cloth 0-913460-49-4; paper 0-913460-50-8
Published by Monad Press for the Anchor Foundation
Distributed by Pathfinder Press, Inc.
410 West Street, New York, N.Y. 10014*

First printing, 1976

Contents

Introduction 7

1. Between Two Revolutions 13
2. Wage Workers and the Civil War 31
3. Class Alignments in the South After Appomattox 49
4. The Rise of Radical Reconstruction 63
5. Class Struggle Under the Radical Regimes 84
6. The Industrial Capitalists Consolidate Their Victory 104
7. Counterrevolution—the Mississippi Model 139
8. The Final Defeat 158
9. The Republican Party's Betrayal 169
10. Industrial Capitalism and Conservative Rule 188
11. Racism and Historical Mythology 207
12. Thermidor 228

Notes 249
Bibliography 255
Index 263

Introduction

This 200th year since the Declaration of Independence also marks the 111th year since slavery was abolished. Yet nonwhites continue to suffer flagrant discrimination throughout America. Although the fact is admitted by almost everyone, there are few consistent explanations of why this injustice persists and seems to many unsolvable.

During the 1950s and 60s the civil rights movement raised the hope that, with the elimination of all laws specifically discriminating against Blacks, a gradual process would set in leading to full equality. Gains were made at various levels through the mass struggle itself. But now, a decade after the crest of the civil rights movement, it is clear that, despite the elimination of anti-Black laws and even passage of laws specifically protecting the rights of Blacks, oppression and discrimination remain with no end in sight.

Recently the disparity in income between Blacks and whites has begun to widen. Black income is now about 56 percent that of whites—that means Blacks live at about half the standard of living of whites. Segregation in housing, jobs, and education is prevalent. Unemployment among Afro-Americans continues at twice the rate for whites, and in some areas the disparity is even greater.

The evils and injustices are indisputable. Yet accredited social scientists seem incapable of explaining the secret of their persistence. This problem, usually called racism, seems to have such a grip on U.S. society that it is able to prevent the discovery of its cause.

The usual explanation given is highly simplistic: namely, the prejudice of whites, especially working-class whites, which liberal politicians, commentators, and sociologists are constantly bemoaning. We are told that, for some unaccountable and perverse reason, people with white skins seem determined to dislike those with darker skins. Why this is so and why it is so persistent is shrouded in mystery. Not knowing the source of the problem, the liberals find themselves unable to offer an adequate solution.

If an individual, brick in hand, waited in front of a school to kill or maim a child because of the child's color, such a person would be considered deranged, arrested, and sent to a mental institution. But when a few hundred stand together with bricks and bats yelling "kill niggers," that is considered a political protest. What this proves is that this psychotic disorder is generalized and has its source, not in an individual aberration, but in the social structure.

What are we to conclude when mayors, governors, and even the president of the United States, as well as the editors of many major dailies, express sympathy with the goals of these psychotic people? Of course, these notables, like Pontius Pilate washing his hands of the affair, dissociate themselves from the "methods" used. Clearly the matter goes far beyond considerations of individual psychology and political hypocrisy. The mentally disturbed few who are impelled into the streets consciously seeking to harm Blacks, and the condoning officials, are but by-products of the larger and more powerful socioeconomic forces that give rise to racism, forces that derive enormous material benefits from the perpetuation of racism.

Racism to one degree or another exists in all advanced capitalist nations, including Japan. But the extreme forms of racism found in the United States have been matched only in Nazi Germany and South Africa. As recently as the 1930s the phenomenon of public lynchings still existed here. Thousands of people would gather to watch another human burned alive or tortured to death. Elected representatives and law enforcement officials would often participate in these Roman holiday events. Sometimes Democratic Party officials would address these gatherings—not to halt, admonish, or recommend psychiatric help—but to encourage the lynchers. When the schedule of a lynching was known far enough in advance, newspapers and radio stations often would announce the time and place. There were even instances when the railroads ran special excursion trains to the scene. The federal government, whether under a Republican or such a liberal Democrat as Franklin D. Roosevelt, would always refuse to interfere.

Although the political climate today, thanks primarily to the mass civil rights movement of the 1950s and 60s, has caused this particular form of murder of nonwhites to lapse, we must ask ourselves how such racist atrocities, as well as the current forms of racism, can be explained.

Marxists and most serious non-Marxist historians recognize that racism had its origin in the establishment of chattel slavery in the early stages of the development of capitalism. While slavery had generally disappeared in Europe during feudalism, it took a new lease on life in the West as commercial capitalism grew. Slavery was introduced into the New World colonies to solve the problem of an acute labor shortage. Racism, the theory that those with white skins are superior to those with black skins, was gradually elaborated to justify this chattel slavery. First came slavery, then racism. Racism also played its part in justifying the clearing of the land of the native populations through wars of genocide.

This historical fact poses the question: Why has racism and racial oppression survived the abolition of the original cause, chattel slavery. What is responsible for its perpetuation? This question is particularly crucial for the study of American history because chattel slavery was ended in such a cataclysmic manner.

The existence of slavery in the southern part of the United States created a social formation which found itself in conflict with the development of industrial capitalism. The struggle for supremacy between the two finally led to a military showdown and a titanic civil war, the most momentous event of the nineteenth century.

In that conflict the deaths on both sides totaled 623,000. This is a figure only slightly less than all the deaths sustained by the United States in World Wars I and II, the Korean War, and the Vietnam War, combined. If the wounded are added, the casualties reached 1,094,453. For the Union, which had 22 of the 31 million population at that time, this meant one out of every ten adult males was a casualty, and for the Confederate states (including the Black population) it meant one out of four.

A conflict of such magnitude had a profound effect on the entire population. Existing attitudes of whites toward Afro-Americans were especially shaken by the fact that the decisive turning point in the conflict was the freeing and arming of Blacks. This great revolutionary war destroyed chattel slavery forever in the United States. That development in turn confronted American society with a most formidable problem: What would now happen with the Afro-American people and other nonwhites? Would they be considered equal to whites and assimilated as those from Europe—Irish, Germans, Scandinavians and Italians—had been and would be? For a short period significant steps were taken in this direction. Then the course of the nation was sharply reversed.

The interconnection of events in the phases constituting this second American revolution and its aftermath are not as confusing and impenetrable as most historians like to make out. Why racism survived slavery can be concretely and scientifically explained. The reason our present society has so difficult a time with this problem is that an honest accounting points the finger of guilt directly at the present capitalist system and its ruling class. The same social system that gave rise to chattel slavery found it necessary to abolish it, but it also found the by-products of slavery—racial oppression and the ideology of racism—extremely valuable for further use.

Just as chattel slavery was originally established because it was profitable and produced racist ideology as its justification, the racial oppression of our epoch owes its strength to the profit motive and it, in turn, has promoted racism for ideological support.

Historians try to convince us of the reverse. Most often they begin by complaining that racist ideology among the mass of whites, especially uneducated plebian whites, made it impossible to do away with the peculiar circumstances of Black oppression. To this argument they usually add that, since the Blacks had just emerged from slavery, they were not educationally qualified for a status fully equal to that of whites. Liberal historians generously concede that this was not the fault of the Blacks.

A look at the facts points to exactly the opposite conclusion. The racism of the white masses showed signs of disintegrating under the impact of revolutionary events. The industrial capitalists who came to control and dominate American society, including the two big political parties, had to wage a long campaign, which included an armed counterrevolution and an enormous propaganda effort involving the rewriting of history, to assure the continuance and reinforcement of racism.

From the end of the Civil War into the 1880s it was demonstrated again and again that the most successful tactic for winning votes among plebian whites in the North was an appeal against the mistreatment of Blacks in the South.

The turn towards granting the ex-slaves equal rights with whites in 1867 had the support of the majority of white workers and farmers in the nation. This was indicated by the triumph of the Radical Republicans in the decisive elections of 1866—before Blacks could vote. It did not mean that the mass of whites had abandoned racist attitudes but that such attitudes had been greatly weakened and a strong antiracist current was flowing. The later revival and strengthening of racism was rooted in socioeconomic factors much more powerful than the ideological carry-over from pre–Civil War times.

An understanding of the rise and fall of Radical Reconstruction is therefore essential for understanding why racial oppression and racism have become integral parts of present-day society.

This book had its origin in a series of lectures delivered at a Young Socialist Alliance educational conference at Oberlin, Ohio, in the summer of 1974. It is only a partial contribution towards a full analysis of Radical Reconstruction, which in itself would be but part of a needed Marxist analysis of the second American revolution as a whole.

This work does not offer any original research. The information contained in it is taken from the books, pamphlets, and articles listed in the bibliography. Only its interpretation of the data is new. In one sense it is a defense of the contributions made by C. Vann Woodward in his *Origins of the New South, 1877-1913* and *Reunion and Reaction*, since its thesis is based on Woodward's important factual findings. The book concentrates on explaining why Radical Reconstruction began and especially why it was overthrown. The first two chapters present the historical background against which these events took place.

Although much of the factual information used in this work is taken from the school of the self-styled revisionist historians, I reject their claim to have disproved the basic outline of Charles and Mary Beard and Howard K. Beale's economic determinist interpretation, which was so illuminating despite its one-sidedness.

My goal has been to bring together in an integrated interpretation what others have seen as separate and unconnected developments in the United States between 1861 and the 1890s. This picture in turn has been placed within the broader international view of the meaning of the second American revolution best expressed in the articles of George Novack in *America's Revolutionary Heritage* and his book *Democracy and Revolution*. Unfortunately the contributions of this outstanding Marxist scholar are not well known among academic historians.

Arthur Lobman, a longtime student of Southern history, assisted Jon Britton of Monad Press in editing the manuscript. George Weissman, an active socialist for over forty years who is widely read in American history, also reviewed the manuscript and gave much helpful advice.

PETER CAMEJO
May 1, 1976

1

Between Two Revolutions

In the sixties and seventies of the last century, the industrial capitalists of the United States brought together other elements of the population in a new party and led a titanic military struggle which destroyed chattel slavery and with it the slaveowning class—the slavocracy. At the end of that great Civil War there opened up the possibility of ending oppression of Blacks based on race. The triumphant industrial capitalist class took steps in that direction in the years between 1867 and 1877, the period known as Radical Reconstruction. Then it stopped, turned around, reinvoked racism, and reestablished racial oppression with a vengeance. The paradox and tragedy of Radical Reconstruction is that the principal force that brought it into being was also responsible for smashing it. It was a betrayal of the Afro-American people by those who appeared at the time to be their greatest ally.

Understanding the Civil War and Radical Reconstruction, which together constitute the second American revolution, requires tracing the course of events leading up to them. For this we must begin with an examination of the origins of the coalition of social forces which destroyed chattel slavery, a coalition born in the rapid changes that dominated the period between the first and second American revolutions.

Within a few years after the American colonies won their independence from Great Britain, the dominant class in the South, the slaveowning planters, and the moneyed class in the North—merchants, bankers, and to a lesser extent manufacturers—agreed to establish a partnership government for the new nation.* The basic structure of this government was worked out by representatives of this small but wealthy minority of the population at a closed convention in 1787 in the form of a written agreement—the Constitution of the United States.

The framers of this document had two basic problems to solve. First, to gain acceptance from the independent farmers and small artisans—the majority of the population—the Constitution had to have the appearance of providing for government by the people, but at the same time its framers intended that it put control safely in the hands of the owning classes of the North and South. The common people had just been through a revolution that imbued them with radical ideas about democracy; they were heavily burdened with debt because of hard times and were showing themselves throughout the land to be a danger to the creditor and propertied classes. In Massachusetts farmers led by veterans of the Revolutionary War had taken up arms, in what was known as Shays's Rebellion, to stop the courts from foreclosing mortgages and enforcing the penalties for nonpayment of debts. Even after an army had smashed the rebels, Shaysites found sanctuary in Vermont and New York and made guerrilla raids into Massachusetts. In Rhode Island the farmers had won control of the legislature and were passing laws providing for the issuance of "soft" or cheap money, making it legal tender for the payment of debts.

Secondly, each of the partners—the Southern slaveowners and the Northern capitalists—wanted the Constitution to contain provisions guaranteeing that neither could achieve such complete control of the new government that the basic interests of the other were threatened. For, while both partners had much in common as propertied classes, the forms of their property were different and hence their interests diverged on a series of points.

---

* Although slavery is historically a precapitalist form of labor, the plantation owners of the South operated as part of the world capitalist system and can be treated as a section of the capitalist ruling class as a whole. In this chapter the word "class" is used in this broad sense, embracing both Northern merchants and Southern planters in one economic category, as well as a narrower sense, in which the two are distinguished from each other on the basis of their different forms of capital investment. See George Novack's discussion of hybrid formations in *Understanding History* (New York: Pathfinder Press, 1972).

To solve these problems the Constitution provided for a federal government divided into three counterbalancing branches, along with an intricate system of vetoes and checks and balances. These kept popular rule to a minimum and gave the two wings of the ruling class a system for working together while protecting their separate interests.

Of the three branches of government only part of one, the lower house of Congress, was to be elected by popular vote. The Senate (undemocratic in its very concept since, regardless of population, each state would have but two representatives in it) and the president were to be selected by indirect election. Members of the Supreme Court were to be appointed for life. There was no way for the people to remove or recall any elected or appointed official from office. Minority rule over the majority was further reinforced in the various states by the denial of the vote to women, Blacks, and those not meeting property-owning or religious qualifications.

There were also devices in the plan to give minorities in the government itself a veto power. An act of Congress passed by majorities in both houses could be vetoed by the president; a two-thirds majority in both houses was required to override a presidential veto, i.e., one-third in either house could prevent the overriding of a veto. Furthermore, the Supreme Court had the power to nullify an act of Congress as conflicting with the Constitution (implicit in the document drawn up in 1787, this power was made explicit by the Supreme Court's decision in *Marbury* v. *Madison* in 1803). And to make any alteration or amendment of the Constitution, approval by three-fourths of all the state legislatures was necessary.

To induce the slavocracy to bring the Southern states into a federal union with Northern states whose white population was larger, it was agreed that for purposes of representation in Congress and in the Electoral College (which chose the president) slaves would be counted as three-fifths of a person; Indians were not to be counted at all.

There was widespread opposition to the Constitution because of its undemocratic features. In order to secure its acceptance by the required number of states, its backers had to promise to accept the ten amendments known as the Bill of Rights. These, however, were guarantees of specific liberties and prohibitions of particular acts of tyranny; they did not alter the basic setup or inner mechanics of the new plan of government.

16 *Racism, Revolution, Reaction*

With the passage of time, the ruling class found it unnecessary to continue a number of the undemocratic devices to maintain its control and under mass pressure accepted some reforms. Virtually direct election of the president and universal franchise for adult white males were conceded in the period between the first and the second American revolutions. Direct election of senators came in 1913, and the vote for women in 1920.

George Washington was inaugurated as president of the new government in the spring of 1789. During his administration it became quite evident that despite all the checks and balances the merchant capitalists of the North dominated the government and had established policies which primarily benefited themselves. For example, an excise tax was levied domestically and tariffs were imposed on imported commodities. The settling of lands on the western frontier was slowed lest it excessively tighten the labor supply in the East, thus facilitating workers' demands for higher wages. A national bank, four-fifths of whose stock was held by private investors, was chartered. The Northern capitalists were also able to push through an assumption and funding of debts of the previous government, which had carried on the Revolutionary War, and the debts of the states. This measure, by conservative estimates, increased the value of long depreciated notes and nearly worthless currency by at least $40 million, a huge figure for that age when one realizes that it equaled one-tenth of the total taxable value of land in the country. Practically all of this depreciated paper had been bought up by capitalists and wealthy speculators with advance knowledge of what was to come.

Frontier farmers in western Pennsylvania especially resented the excise tax on whiskey because the mountains prevented them from getting their grain to market in any other form than easily transportable whiskey. In four counties they held angry demonstrations and refused to pay, driving off the tax collectors. As an object lesson to all dissatisfied farmers the new government sent an army of 15,000—almost the same size as the combined American-French army that had compelled Cornwallis's surrender at Yorktown, ending the war with Britain—against the recalcitrants.

The dissatisfaction of the small farmers—the overwhelming majority of the population—was soon exploited by the slavocracy for its own political ends. As a class whose income was also derived from agriculture, the slaveowners joined with the farmers in opposing a number of the measures enacted by the new government. The merchant capitalists were not socially or politically strong enough to withstand this coalition of the plantation owners and the small farmers, and in 1800 they lost control of the federal government in the election that brought Thomas Jefferson to the presidency.

While Jefferson pursued policies benefiting the agricultural slavocracy, the merchants were not totally excluded from participation in the federal government and some of their proposals were accepted. For instance, the national bank was permitted to continue in operation until its charter ran out in 1811. The difficulties in financing the War of 1812 with Britain and the chaotic condition of the currency led the Republicans, as the Jeffersonians called themselves, to charter a second national bank in 1816 for another twenty-year period.

The Louisiana Purchase brought over one million square miles into the United States in 1803. Although the War of 1812 failed to add new territory, the slavocracy had only to wait five years until its prime object in that war—Florida—was acquired by purchase. The expansionist slavocracy, backed by the land-hungry frontier farmers, kept seeking opportunities to acquire new territory—by pushing the Indians off their land and later grabbing Mexico's northern and western provinces.

After the War of 1812, important changes began taking place in the North, South, and West. One of these was the rise of cotton. The cotton gin, invented in 1793, was perfected by the turn of the century, giving rise to an enormous expansion of cotton production. In 1790 the United States had exported the insignificant total of 81 bags of cotton. By 1810 this had risen to 93 million pounds. And in the period of peace that followed, cotton replaced other Southern crops, becoming the single most important crop not only of that region but of the entire nation. The "Cotton Kingdom" spread rapidly over a territory of 400,000 square miles. It produced the overwhelming bulk of the world's cotton and accounted for the major part of U.S. exports.

Though the U.S. would remain a primarily agricultural society until after the Civil War, there was a steady development of manufacturing (and with it a proletariat), particularly in the Northeast, in the years between the founding of the republic and the great conflict.

Of course some manufacturing had existed from the colonial days—the processing or preparing for shipment of the products of the forest and the sea, and of agriculture (such as milling and meat packing). In addition there was the production of articles of consumption by household industry and by artisans. These forms of production reproduced themselves on the frontier as they were displaced by more modern forms in the older states.

Since most manufactured articles were imported, any cutoff of overseas trade was a spur to manufacturing in America. This happened during the War of 1812, as well as during the Embargo of 1807 and the various Nonintercourse Acts which preceded the outbreak of hostilities.

This period saw the birth of the factory system in the U.S., though at first it did not fully cut the umbilical cord to merchant capital and the more primitive forms of production. For example, initially spinning was done in factories but weaving was done in households, with the distribution of the yarn and the collecting and sale of the cloth done by merchants (the "putting-out" system).

From around 1815 to 1840 small factory production grew rapidly. By 1825 there were 60 textile mills, over 300 tanneries, over 200 bark mills, and some 10 paper mills in New Hampshire. The 161 mills and factories in Massachusetts represented a capital of $30 million. Providence, Rhode Island, claimed to be the richest city of its size in the world, for in and around it were 150 manufacturing establishments, employing 30,000 men and women. The Hudson River Valley from New York City to Albany is described by writers of the period as "teeming" with factories. Coal and iron industries were developing in Pennsylvania, with Pittsburgh already the great manufacturing center for the Mississippi Valley. From Maine to Maryland, and out west to Missouri, new industries of a hundred types were springing up.

The period from 1840 to 1860 saw an accelerated growth of manufacturing in the Northern states and the introduction of steam power. The rise of railroads made the distribution of commodities even cheaper than canal transport had been in the preceding period. Mills began to manifest the features of modern factories. Artisans' shops developed into mills. Manufacturing ceased to be an adjunct of merchant capitalism and large amounts of merchant capital were transferred into manufacturing.

Another striking development in this period was the rapid settlement of western territories. First settled were Kentucky and

Tennessee, by streams of poor white farmers, mainly from Virginia and North Carolina, pushed off their land or bought out by the expanding plantation system. Both Kentucky and Tennessee were populous enough to be admitted to the Union as states before the turn of the century. As the plantation system spread into these new states, the pioneer farmers were again driven onto poorer or mountainous land. Large numbers of these Kentuckians and Tennesseans sought new lands and a better life north of the Ohio River, where they came to constitute an important element in the population of what would become the states of Ohio, Indiana, and Illinois.

A similar process had taken place in the old Southwest (Georgia, Alabama, and Mississippi). Frontier farmers had cleared the land only to be pushed out or bought out by the advance of the slaveholders who, forsaking the exhausted soil of the old Southeastern states, were extending the voracious Cotton Kingdom to the Mississippi. The poor white pioneers again were driven to the hills and mountains of the area or pushed across the Mississippi to clear new lands.

In the settlement of the old Northwest (Ohio, Indiana, Illinois, Michigan, and Wisconsin) the poor whites from the South, many with Presbyterian and Quaker backgrounds, mingled with immigrants from the Middle Atlantic states and New England, developing communities of small freehold farmers where slavery was forbidden. In addition there was a large European immigration into the area, with Germans predominating—over half a million immigrants settled there between 1830 and 1850, and another million in the next decade.

In 1775 there had not been—outside New Orleans—more than 5,000 white settlers, mainly French, in the area drained by the Mississippi; the census of 1830 gave populations of 937,000 to Ohio, 348,000 to Indiana, and 157,000 to Illinois.

The river network of the Mississippi was a natural system of transportation southward for the produce of these small farmers. They grew food and raised livestock for sale to the cotton plantations of the old Southwest. (In their race to maximize cotton production these new plantations were slighting the growing of corn and instead were buying corn and pork—the staples of the slave diet—on the market.) New Orleans was the receiving point for the agricultural production of the old Northwest for distribution to the cotton plantations or transhipment to Europe.

Everything was geared to cotton production: the Midwest farmers raised food for the slaves, Northern merchants helped finance and export the cotton crop, while Great Britain's factories fabricated it into cloth. The British capitalists also provided credit to the Northern merchants who handled the export of cotton and the import of British manufactured goods.

The growth of cotton production consolidated the grip of the slavocracy on the federal government. The slavocracy-farmer coalition now expanded. It drew into its ranks the merchants whose interests were tied to cotton. The numerical growth of the small farmers forced the party of the slavocracy, the Democratic Party, to step up its demagogy as the party of the "people."

Almost alone in opposition stood the rising industrial interests. They wanted tariffs to protect their factories against British industries. The slavocracy at first had entertained hopes of a growth of industry in the South, but they put all their capital into cotton raising and slaves and soon realized that tariffs only meant higher prices for manufactured goods. American industry also wanted the federal government to build or subsidize such internal improvements as roads, canals, and railroads that would permit its products to flow westward to the growing farm population of the Midwest. The slavocracy saw nothing to gain from such projects and opposed them.

Small farmers in the East who provided foodstuffs for the growing urban centers of the seaboard often backed the industrial capitalists. The workers and artisans were divided. The Democratic Party paralleled its plebian demagogy among the farmers with the championing of some reforms at the expense of factory owners to attract the workers of the North. A labor party that appeared in the 1820s was soon co-opted by the Democrats.

Through the Democratic Party coalition with small farmers, merchants, and some workers, the slavocracy maintained decisive control of the federal government up until 1860. Most of the time the White House, the Congress, and the Supreme Court were directly under the control of the slavocracy.

But while cotton was king, several processes were in motion which would result in a reshuffling of class alliances and a new, revolutionary coalition. In fact the very success of cotton helped spur changes that led to its dethronement. In the Midwest the cotton economy's demand for foodstuffs stimulated a rapid expansion and westward migration of the free farming class. In the Northeast the impact of this agricultural growth was a continuing expansion of industry, until by the 1840s the industrial bourgeoisie had economically surpassed the merchant bourgeoisie.

In spite of the federal government's refusal to subsidize canals, new roads, and railroads, some were built anyway, such as the Erie Canal, which began carrying goods from the Midwest to the East, much of it foodstuffs destined for consumption in the East and for export to Europe. The main trade route for the Midwest became the railroads to the East Coast rather than the Mississippi River to New Orleans.

Along with this economic shift came a new problem for the slavocracy. Its political ally up to that time, the small farmer of the Midwest, was trying to acquire the same lands it wanted for the expansion of the Cotton Kingdom. This competition became so intense that for a time it dominated national politics. In Kansas the struggle turned bloody in the 1850s, with John Brown waging guerrilla warfare against the proslavery forces.

These developments had their ideological and political reflections.

The Abolitionists

After the first American revolution, antislavery sentiment was widespread among both farmers and the upper classes. Successively the Northern states abolished slavery, and even among Southern slaveowners many envisioned some eventual emancipation. Although the Constitution condoned slavery—"persons held to service or labor"—and permitted the slave trade from Africa (with a tax not to exceed ten dollars per slave), it also set 1808 as the year when the importation of slaves could be ended by a majority vote in Congress.

It was the hope of the ruling-class critics of slavery that by ending the slave trade they could bring about gradual emancipation. But the spectacular rise of cotton production killed that illusion. Though Congress declared the importation of slaves illegal in 1808, this neither stopped the traffic nor fostered any interest in gradual abolition. With slavery more profitable than ever, new ideological justifications for it were soon advanced, replete with religious, biological, and political "proofs" of its morality and benefits.

The antislavery movement had two waves in American history. The first rose prior to the invention of the cotton gin, reaching its height with the radicalization of the first American revolution. The second mounted as the conflicts between the slavocracy and industrial capitalists grew more frequent and intense. From about 1810 to 1830, antislavery sentiment and activity almost disappeared among whites. Those few heroic individuals, both Black and white, who publicly called for an end to slavery were isolated and treated as crackpots.

Most historians trace the beginning of the second wave from William Lloyd Garrison's return to the North in 1830 from Baltimore, where bold antislavery writing had earned him a jail sentence for libel and a certain amount of notoriety. While in jail he had prepared a series of lectures calling for the immediate abolition of slavery and attacking the American Colonization Society, the organization which claimed to deal with the slavery problem from moral and philanthropic motives by sending free Blacks to Africa. Blacks in Baltimore had convinced Garrison that the organization's real purpose was to assuage Northern whites' consciences regarding slavery, and that it was the enemy of free Blacks whom it libeled as an undesirable and unassimilable element in the American population.

Garrison's lectures in the North were only a partial success. In Philadelphia he received a welcome only from the free Blacks— who had heard about him and were enthusiastic over his ideas— and a few Quakers. In New York the free Black community received him as a hero, but again there was little interest on the part of whites. So it went in the other cities.

The abolitionist movement grew very slowly at first against general hostility. Originating among the free Blacks, its base eventually expanded among the middle classes of the East, especially in New England, and the small farmers of the Midwest. The 1831 slave insurrection in Virginia was blamed by the slavocracy on the new abolitionists, and soon throughout the South a permanent witch-hunt against suspected abolitionists was instituted, which continued until the end of the Civil War. This virtually prevented a Southern-based abolitionist movement from developing.

The personal dedication and sacrifice of abolitionists both Black and white is one of the great revolutionary traditions of the American people. The exploits of Harriet Tubman, who repeatedly went South to help slaves escape, and the hundreds of others who served as links in the Underground Railway, as well as the brilliant oratory and writing of Frederick Douglass and Wendell Phillips, are still models for those struggling against social injustices in our day.

The work of the abolitionists and their influence cannot be measured by membership figures alone. They affected the thinking and helped set the mood which led to the rise of the Republican Party, and their participation in the Civil War helped to turn it into a crusade against slavery.

In addition to the members of the various wings of the abolitionist movement, there came to be numerous individuals persuaded by or influenced by their propaganda who did not join the movement, or who had given up organizational connection with it, but who took antislavery positions within their own organizations and parties. These included a small but growing number of men in Congress. They opposed the extension of slavery into the Western territories and supported some of the demands raised by the abolitionists—for example, ending slavery in the District of Columbia and opposing stricter fugitive slave laws.

The Rise of the Republican Party

The industrial revolution achieved its fastest growth on a world scale between 1850 and 1870. In the United States the growth of industry combined with other factors in the 1850s to decisively alter the socioeconomic relationship of forces against the slavocracy. Politically this shift was expressed in the rise of a new party, the Republican Party, which in essence was a new coalition between industrial capitalists, the Midwest farmers, and certain layers of the artisans and workers. To consolidate this bloc the industrial capitalists offered an important inducement to the farmers: stopping the expansion of slavery and giving free land to settlers through the Homestead Act. The bloc was built around the slogan "free soil," which completely dominated the pre-Civil War Republican election campaigns. The fact that the program also called for high tariffs was naturally not publicized in rural areas with the same vigor.

By the 1850s the Midwestern economy had grown enormously. The census of 1850 shows that the combined market value of all Southern staples—cotton, tobacco, rice, hemp, and sugar—was equaled by the hay crop alone of the North. The shift of a substantial sector of the farmers of this region from a political bloc with the slavocracy to one with industrial capitalism brought the country to a political crisis. The economic depression of 1857 helped force the conflict to a head.

The impending conflict had more than national implications. Concealed in it was also a struggle between American and British industry. The basic economic question posed was whether American agriculture would be an adjunct to British or American industrial growth. Historically, the question of who would dominate world imperialism in the twentieth century was to be settled in this war.

After the Civil War, Britain and other European countries remained a crucial market for both cotton and foodstuffs produced by American agriculture, but now it was American industry which fattened on this produce. European investors continued to finance the expansion of American capitalism until World War I, when finally the United States ceased to be a debtor to Europe and reversed the roles.

Secession and War

With the election of Lincoln, the Republican Party candidate in 1860, the control of the executive branch of the federal government changed hands. Even though it had not yet lost control of Congress or the Supreme Court, the slavocracy could read its political future and chose to break the seventy-year-old constitutional agreement for a joint government. The period of struggle in the sphere of elections and parliamentary maneuvering was over. The federal government had to acquiesce to secession or use force to stop it.

Within the opposing camps differences existed over what policy to follow. In the North many of the commercial capitalists, especially those around the port of New York, vacillated, fearing that war would be disastrous to their trade with both camps and internationally. In the South among some of the farmers who did not hold slaves and in the embryonic industrial capitalist class, there was opposition to a military showdown. The resistance to secession was so substantial in some Southern states that it became necessary for the slavocracy to carry out virtual coup d'etats to impose its will. In the slave states of Missouri, Kentucky, Delaware, and part of Virginia, its secessionist campaign failed altogether. But once the test of strength was actually begun with the firing on Fort Sumter, the war factions on both sides rapidly became dominant. In the North the Republican Party was gradually transformed from a simple electoral political party into a powerful machine, a revolutionary instrument wielding increasingly centralized power.

The industrial capitalists of the North, feeling national political hegemony within their grasp, could not tolerate the prospect of a new nation appearing on the continent, particularly one led by their opponents, which would remove one-third of the territory and population of the home market. The separatist Confederacy, moreover, would be financially tied to Britain and would be able to draw from it the political and military backing to continually threaten what remained of the old American Union and to keep it weakened.

Finally, Northern industrialists of foresight were aware that the new Confederacy ultimately would have to expand or die. Economically inferior and outnumbered in population by the North, it could at best hope by its war of secession to weaken the United States sufficiently to force a stalemate; and during a temporary peace to build itself up with British aid for the acquisition of new lands for its plantation system. Such new lands could only be gained by wars of conquest in U.S. territories, the Caribbean, Mexico, or South America.

Once hostilities broke out, the North—despite its advantages and Britain's initial policy of waiting to see if the Confederacy could hold out—found it hard to defeat the South. There were various reasons for this.

First, the capitalist rulers, seeking to prevent the war from turning into an open class struggle in the South, took a stand in favor of slavery. Just prior to the outbreak of war, Lincoln and the Republicans went so far as to push through Congress and start ratification by the states of an amendment to the Constitution guaranteeing Southern slavery forever. That would have been the Thirteenth Amendment! With the firing on Fort Sumter that offer was dropped, but the proslavery line continued with Lincoln's policy of reassuring pro-Union slaveholders in the border states. And when slaves fled into the Union army's lines they were returned to their masters.

This course blocked the potential uprising and other pro-Union activity of 40 percent of the people behind the enemy lines—the Black labor force of the South. It also meant failing to tap to its *full* potential the enthusiasm for the war that an avowedly antislavery stand would have evoked from the abolitionist-minded layers of the middle classes of the East, the small farmers of the Midwest, and the many immigrant workers of European origin. Lincoln's course also delayed and limited the role of international solidarity with the Northern cause, which nonetheless had an important political effect, especially in Britain where the very textile workers thrown out of work by the war demonstrated against slavery and the threat of British intervention on the Confederacy's behalf.

The Northern capitalists were incapable of subordinating their individual greed to the needs of the struggle, and the whole war was a saturnalia of corruption. It reached right into the cabinet with scandals involving graft on army supply contracts and the commissioning of officers, and Lincoln was forced to ease out Secretary of War Cameron by sending him off to Russia as ambassador.

Incompetents were given army commissions—generals were appointed by the hundreds on the basis of bribes or their connections in the ruling class. The top command was totally disorganized for a period. Internal differences and intrigues within the ruling class led to confusion, vacillation, even contradictory commands. Such errors were paid for in blood by the plebian farmers and workers in uniform and caused widespread demoralization.

The South had certain military advantages, such as more graduates of military academies and more officers with command and combat experience in the old federal army. The Southern states also had a martial tradition, and because of the constant need to police the slave population, practically all white men there were trained in the use of weapons. Finally, the Confederates were fighting a defensive war on their own soil with interior lines of communication and supply.

As the war dragged on, casualties mounted. Disaffection and discouragement grew in the ranks. It became harder and harder to replenish the losses. Volunteers became scarce. The draft, resorted to by both sides for the first time in American history, met popular resistance and resentment.

A New Force Enters the Revolutionary Coalition

Under these pressures the Republican Party divided into radical and moderate wings. With their policies gradually becoming dominant, the Radicals called for subordinating everything to the war effort, turning the war into a war for emancipation, and bringing Afro-Americans into the army. The Republican Party grew in numbers and power and became closely tied to the military machine and through the crisis of war consolidated its power.

Eventually the pressure from the Radicals forced Lincoln, a moderate who vacillated between the two wings of his party, to turn the war into a crusade against slavery. Lincoln, who had always opposed the abolitionists, personally possessed the racist prejudices of his Kentucky and downstate Illinois background. When the end of the war was in sight he considered schemes for deporting Blacks from the country, believing it impossible for free Blacks to live harmoniously among whites. These views, not fitting the needs of any class or social layer, were not taken seriously beyond the confines of a small group and died along with the white-supremacist "Great Emancipator," save for a weak echo in Lincoln's successor, Andrew Johnson.

As the war continued, the government's position towards Blacks gradually changed. Escaping slaves were no longer returned by the Union army to their Confederate owners, but were kept as "contraband of war" and put to work on fortifications or as teamsters, etc. Then Blacks were accepted into the army and formed into regiments. Some 80,000 from the North and 125,000 from the slave states served in the Union forces.

War Department records show that a month after Lee's surrender there were 166 Black regiments in the Union army— 145 infantry, 7 cavalry, 12 heavy artillery, 1 light artillery, and 1 engineers. The enlistment records (apparently incomplete) showed 178,975 enrollments, approximately one-eighth of the entire Union army.

Service in the U.S. Navy, which from its beginning had accepted free Blacks, was proportionately much higher. From 1861 on, official Navy policy had been to "fill up the crews with contrabands," and the records show that during the war there were 29,511 Black enlistments, about a quarter of total naval personnel.

As W.E.B. Du Bois pointed out: "In proportion to population, more Negroes than whites fought in the Civil War."[1]*

But that is still not the complete picture. An unrecorded number of Blacks, estimated variously as 300,000 and 400,000, served the

---

* Notes on sources begin on page 249.

Union forces in myriad occupations—as laborers, carpenters, fortification builders, teamsters, scouts, and spies. In addition there were the unpaid multitudes that accompanied the advancing Union armies doing volunteer work.

In answering Democratic Party criticisms of his policy of taking freed slaves into the army, Lincoln gave the following testimony as to the crucial role they were playing: "There are now in the service of the United States near two hundred thousand able-bodied colored men, most of them under arms, defending and acquiring Union territory. . . . Abandon all the posts now garrisoned by black men; take two hundred thousand men from our side and put them in the battlefield or cornfield against us, and we would be compelled to abandon the war in three weeks. . . . My enemies pretend I am now carrying on this war for the sole purpose of abolition. So long as I am President, it shall be carried on for the sole purpose of restoring the Union. But no human power can subdue this rebellion without the use of the emancipation policy, and every other policy calculated to weaken the moral and physical forces of the rebellion. Freedom has given us two hundred thousand men raised on Southern soil. It will give us more yet. Just so much it has subtracted from the enemy."[2]

And in an August 26, 1863, message he sent to be read "very slowly" to a mass meeting in his own Springfield, Illinois, Lincoln said:

"I know as fully as one can know the opinion of others, that some of the commanders of our armies in the field, who have given us our most important successes, believe that the emancipation policy and the use of colored troops constitute the heaviest blow yet dealt to the rebellion, and that at least one of these important successes could not have been achieved when it was but for the aid of black soldiers. Among the commanders holding these views are some who never had any affinity with what is called Abolitionism, or with Republican party politics, but who hold them purely as military opinions."[3]

More decisive military measures were taken. General Sherman broke with the tradition of long supply and communication lines, which limited an army's maneuverability. After the capture and burning of Atlanta, he struck out directly through Georgia on his march to the sea. The military feat of marching an army of 65,000 men for four weeks through enemy territory, cutting a sixty-mile-wide swath of scorched earth, and living off the land, was made possible in no small measure by the tens of thousands of freed slaves who greeted the Union forces and accompanied them, guiding them, literally unearthing hidden supplies, finding mules, horses, and livestock as well as foodstuffs. Sherman's logistic miracle could largely be found in the Black volunteers who accompanied and led his famous foragers or "bummers." And they took up arms and fought alongside the Union soldiers when they ran into Confederate ambushes or skirmishers.

The coalition of industrial capitalists, Midwest farmers, and Northern workers which had built the Republican Party had been expanded to include the Afro-American people. It was this revolutionary coalition led by the Republican Party, itself transformed into a massive apparatus with a powerful if not always dominant Radical wing, which forced the slavocracy to its knees at Appomattox in 1865, ending slavery and opening a whole new period of American and world history.

A Note on Native Americans and the Civil War

Both the Union and the Confederacy sought to gain the support of the Native Americans. Neither met with much success. The Confederates made more headway because of a combination of factors. Most of the Indians who became involved in the Civil War lived in areas contiguous to Confederate territory. There were some Indian groups which owned Black slaves and the slavocracy was able to appeal to them on that basis. Another consideration favorable to the Confederates that carried weight with some Native Americans was that a divided white world would make it easier for them to protect their own lands.

The Kiowas, Comanches, Choctaws, Chickasaws, most Seminoles, and some Cherokees fought for the Confederacy. Some 3,000 Indian troops, including some Cherokees and over 600 Iroquois, fought for the Union.

Some Cherokees took advantage of the war to make their own declaration of independence from the United States. The Apaches refused to support either side and, like many other Indian peoples, took the offensive instead against both sides to protect their own interests. In 1862 starvation conditions in Minnesota brought on by thieving white traders and broken agreements by the Union government led to an uprising of the Sioux. They fought to get supplies on which to survive the coming winter. They killed 400 white settlers and drove off 20,000 others. The Union army was forced to take troops from the Southern front and send them against the Sioux.

In what is today called the Southwest, both Confederate and Union troops raided the Indians, stealing cattle, other livestock, and crops. As the Indians fought back, the Union found itself again forced to send troops westward to fight the Navajos and Cheyennes, as well as the Apaches and Sioux.

The Civil War historically began the last wave of the long genocidal war against the Native Americans.

The Union offered Confederate prisoners freedom if they would volunteer to fight the Indians. After the war many Union soldiers deserted to avoid having to fight in the West. The army, drawing on both Union and Confederate veterans, sent large numbers of troops, including even one all-Black regiment, west. The generals involved in the westward turn of the army after the Civil War included the top commanders, such as Generals Grant, Sherman, and Sheridan. General W. S. Hancock, who stood by while Blacks were murdered by terrorists in the region his troops occupied in the South after the war, became notorious in 1867 for burning Cheyenne, Arapaho, and Sioux villages. He topped off his record by murdering workers back East in cold blood in the 1877 strikes and, as a reward for all his services, was given the presidential nomination of the Democratic Party in 1880.

In the general radicalization at the end of the Civil War, demands arose for more humane treatment of the Indians, but not much came of this reform movement. Later, as reaction triumphed throughout the country, the drive for an openly genocidal policy gained momentum. From 1866 to 1876 some 200 military engagements, primarily with the Sioux, took place. In 1877 the Nez Percé rose up under Chief Joseph and made their heroic 1,000-mile retreat, pursued by three white armies, to within fifty miles of the Canadian border and the hoped-for sanctuary, before they were defeated. Thereafter there were fewer battles, most of them against the Apaches. On December 29, 1890, came the brutal massacre of Sioux at Wounded Knee, South Dakota.

To the new industrial capitalist rulers, Native Americans, like the slavocracy, represented an obstacle to their total triumph and unrestrained exploitation of the entire country from one shore to the other.

2
Wage Workers and the Civil War

To see what the working class's attitude toward the antislavery movement and the Civil War was, and to understand the reasons for it, we have to look at the development and circumstances of wage workers in the United States.

Of course there had been wage workers in the American colonies almost from their beginning. Most of these were former indentured servants who, having completed the legal period of their servitude, continued to work as laborers or in the crafts they had learned. In a craft shop, there would be the master, who owned the establishment, and perhaps several apprentices and hired workers, who looked forward to the day when they could in turn become small masters. In addition, in important seaports there were merchant seamen and workers in the various waterfront trades (shipbuilding, sail making, rope making, etc.). These latter played an important role in Boston as the militant nucleus for the actions led by Sam Adams and other radicals in the events leading to the outbreak of the first American revolution.

But absolutely and proportionately the workers were a tiny class in colonial and revolutionary America. For this was overwhelmingly a society of independent producers, that is, small proprietors or, to use scientific terminology, petty bourgeois who owned their means of production. Most of these were, of course, small farmers, but in addition there were artisans who owned their workplaces and tools. Often they hired a few workers; but many, such as blacksmiths and wagoners, did all their work alone or with their families. This preponderance of independent producers held for all the states which formed the Union after the victory of the first American revolution save in the South, where planters, whose property in land and slaves represented a considerable capital investment, dominated the economy and society.

There was a slow but steady growth of the economy after the revolution, with seaboard cities increasing in size and a corresponding increase in the number of craftsmen, artisans, and workers. But it is not until the period of the Napoleonic Wars in Europe and the consequent shutting off of imports of manufactured goods, through the Embargo and Nonintercourse Acts and the War of 1812-15, that the industrial history of this country, and thus of the American working class, really begins.

To take advantage of the great demand for textiles and other manufactured goods, which previously had been supplied by England, Northern merchants and bankers began to introduce the factory system, utilizing the newly developed machinery of the industrial revolution. Whereas in Britain the capitalists had been able to draw their work force from the great mass of dispossessed peasants and ruined handicraft workers with nothing left to sell but their labor power, there was no such pauperized reservoir of labor in the United States. To induce skilled, and particularly unskilled, labor to work in the new factories, and to induce new sectors of the population—mainly the daughters of New England farmers—to enter the work force, the founders of American industry had to offer relatively attractive wages and working conditions. Thus the horrors in working conditions, housing, and wages that made the workers' lives an earthly hell in Europe were relatively absent from the factory system in its early period in America.

The new factories, however, were not built in the cities, but on the available waterpower sites in outlying, usually rural, areas. Thus these new concentrations of workers were largely isolated from the older city working class.

For several generations the working class saw itself in local or at the most regional, rather than national, terms. This was due not only to isolation because of the poor conditions of travel and communication but also to parochial attitudes, dating from colonial times, based on the diverse origins and religions of the settlers. As the growth of the economy and the improvement in communications tended to counteract these prejudices new immigration tended to produce others.

In 1790 the U.S. population was less than 4 million (of whom three-quarters of a million were slaves); by 1820 it had risen to over 9½ million (of whom over 1½ million were slaves). Besides the natural increase, there had been an immigration of some 200,000 in the period. From this time on, more or less accurate official records of immigration were kept. Fluctuating with economic conditions here and in Europe, immigration rose steadily from less than 10,000 a year in the early 1820s to 79,000 in 1837; the greatest influx of immigrants in proportion to the existing population in all U.S. history came in 1845-50, reaching well over 350,000 for the last-named year. This was because of floods and crop failures on the Continent, the potato famine in Ireland, and the defeated revolutions of 1848-49. All told, between 1820 and 1860 more than 5 million immigrants came to the United States.

While almost all the countries of Northern and Western Europe contributed to the flow of immigrants, the largest contingents came from Germany and Ireland. Many of the Germans were peasants and came with enough savings to buy land in the West and start farming. But many had been skilled workers and they remained in the cities and soon became an important element in the working class, often dominating various crafts. Though most of the Irish immigrants had been peasants in the old country, most arrived too poverty-stricken—especially those driven onto the immigrant ships by outright hunger during the famine years—to do anything but seek immediate employment. Since few had any skills they came to furnish the bulk of the laborers—the ditch and canal diggers, the railroad construction crews. All the Eastern seaboard cities came to have large populations of impoverished Irish laborers and their families, just getting by when they had work and dropping below the hunger line when jobs were scarce.

Thus the working class in the United States prior to the Civil War was very heterogeneous. Besides the regional and religious differences among the native born, there was the division of native born versus immigrant, and divisions among the immigrants themselves on national and religious lines. Finally there was a small free Black population in the North who were discriminated against because of the racism that had been inculcated into the native-born white population in the period when slavery had existed in the North and which was continually reinforced by the existence of slavery in the South.

There were wage workers in the South, too. But as a class they were much less significant than the workers in the free states. The fact that slaveowners could train their own slaves to be skilled workers, or could buy skilled slaves for particular projects, lessened the job opportunities for free workers. Moreover, the practice of slaveowners "hiring out" their skilled slaves threatened the job security of the white workers in their traditional occupations in the few cities of the South. White workers tried to prevent the entrance of slave labor into their trades because the slaves, not being free agents, could not join them in demands for better wages or working conditions but had to accept whatever their owners ordered them to. Thus the action and anger of the white workers in the South became diverted away from the slave-owning class to the Blacks, the victims of that class, and reduced to its simplest terms became a campaign to keep Blacks out of what should be "white men's jobs." Frederick Douglass, among many other former slaves, tells of the hostility he met from white workers in Baltimore when, as a skilled slave, he was employed in a shipyard there.

Because of the low level of industrial development and the disadvantage of competing with slave labor, the working class remained small in the South and only a trickle of the great wave of immigration went to that part of the country. But there were some jobs for which the slaveowners preferred to use free white laborers—these were jobs on which it was too costly to risk slaves, who represented a capital investment. Thus for ditching and draining malarial swamp areas and for the dangerous jobs on the river steamboats, Irish laborers were preferred. Their death or disability cost the employer little or nothing.

Save in periods of financial panic or depression, there was a chronic shortage of labor in the U.S. until the 1840s. Consequently, labor was paid better here than in Europe. It is estimated that wages of unskilled labor here were between one-third and one-half higher than in Britain, and those of skilled labor higher by not quite as much.

Though the period from 1837 to 1852 has been called a "long depression" it was actually a period of alternating prosperity and minor depressions. But it is the decade of the 1840s which brought a marked change in the situation of workers in America. The increased immigration crowded the cities and the resulting competition among workers allowed employers to reduce wages; at the same time it was a period in which the cost of living, especially in the cities, rose. Horace Greeley, publisher of the *New York Tribune*, calculated the rise in the cost of living in New York City between 1843 and 1850 at 50 percent. And in 1851 he set the minimum necessary budget for a family of five at $10.37 a week; but skilled workers in the construction trades at that time averaged only around $10 per week; and the majority of hatters, painters, cabinetmakers, and other skilled workers were earning between $4 and $6 per week. One observer in 1845 estimated that one out of every seven persons in New York City was a pauper. And in the mill towns of New England the "golden age" of the initial years when the employers had behaved paternalistically, offering relatively decent wages, working conditions, and housing to induce young farm women into the new factories, had passed. Most of the women had left after the failure of prolonged struggles and strikes to maintain their standards and had been largely replaced by immigrants and an increased number of child laborers.

There are records of concerted action by workers as early as the colonial period, and during the Revolutionary War they protested the rise in the cost of living relative to wages. Between 1790 and 1825, there were sporadic appearances of unions and strikes in one or another city or in a single trade. But it is after 1825 that the labor movement really begins. The Eastern seaboard cities became the scene of the creation of unions in various trades and their linking together in a single city and then establishing connections with similar unions in other cities. In 1827 a carpenters' strike in Philadelphia for a ten-hour day spread to other building crafts and resulted in a Mechanics Union of Trade Associations. Soon thereafter in more than a dozen Eastern and Midwestern cities similar associations of local unions were formed.

In 1828 the Philadelphia unions formed a Workingmen's Party and won the balance of power in the city council. Similar parties quickly sprang up in New York and New England. They did not last long—either splitting into impotence or being co-opted by the Democratic Party, which dealt heavily in plebian demagogy. Despite their titles they were not true class parties, since "workingmen" included not only wage workers then but farmers, master craftsmen, even manufacturers—only those considered nonproducing parasites, such as merchants and bankers, were excluded.

The labor movement of the 1830s and 1840s not only sought to win better working conditions and wages—the call for a ten-hour work day was raised in this period and would long continue as the most important labor demand—but supported demands for numerous social and political reforms. It sought to expand and implement the democratic rights promised by the first American revolution: extension of the franchise, an end to religious qualifications for officeholding, the abolition of imprisonment for debt, free public education, a mechanics' lien law (so that when an employer went bankrupt wages due the worker would have first claim on the assets), reform of the militia system (which fell heaviest on workers since the rich could escape compulsory drill and service merely by paying a fine for nonappearance).

In this period, and particularly in the 1840s, American workers considered and often were attracted by numerous proposals and panaceas for deepgoing social reforms such as the abolition of inheritance of wealth, the formation of utopian socialist colonies, consumers' cooperatives and producers' cooperatives (often the last desperate resort of a union which had lost a strike), and land reform which would stop the sale of public land to companies and speculators and give it free in small holdings to actual settlers.

Financial panics and periods of depression wiped out existing unions or reduced them to impotence. It was in such periods that workers thought most about deepgoing economic and social reforms and were most attracted to radical proposals. With the discovery of gold in California in 1849 and the breakneck pace of railroad construction, business prosperity returned in the 1850s and workers, concentrating upon the now possible improvement of wages and working conditions through union action, turned away from visions of fundamental social change. Though the panic of 1857 destroyed most unions, a few survived nationally and the ten-hour day had been established fairly widely by the beginning of the Civil War.

The early years of the parallel existence of the abolitionists and the laborites are marked by frequent appeals from one side to the other to merge, since both were dedicated to the cause of reform. But what the appeals really came down to was the demand by each that the other accept its organization and program. Whereas for the labor reformers antislavery was but one of a number of issues—labor reform, anticlericalism, and free education being equally or more important—for the Garrisonians the abolition of slavery had top—almost exclusive—priority.

The *New England Artisan*, publication of the New England Association of Mechanics and Workingmen, labeled slavery a "national curse" and proposed that working people petition Congress to abolish it immediately, with the expenses of compensation to be paid from the sale of public lands and other federal revenue. But while endorsing the efforts of abolitionists to arouse sympathy for the enslaved Blacks, it admonished them not to overlook the daily sufferings of the white workers. "We see oppression all around us," declared the paper, "and what is still worse, we see it often inflicted by those very persons who profess to have the most pity for the slaves of the South."[1]

Orestes Brownson, then in his phase of radical labor reformer, called the wage system "a cunning device of the devil, for the benefit of tender consciences, who would retain all the advantages of the slave system, without the expense, trouble, and odium of being slaveholders."[2]

Albert Brisbane, the foremost popularizer of the ideas of utopian socialist Fourier in this country, wrote in *The Liberator* of September 5, 1845:

"Slavery of capital, under which man is the dependent drudge, and the menial of the power of money, and must sell his time, labor and talents—which is equivalent to selling himself day by day, or by retail—to him who has the means of buying them. . . . This miserable system, which wears out the souls and bodies of the working classes enriching the few, and leaves them and their families to starve in sickness and old age, is only a modification of serfdom and one degree above slavery; it sways with iron rule the destinies of the laboring classes, where slavery and serfdom no longer crush them to the earth.

"If there is a reform which is imperiously demanded, it is a reform of this *servitude to capital*. . . . It would be a noble step, it strikes me, if the advanced guard of the Abolitionists would include in their movement a reform of the present wretched organization of labor, called the wage system."[3]

But there were less sweetly reasonable exchanges between prolabor reformers and the abolitionists. Horace Greeley, in declining an invitation to an antislavery convention in 1845, wrote: ". . . If I regard your enterprise with less absolute interest than you do, it is not that I deem Slavery a less but a greater evil. If I am less troubled concerning Slavery in Charleston and New Orleans, it is because I see so much Slavery in New York, which appears to claim my first effort. In esteeming it my duty to preach Reform first to my own neighbors and kind, I would by no means attempt to censure those whose consciences prescribe a different course. Still less would I undertake to say that the Slavery of the South is not more hideous in kind and degree than that which prevails at the North. . . . But how can I devote myself to a crusade against distant servitude, when I discern its essence pervading my immediate community and neighborhood?"[4]

The dispute frequently degenerated into hostile acts and mutual accusations of hypocrisy. Thus at the mass meeting of the Labor Reform League of New England, held in Boston in 1847, the Garrisonians packed the hall and voted down a resolution calling for the abolition of *all* slavery and voted a substitute that chattel slavery had to be abolished "before that elevation sought for by the laboring classes, can be effected."

The abolitionists tried to shame the laborites by charging them with inhuman selfishness for striving to better their own conditions while Blacks languished in slavery in the South; prolabor speakers accused the abolitionists of melting with sympathy for the plight of the distant slaves while being willfully blind to and hardhearted about the sufferings of workers in the North.

George Henry Evans, who came from the original circle around the utopian socialists Fanny Wright and Robert Dale Owen, and who became famous for his panacea of free land, which he propagated with singleminded fanaticism, wrote of those well-to-do people becoming influenced by the abolitionists: "When they shall have ceased to oppress and grind in the dust the widows and orphans whom Providence has placed at their mercy—when they convince us that the laborers in their factories are better clothed and fed, and in truth enjoy the boasted rights of free-men in a greater degree than the slaves of the South, we will give them that credit for sincerity, and honesty of purpose which we cannot now award to them."[5]

Behind the dispute and embittered relations lay the differences in the composition and basic motivations of the two movements. Save for the Blacks, none of the abolitionists had a direct material interest in the emancipation of the slaves; that is, they did not stand to benefit directly. Their motivation was a compound of democratic and humanitarian idealism, and only indirectly expressed the needs of the rising industrial capitalism. On the other hand the labor movement, though many of its intellectual leaders had been drawn to it by idealism, was overwhelmingly a movement of workers being lashed into class consciousness by exploitation, economic misery, and harsh social conditions. Their material needs spurred them to collective action against their employers and in addition, particularly in periods of depression, to look for radical schemes to transform the whole social system. While many despised slavery and favored emancipation of the Blacks in the South (though no one, including the abolitionists, advanced any practical proposals as to how that could be accomplished), they were not "high-minded" enough to regard their own plight dispassionately and to assign top priority to the demand for abolition. When antislavery issues did arise that seemed to them to have a direct bearing on their own interests, as in the case of whether slavery should be permitted in the new territory acquired in the war with Mexico, the workers of the North, particularly of New England, took an antislavery stance by backing in this instance the Free Soil Party. For they knew that slavery was inimical to free labor wherever they coexisted. They knew furthermore that the slavocracy would, unless prevented, preempt vast tracts of the best land there. And Evans and other labor reformers had convinced them that a policy of free soil and free homesteads for actual settlers was the best policy for the workers and—who knew?—maybe they or their children might be able to get such a homestead.

The creation of the Free Soil Party at the end of the forties was a preview of the founding of the Republican Party in the mid-fifties, and in the secession crisis which followed Lincoln's election the workers, again feeling their direct interests were involved, rallied to support the war for the preservation of the Union.

But many workers were also the victims of manipulation in the political struggles between the various wings of the capitalist class. This was due to their own lack of consciousness as a class and their illusions about the true class character of the capitalist parties. The Democratic Party had long been, and would long continue to be, expert in such manipulation, combining anticapitalist demagogy with racism.

In forming the new national political coalition that won the 1860 election, the Republican Party had offered specific benefits to the manufacturing wing of the capitalist class in the form of promises of a protective tariff and other pro-industrial measures. To the farmers it promised to keep slave-tilled plantations out of the western territories, whose land would go instead without payment to actual settlers through the Homestead Act. But nothing specific was offered to the workers.

True, such a land reform proposal had originated in the labor movement and workers undoubtedly favored it. Some no doubt cherished dreams of leaving their ill-paid jobs and becoming independent farmers. But the actual facts and figures show that relatively few workers did so. Those who were skilled had invested years in acquiring their skills but rarely had any farming experience. Few had the considerable funds needed for such a step. Even with the land free, enough savings were required to defray the costs of the move, the purchase of necessary equipment and livestock, and money to live on while the shelters were being built, the land cleared and a first crop planted and harvested. For the unskilled, who lived a hand-to-mouth existence, it was usually out of the question. Those able to take advantage of the Homestead Act were mostly farmers, who sold existing farms and moved further west, the grown children of farmers, and immigrants who had farming experience and sufficient means for the move west and the initial expenses. Nonetheless, even those workers who could not take the step favored the measure as relieving the labor market from even more overcrowding by draining off from the countryside and immigrant flood people who would otherwise have come into the cities competing for jobs and thus driving down wages. Though not offered any direct economic benefits by the Republican platform, many Northern workers supported that party on general considerations; and when the slavocracy actually began the war, the overwhelming majority—whether they had voted Democrat or Republican—supported the Union.

Among the reasons why this was so was that the Northern wage worker regarded the United States with all its faults as the most democratic nation in the world. While workers in Europe were seeking to throw off kings and emperors and to win elementary democratic rights, such as manhood suffrage, workers in the U.S. not only had these rights but could establish newspapers and parties and, despite some legal hindrances, could organize into unions. Moreover, it was a country where people could rise from the lower classes; there were innumerable examples of workers who had become independent farmers, shopkeepers, small employers, or even industrialists. This all applied to the North; the South was looked upon as very different. There slavery had brought a sharp curtailment of freedom for plebian whites. The slaveowners monopolized the best land; poor white farmers were forced to the less fertile areas or the mountains. In the cities workers' wages were low; conditions were poor. The South was a region that knowing immigrants avoided.

Of course, economic processes were at work in the North which would in time slow and then reverse the upward social mobility. Then there would be far more examples of independent artisans, master craftsmen, and farmers becoming propertyless wage workers than vice versa. Indeed, the radicalism of skilled craft workers in the cities in the decades before the Civil War was a response to the erosion of their economic and social status and opportunity to rise. But in 1860 the trend was far from obvious for most, its manifestations being regarded as aberrations rather than the wave of the future.

On the surface the trend seemed to be just the opposite. Industrial progress appeared to most as the story of the rise of the ambitious worker to capitalist. Typically, a farm youth or immigrant would become an assistant to an artisan, learn the requisite skills, then in the rapidly expanding economy open a shop—possibly in the Midwest, where opportunities were greater—and finally, hiring a few workers, set out to become a capitalist.

The belief that ideally every adult male should own property and be an independent producer remained a powerful ideological force among American workers. This not only took the form of hoping for one's own farm but was also wishfully seen as a potential outcome of the growth of industry. This underlay much of the interest and illusions among workers about utopian socialist colonies and producers' cooperatives, where all would be equal producers and owners.

The small scale of industrial production lent itself to such illusions. The average investment per manufacturing establishment as late as 1870 was only $8,400, with the average establishment having eight workers. Mines in Pennsylvania and mills in New England might employ in some instances hundreds or even a thousand workers, but even in textile-manufacturing Massachusetts the average investment per manufacturing establishment (twice the national figure) was only $17,536. Midwest industry was qualitatively smaller—Ohio's 22,773 manufacturing establishments outnumbered Massachusetts' by 9,000 but employed only half as many workers.

Another contributing factor to the worker's outlook in this period was the rural nature of the North in 1860. In that year only 19.7 percent of the population lived in an urban environment; and by urban was meant a town of 2,500 or more—by our standards today a mere village. Though urbanization was proceeding rapidly, by 1870 there was only 25.6 percent of the population in towns of 2,500 or over. This did not mean that the U.S. was overwhelmingly agricultural, for already in 1860 41 percent of the population were in nonagricultural types of work (by 1870, 47 percent). It must be concluded that a large part of the nonagricultural population lived in a rural environment and was in close contact with the farming population. Most of this nonagricultural portion of the population consisted of wage workers.

What today would be called blue-collar workers and their families are estimated as constituting 27.4 percent of the U.S. population by 1870. The number of actual industrial workers was somewhat less; of the 3½ million blue-collar workers in 1870 just over 2 million were industrial workers. This figure represents more than a 50 percent increase over 1860, when there were 1,300,000 industrial workers.

On the eve of the Civil War one-third of the nonagricultural wage workers in the U.S. were foreign born. They were concentrated in the larger cities. They formed a majority in New York and Chicago. In St. Louis, already an important city, there were more workers who had been born in Germany than those born in the U.S. Of the six biggest cities only in Philadelphia did American-born workers outnumber immigrants.

Germans and Irish constituted the bulk of the foreign born. Many of the Germans had come after the defeat of the 1848 revolution and were imbued with advanced ideas about democracy, unions, even socialism. Among them were some associates and disciples of Marx and Engels who played a part in orienting the German community against the slavocracy and towards participation in founding the Republican Party, as well as defense of the Union when the war came. Regiments of German workers from St. Louis, for example, kept Missouri (a slave state) in Northern hands. Many of the Germans who had military experience became officers in the Union army, as, for example, Joseph Weydemeyer, once an artillery officer in the Prussian army, and an old colleague of Marx and Engels.

The Irish, who had emigrated in the Famine years ragged and hungry, crowded into the big city slums in the Eastern seaports. While canal and railroad building had distributed many Irish throughout the entire North, where they usually inhabited shanties along the railroad lines, about five-sixths of them remained east of the Appalachians in the big urban centers. They constituted a huge reservoir of unskilled and menial labor. In social status they were closest to the discriminated-against free Blacks, with whom indeed they competed for jobs as unskilled laborers or domestic servants.

The conditions they were subjected to may be gleaned from the comment of Ralph Waldo Emerson, the great American philosopher and man of letters of the period. After registering approval of the railroad building going on, he added:

"Our hospitality to the poor Irishman has not much merit in it. We pay the poor fellow very ill; To work from dark to dark for sixty or even fifty cents a day is but pitiful wages for a married man. It is a pittance when paid in cash, but when, as generally happens, through the extreme want of one party, met by the shrewdness of the other, he draws his pay in clothes and food, and in other articles of necessity, his case is still worse. . . . Besides, the labor done is excessive; and the sight reminds one of Negro-driving. Good farmers and sturdy laborers say that they have never seen so much work got out of a man in a day. Poor fellows!"[6]

Whereas the Germans had formed their own craft unions and social and political organizations, the Irish immigrants in the big cities were organized by the racist Democratic Party machines, such as Tammany in New York. By affording them a certain protection and granting some economic crumbs in the form of strategically distributed patronage jobs, election day payoffs, etc., the machines manipulated the Irish for their own ends. They also played on their Irish nationalism and fierce hatred of Great Britain. In this fashion the Democratic machines sometimes stirred them to actions against the Abolitionists, who were pictured as British agents because of their close ties with the British anti-slavery societies, and as a threat to the employment of Irish because of their championing of Blacks, who would compete for the same type of jobs. Finally it was emphasized that a large section of the newly founded Republican Party consisted of a wing of the recently deceased American Party (the Know-Nothings), the bigoted opponents of foreign-born workers, especially of the Roman Catholic Irish.

When the secession crisis came to a head with the Confederate firing on Fort Sumter, the workers of the North rose in their overwhelming majority to defense of the Union. Native and foreign-born workers responded enthusiastically to Lincoln's call for volunteers. Some unions organized their members and volunteered as military units, posting "closed for the duration" signs on their headquarters. All-German, all-Irish, even all-Polish and all-Italian units were enrolled. Free Blacks volunteered their services from the beginning but because of race prejudice and the federal administration's timidity were refused.

As to the actual composition of the soldiers in the Union army, it is calculated that 48.7 percent came from agricultural backgrounds and 42.1 percent were laborers and mechanics.[7]

The early enthusiasm for the war gradually cooled with the passage of time and the worsening of the workers' living standards. Because of inflation and the depreciation of the "greenbacks" (paper money issued without the backing of gold), real wages dropped drastically. Manufacturers, farmers, and other independent producers did not suffer, but profited, from the inflation since they received ever higher and higher prices for their products. Measured against gold, the wages of workers in 1863 were only 76.2 percent of what they had been the year before the war began (1860), and by 1865 the figure stood at 66.2 percent. While workers and soldiers were paid in depreciating greenbacks, the purchasers of government bonds were guaranteed payment of the interest in gold. Nor did workers benefit from the labor shortage due to the large number of men taken by the armed forces; during the war 800,000 immigrants arrived, filling the gap left by those who had donned uniforms.

Working women, especially seamstresses, whose men were in the army, had a particularly difficult time because of low wages. The average in 1865 for women working for contractors on army clothing was $1.54 per week. Of course some received money sent home by their husbands or sons in uniform, but since the ordinary soldier was paid only $13 a month (raised in the middle of 1864 to $16) this was not much.

While their living standards were deteriorating the workers could see about them the orgy of profiteering and graft that was enriching the employing classes as never before in U.S. history. Millionaires had been a comparative rarity in pre–Civil War America, now they were sprouting up like mushrooms after a rainy spell. Manufacturers of war materials, shoddy uniforms, shoes that fell apart after a few marches, piled up profits; railroad manipulators were grabbing off huge tracts of land which were supposed to have gone to actual settlers under the Homestead Act. The orgy of lavish and conspicuous spending by profiteers made more bitter the sufferings of the workers.

The war brought to the surface the class antagonism between wage workers and their exploiting employers. Discontent rose rapidly. Strikes to maintain the standard of living were met with vicious repression, with the employers and government using the war and patriotism as justification.

The Radical Republicans had emerged on the program of employing the sternest necessary measures all up and down the line for the war effort. This included disciplining the workers and crushing strikes. The Radical Republicans were not "radical" in the sense that most people use the term today when the struggle between the workers and capitalists dominates society on an international scale. The Republican Radicals were bourgeois radicals, many of them capitalists themselves, as was their great leader Thaddeus Stevens. They favored a bourgeois revolution, that is, the triumph of American industrial capitalism, and the elimination by decisive measures of all obstacles in its way. They saw no justification for workers' resistance to the prevailing economic situation; they condemned it as aid to the enemy and sought to treat strikers as betrayers of the Union cause.

That is why the Radical Republicans could at the same time be for emancipating the Blacks of the Rebel slaveowners, driving the Indians off their lands in the West, using the army to break strikes, and reestablishing servitude for immigrant workers. Though this latter—the Contract Labor Law—was soon repealed as unnecessary, when it was passed it had the support of many Radical Republicans.

In addition to the passage of special antilabor legislation by various states and the use by some generals of troops against strikers, employers used strikebreakers. Sometimes these were indentured immigrants brought in under the Contract Labor Law, sometimes they were Blacks who, logically, had no scruples about taking jobs from which employers and prejudiced white workers had previously barred them.

The Democratic Party and its newspapers especially played on the fears of white workers that "great hordes" of freed Blacks would stream up from the South to drive down wages and take away jobs. For example, in the summer of 1862 Blacks were hired to work on Ohio riverboats for $30 a month, undercutting the prevailing rate of $40 to $75 a month. The *Cincinnati Enquirer* reprinted a scare article from a Philadelphia paper stating that Black labor there was driving down wages and that Negro workers were streaming in from the South willing to work for ten cents a day. In a few days white boatmen in Cincinnati, mostly

Irish, attacked the Blacks and for five days rioting raged on the riverfront.

Packinghouse workers in Chicago denounced a plan by employers to "crush out the free white working men of Illinois, by thus seeking to bring free negro labor into competition with white labor" and threatened to strike if the plan was put into effect. In the spring and early summer of 1863 there was fighting between Irish and Black longshoremen on the waterfronts of Chicago, Detroit, Cleveland, Buffalo, Albany, New York, and Boston, caused in almost all cases by the employers' use of Blacks as strikebreakers. In June 1863 when 3,000 white longshoremen in New York City struck for higher wages, Blacks under police protection were brought in to take their jobs.[8]

For the first two years of the war, recruitment for the Union army had depended on volunteers, but in March 1863 Congress passed the first conscription act. Leaders of organized labor accepted the measure as a wartime necessity but bitterly opposed its provision by which a draftable person could purchase exemption by paying $300. While such a payment was within reach of the middle class and a mere trifle to the wealthy, it was beyond the means of workers—particularly unskilled workers with families to support.

For example, Jonathan Fincher, leader of the Machinists' and Blacksmiths' Union and editor of a labor paper, declared:

"We cannot silently see the poor conscript torn from family and friends, and forced to the ranks, while the worthless drone upon society, a rich man's son, can, by paying the cost of a week's debauchery, be relieved from the hardships and dangers of a soldier's life. . . . For the sake of the country let the conscription come. But let it come alike upon the rich as well as the poor. No exemptions! No, not one—either for worth or worthlessness, distinction or obscurity, wealth or poverty."[9]

When the authorities began to put the draft into operation in July, the workers' frustrations exploded in a spontaneous uprising in New York City which spread on a smaller scale to several other cities.

The workers' long pent-up anger had numerous causes: increasing poverty due to the reduction in living standards by inflation, class hatred of the capitalists' war profiteering and the rampant political corruption, bitterness at the heavy casualty rate in the war, and the recent defeat of a series of strikes for higher wages. The anger of the workers centered around their living conditions but the spark which touched off the explosion was the implementation of the draft with its exemptions for those with higher incomes. Because of this, historians have called the uprising the "draft riots" and have presented it in a one-sided manner.

On Monday, July 13, 1863, a spontaneous protest demonstration began in the streets of Manhattan. Workers began marching from factory to factory calling out an ever increasing number to join them. They sought out ruling-class targets on which to vent their feelings. The police tried to disperse them, but instead of fleeing they stood their ground and dispersed the police. In some cases the police fired into the demonstrators' ranks. As word of these killings spread, reprisals against the police began. Individual policemen, particularly commanding officers, became the objects of the workers' wrath.

As the fighting intensified, the workers sought to arm themselves. They broke into armories and gun shops, seeking weapons wherever possible. Soon thousands of armed workers had taken over the streets of New York. They had no organization leading them, though the fire-fighting companies (in that era strictly volunteer) initially furnished something of an organizational framework and leadership.

The battles with the police continued for days and swept throughout the city. Manhattan's Lower East Side as far north as Twenty-third Street was the focal area of workers' strength. Battles raged up and down Bleecker Street and as far north on the West Side as Forty-second Street. The police suffered defeat after defeat until they had been driven back into their station houses, where they successfully withstood sieges in some cases and were overrun and overwhelmed in others. According to some reports, there were at times as many as 10,000 armed workers parading in a single demonstration.

With the defeat of the city's police force, the ruling class called for troops, and 10,000 soldiers with artillery were withdrawn from the Southern front and marched into New York. The workers courageously resisted the army, even standing up to artillery firing grapeshot point-blank. But by Friday they had been crushed. It is not known just how many were killed, but at that time there were 100,000 workers in New York and most estimates put the death toll around 1,000. The sympathy risings in other cities were more easily put down.

The New York City uprising was the high-water mark of the

internal conflict between the workers and capitalists during the war. It involved huge numbers of Irish-American workers who, save for the small Black population, were by far the poorest of the city's workers. No proof exists that these demonstrations were motivated by sympathy for secession or the Confederacy. In fact the Irish-Americans had provided more volunteers proportionately for the Union army than had native-born Americans.[10] Yet historians, in order to discredit the uprising, have concentrated their attention on a reactionary aspect of these stormy events— the racist episodes. On this basis they have generally depicted the "draft riots" as antiwar, anti-Black, pro-Confederate demonstrations.

To New York's Black community the uprising was a pogrom. In their confused consciousness many Irish workers amalgamated exploiting capitalists with Republican abolitionists and Blacks, all as one threatening force. In no small measure responsible for the pervasive racism were the employers, such as those who had used Black workers to break strikes, who had long worked hand in glove with the Democratic Party's campaign to inflame race hatred against Blacks, thus diverting the hostility of the Irish and other workers from the rich to Blacks.

About twenty Blacks were killed by whites during the five-day struggle. A hastily evacuated Black orphanage was looted of cots and bedding and then burned. Beatings and other atrocities took place. The overwhelming majority of the workers participating in the uprising were not involved in any anti-Black attacks but concentrated their fury on the police and targets directly connected with the rich. However, there is no record of any tendency among the workers to oppose the racist acts that took place.

No organized socialist current with a clear antiracist and pro-working class outlook then existed. What few revolutionary socialists there were at that time were concentrating their efforts on the defeat of the slavocracy, realizing that such a defeat was a prerequisite for the growth of the workers' movement.

The overwhelming majority of Northern workers supported the war, but their clashes with the new industrial rulers forewarned that another "irrepressible conflict" was already gestating during the war itself.

3

Class Alignments in the South After Appomattox

The Confederate surrender at Appomattox in April 1865 ended the slavocracy. The freeing of the slaves meant the expropriation of $2 billion, approximately half the slavocracy's capital. But this was not the entire loss suffered by the slaveowners. The war had brought a disastrous drop in the value of their land—to one-third of its previous value, on the average. Also it had destroyed much of their fixed capital, buildings, and machinery. Most of their liquid funds had been put into financing the Confederate war effort. Unlike the Northern capitalists whose war loans would be repaid with interest, holders of Confederate bonds and currency found that they were only worthless paper. The Confederate debt was no small amount for that era but totaled some $1.5 billion. Added to this was the fact that the debts to Northern businesses and individuals, repudiated by Southerners upon the outbreak of the war, were now collectible.

The great majority of slaveowners had owned only a few slaves; after the war they remained small—but poorer—farmers. But the 1,733 families which had each owned over a hundred slaves and had dominated antebellum society in the South suffered an economic deathblow. To raise capital to continue farming they were forced to sell huge tracts of their land or to go deeply into debt. Many abandoned their plantations and sought livelihoods elsewhere. Some became lawyers or agents for Southern branches of Northern corporations; others sought security in governmental posts; still others were driven down to the status of proprietors of small family-run farms.

The former slaveholding aristocracy had simply ceased to exist as a class formation. Comparing the completeness of the triumph of the Northern capitalists with the English and French revolutions, historians Charles and Mary Beard write: "Their planting opponents were laid lower in the dust by one revolutionary stroke than the nobility of France or the landed gentry of England. . . ."[1] They further note that among the capitalist plutocracy that emerged nationally in the years between the Civil War and the end of the century not one important figure came from this once dominant class. C. Vann Woodward, the historian of the New South, has further shown that of the industrialist capitalists who arose in the same period in the South itself, those of Southern origin were overwhelmingly from nonslaveholding families.

Real economic power shifted in the postwar South from the landowning to the urban commercial interests, which financed the growing of the crops as well as railroad construction and other industrial undertakings.

The disappearance of the former slavocracy as a social layer is a crucial historical fact for understanding the period. To speak of the ex-slaveowners as a meaningful socioeconomic category after the Civil War is simply false.

Describing planters selling their lands "on the auction block, often at ruinous prices, to capitalists," the Beards cite the statement of Southern historian Philip A. Bruce, who lived through the period, that "the higher planting class . . . so far as it has survived at all, has been concentrated in the cities. . . . The transplantation has been practically universal. The talent, the energy, the ambition, that formerly sought expression in the management of great estates and the control of hosts of slaves, now seeks a field of action in trade, manufacturing enterprises, or in the general enterprises of development."[2]

In 1950 a study entitled *Confederate Leaders in the New South* by historian William B. Hesseltine appeared. It traced the postwar careers of 656 Confederate leaders. While these were mainly political and military figures, 134 of them had been planters or farmers, and what happened to them concretely reinforces the earlier conclusion drawn by the Beards.

After the war "all but a scant handful of them were impoverished," they had no seed, fertilizer, or credits, writes Hesseltine. "For the overwhelming majority" of these ex-Confederate leaders "peace meant months—and sometimes years—of search for new means of making a living." And he continues, "But almost without exception those who achieved prominence in the postwar South were corporation lawyers—serving as counsel, as directors, or as presidents of railroads, mining companies, or manufacturing establishments."³ Invariably these businesses were Northern owned and controlled. Former members of the slavocracy's top command were able to salvage their personal welfare by placing their talents at the service of the victorious Northern industrial capitalists.

This trend prevailed regardless of the political views advocated by the ex-Confederate leaders. Even diehards like General Jubal A. Early, Robert Toombs, and John Cabell Breckinridge, who left the United States rather than accept life under the conquerors, eventually returned to become servants of the new rulers.

Robert E. Lee advised his fellow Confederate leaders to accept the new order. Although he himself turned down many offers to hire out to Northern interests, he finally accepted a $5,000-a-year retainer from railroad interests. Jefferson Davis, who—like Robert Toombs and Jubal Early—maintained he had always been and still was right about secession, tried to return to farming but like most others failed. He supported himself by writing.

Only a few became Radicals; almost all opposed Radical Reconstruction. While remaining in the employ of Northern interests, they opposed Radical Reconstruction even in the period when their Northern bosses were inclined to back it. A good example, whom we shall meet later in this volume, was the 100 percent Confederate, white-supremacist Major General Matthew Butler, who after the war returned to South Carolina with $1.75 in his pocket and debts of $15,000. He worked for Northern interests and remade his fortune, declaiming all the while for Southern "home rule." To Butler's name can be added an enormous list. Former Confederate generals (such as P.G.T. Beauregard), cabinet members, and congressmen loyally served Northern interests while employing anti-Northern rhetoric in their calls for "home rule."

Land, Labor, and Capital

Behind the front ranks of the Union army as it advanced into the South came agents of Northern capitalist interests seeking to buy cotton and to invest in the now extremely cheap land. These interests opposed proposals for the distribution of the plantation land among the ex-slaves. In this they were reflecting the consensus of the Northern business community. They looked upon the newly freed Blacks as a cheap labor supply and at times engaged in brutal exploitation of them.

Although some officers had been radicalized by the war, the army command, except when motivated by military considerations, was only a little more sympathetic towards proposals for a distribution of land among the freed slaves. Even attempts by Blacks to buy land were often blocked. Within the top ruling circles only a small group of Radicals, led by Thaddeus Stevens, favored a general land reform for the benefit of the ex-slaves.

Arguing in Congress for a land reform, Thaddeus Stevens presented the following statistics. The land of the richest 70,000 slaveowners and public lands in the hands of the ex-Confederate states totaled 394 million acres. There were at most one million Black families in the South. To give each 40 acres would thus require only 40 million acres, a fraction of what was available. Stevens proposed selling the remainder to pay the federal war debt.

Even if one were to object that not all 394 million acres of Southern land was suitable for farming or that Stevens's figures were exaggerated, it is obvious that such an expropriation would have provided more than enough land. And it should also be kept in mind that the Western territories were then being opened up for homesteaders (each settler entitled to 160 acres), thus providing additional vast acreages which could make feasible a land reform for the benefit of the ex-slaves. But such a reform ran contrary to the interests of the victorious Northern capitalists.

Historically the capitalist class in its revolutions against the feudal landowners of Europe, especially in France, had promoted land reform to win over the peasantry. Only after consolidating its power did it turn against its own past and oppose bourgeois-democratic revolutions elsewhere.

This process is most clearly seen in the expansion of European industrial capitalism into the colonial areas. While the bourgeoisie had favored land reform, industrialization, and even parliamentary-democratic forms of governmental rule for France, it later opposed all three in its colonies. Vietnam under French control, for example, was denied self-determination, parliamentary forms of rule, land reform, or industrialization. The bourgeois revolution—unlike capitalism—was not for export. The rise of imperialism definitively turned the bourgeoisie against its own revolutionary past.

In the United States the bourgeois revolution took a form quite different in many respects from that in France. It was carried out in two struggles separated by over seventy years and was not fought against a nationally entrenched feudal landowning class. In the United States there never existed a "peasantry" like that in Europe but rather a huge layer of property-owning small farmers. In both the first and second American revolutions the bourgeoisie offered only limited land reform to the small farmers to win their support. During the second American revolution no land-reform measures were offered in the regions previously under capitalist domination.

What land reform was carried through was at the expense of the Native Americans and in essentially unsettled territory. The inducement offered the small farmers was free land through the Homestead Act. This not only benefited the landless farmers but enabled those sinking into debt to sell out for enough money to furnish a stake for a new start in the West. Nor was there any other way to so quickly and effectively settle this area for capitalist exploitation.

After the small farmers settled the West, the inexorable mechanism of capitalist competition brought about their gradual expropriation to the benefit of the bourgeoisie, which turned its back on the very ally that made possible its rise to political power and had assured its victory over the slavocracy. Through excessive railroad freight charges, control of the marketing of the crops, bank mortgages and credit, capitalism ground down the small farmers. By 1890 the records showed that two-thirds of the homesteaders had failed to retain their farms. Moreover, a quarter of all the farms in the U.S. were being operated by tenants—with almost half of these outside the South. Even most of those who still nominally owned their land were being turned, in effect, into laborers for big capital. By 1890 28 percent of all farm holdings in the U.S. were mortgaged. It is estimated that in Kansas, for example, one-half of all farm homes had mortgages on them, many having several.[4] More and more the small farmers were being physically removed from the land to join the urban working class.

Unlike its French forerunner a century earlier, the American industrial bourgeoisie during the second American revolution was already a fully developed class with political hegemony in a substantial sector of the country—and with its opponent class concentrated in a smaller and less developed region. It was this regional character of the second American revolution which permitted the industrial capitalists to mobilize a sufficiently powerful social force to achieve victory while limiting the concessions they offered to the lower strata of the population. The relationship of class forces never compelled the bourgeoisie to add land reform for the ex-slaves to its one truly revolutionary concession—the abolition of slavery.

Upon termination of the military conflict the initial reaction of the ruling class in the North was to bring concessions to a halt. Northern capitalists were decidedly against a land reform in the South. They envisioned instead quick profits from the purchase of plantations and investment in cotton and other staple crops of the region. Southern land looked more promising than that in the West. There would be no problem of bringing new and resistant soil into cultivation but simply of exploiting already improved farmland in a region possessed of the necessary infrastructure of roads, bridges, towns, etc., and of utilizing a labor force already on the scene.

Though the slavocracy disappeared, the plantations not only survived but in some cases grew even larger under new owners. After the Civil War the amount of cotton grown in the South—following a brief period of crises—began rapidly to expand once again even at the expense of other crops. For a long time it remained the nation's largest export product, and as late as 1910 American cotton still represented most of the world's production.

Wage Labor or Peonage

The Northern victors at first sought to make the freed slaves into wage laborers—the type of labor force they were acquainted with. The Freedmen's Bureau, organized by the federal government to aid the ex-slaves, played a double role: on the one hand it protected Blacks from being cheated of their wages and on the other it reinforced their status as a non-landowning labor supply.

"There is no way for you to live but by hard work," was the admonition given to Louisiana's land-hungry ex-slaves by General Fullerton of the Freedmen's Bureau when plantation owners, fearful of land confiscation, petitioned him to intervene. "There is no possible way by which you can procure houses and land for yourselves but by working hard and saving your wages."[5] This was the bureau's attitude throughout the South. It helped force Blacks off lands they had occupied and at times even forced them to perform duties not in their work contracts. Led by Major General Oliver Otis Howard, the bureau sought especially to provide labor for plantations taken over by Northern interests, which included officers of the Union army.

Attempts to establish payment of cash wages was resisted by many of the landowning capitalists of the South, especially those short of liquid capital. They found wage labor unworkable under the economic conditions of Southern agriculture. They sought instead to institute one form or another of peonage, a status between slavery and wage labor.

Using methods of production that were backward compared with those in the rest of the country, the plantations needed cheap labor to remain profitable. The wages the landowners offered were so low that they could not even compete with the starvation wages the railroads were paying Chinese construction laborers in the Far West. The wages actually paid in 1867 were less than those paid for hired-out slaves before emancipation.[6]

To low productivity was added a continued decline in the market and price of cotton. England began to receive increased quantities of cotton from its own colonies, reducing the demand and depressing the price for American cotton. After the quick boom of 1864-65, a result of wartime shortages, the market dropped drastically in 1866-67. One authority estimated that as a consequence in large parts of the South only one in five farmers could plant the next year's crop without going deeply in debt. The trend of lower prices for cotton continued unabated until the turn of the century.

Plantation owners, especially in the area known—because of the fertility and color of its soil—as the black belt, were confronted by the maddening contradiction between an abundance of land and a shortage of labor. For in a wage-labor system a labor shortage enables workers to demand higher wages. Even more important in the South of 1865-66 was the availability of land; if plantation owners were not offering acceptable wages, alternative possibilities, such as farming for one's self, presented themselves to the free laborer. Thus wage labor, free to make choices and possessed of bourgeois-democratic rights, stood in contradiction to the need for cheap labor of a plantation system operating within the economic limits of the capitalist market.

This was the recurrence of an old problem. When colonies were first begun in the American South, those entrepreneurs with enough capital to acquire land for plantations were confronted with the problem of finding laborers. Unlike England, there existed no great mass of dispossessed people hungry enough to work for the cheapest wages. People were scarce in America and the abundance of land enabled the free settlers to become small farmers. They could only be lured to work for an employer if the wages offered were high, and even then usually only long enough to save enough money to quit and set up for themselves.

Plantation owners at first tried to solve their dilemma by importing indentured servants. These were men and women who contracted to work for a specified number of years in return for the cost of their passage to the New World, their keep while working, and a stipulated sum of money at the end of the indenture. While many signed indentures to escape poverty in the old country, many others, convicted of crimes or rebellion, were given the choice between jail and America. Some had simply been kidnapped; ship captains would auction them off along the American seaboard.

But white indentured labor was unsatisfactory from the plantation owners' viewpoint for a number of reasons. First it had to be replaced at the end of the period of indenture, which ran from three to seven years. Then it had to be paid the stipulated amount at the end of the contract. Finally, indentured workers were apt to run off to start farming on their own, blending in without difficulty among friendly poor white farmers or mountain squatters, who in many cases were former indentured servants themselves. Any move by the plantation owners to have indentures legally extended to permanent servitude would have aroused the resistance of the poor whites as a direct threat to their own security.

Nor had attempts to enslave the Indians, which had been successful on the Caribbean islands, worked out satisfactorily. Indians in small numbers had been enslaved in almost all the colonies. But it was soon realized that it was too costly in terms of reprisal and possibly chronic border war with members of the slaves' tribe. Even when the colonists waged total war against a tribe and destroyed it, they deemed it wiser to sell their Indian captives into slavery in the West Indies than to keep them in their own colonies. This was the case in New England with the captives of the Pequot War and King Philip's War, and in the South after the decisive defeat of the Tuscaroras. After all, none of the colonies were isolated islands: enslaved Indians on the mainland had a boundless hinterland into which they could escape. Moreover, they could survive in the woods surrounding the farming areas and there make contact with their own people.

Finally, the importation of slaves kidnapped from Africa provided the solution to the labor problem of the plantation owners of the American South. Such slavery had already been established in the Spanish colonies and in the Caribbean, and was quickly adopted here. The advantages of slavery were manifest. It negated the capitalist law of supply and demand in the labor market. It was permanent and, indeed, even reproduced itself in the form of offspring who belonged to the master. After the initial investment it was the cheapest labor possible, being given only its upkeep, enough to keep it in working order. Moreover, since the slaves were of a color different from the rest of the population, escape was difficult and the great abundance of land was no temptation, not being available to them for their own use.

So it was that a precapitalist form of labor, chattel slavery, became the basis for capitalist development in the South.

With the establishment of slavery came an ideological elaboration of racism by the masters to justify it morally and to protect and reinforce it by co-opting the non-slaveholding sectors of the white population, making them in effect racially prejudiced police auxiliaries. Once established, racial prejudice had its own dynamic independent of its origins and long outlived slavery.

In the post–Civil War South, big landowners—whether old or new, Northerners or Southerners—were busily trying to find solutions to the age-old labor-supply problem. They experimented with Irish workers brought down from the North and Chinese laborers imported from Asia, but all these experiments failed.

Their staple crops had periods in which intensive labor was necessary or the crop would be lost. This made them vulnerable to strikes. There were cases where Northern workers brought South forced big pay increases by striking at the crop's critical moment.

In a society where workers enjoyed bourgeois-democratic rights, the only workable solution would have been to expropriate the ex-slaveowners' plantations, break them up into small units, and establish a broad layer of small farmers, both Black and white. Such a revolutionary solution would have resulted in a completely different history for the Afro-American people and for the South as a region.

The alternative was to deny Afro-Americans the status of wage laborers possessed of democratic rights and to force them into a caste labor system resembling peonage, in which the laborer is bound to servitude to a landlord-creditor until his or her debts are paid. Keeping the laborer destitute and in debt is brought about by a combination of laws, economic mechanisms, outright cheating, and measures of legal and extralegal violence. Only under such a system could the ex-slaves be forced to work on the landlords' terms.

The Black Codes, passed by the state governments organized immediately after the war under the so-called Reconstruction policy of President Andrew Johnson, were the first attempts to establish a caste labor system. Though these laws varied somewhat from state to state, in general they did the following: They declared any Black without employment to be a vagrant who could be arrested and hired out to the highest bidder. Blacks were forbidden to leave jobs before the expiration of the period they had been hired for. Some states authorized employers to inflict corporal punishment on Black employees. In addition, the codes deprived Blacks of the right to vote, sit on juries, or give testimony against whites. Schedules of punishments for the same crimes and misdemeanors were more severe for Blacks than for whites.

The immediate postwar period saw bitter class struggle in the South. Blacks, clamoring for a land reform, fought for their democratic rights as the means of self-defense against property owners seeking to force them into peonage. The Northern capitalists at first had no clear position. They had introduced wage labor into the situation but beyond that they were divided over what policies to carry out in the South.

Finding it difficult to institute peonage legally because of the overall political situation nationally, and fearful of the growing organization and self-assertion of the Blacks, the propertied classes in the South resorted to terrorism. In this struggle emerged the Ku Klux Klan and similar secret semimilitary organizations, organized by landowners, on the one side, and the Union Leagues, based on Black laborers, on the other. But the decisive forces which would determine the outcome of this struggle were not to be found in the South. The struggle there had become intertwined with the developments unfolding on a national scale.

The First Southern Governments

At the end of America's bloodiest war, the victors showed remarkable forbearance, which still has not ceased to bring the plaudits of liberal historians. The insurrection of the slaveholders—their treason, in legal terms—was allowed to pass almost unpunished. A few officers of the Confederacy were arrested, but soon released. Only one, Captain Henry Wirz, rendered odious in the North by horror stories of conditions in the prisoner-of-war camp at Andersonville, Georgia, of which he had been the commandant, was executed. Jefferson Davis, president of the Confederacy, sat in jail for two years and then was bailed out by the famous Northern editor Horace Greeley, who had prodded Lincoln for his slowness in proclaiming emancipation; there was no subsequent prosecution of Davis. After surrendering at Appomattox, General Lee, the Confederate commander in chief, simply mounted his horse and rode home to live peacefully ever after.

For comparison with other instances of the bourgeoisie's treatment of defeated class enemies, one should consider the massacre only six years later of the workers of Paris who had risen in an insurrection lasting only a few months. After the Paris Commune was crushed, hundreds of workers were executed without trials and thousands were deported to concentration camps in the colonies for long sentences. And as evidence that kindheartedness wasn't an inherent quality of the American ruling class, one should recall the grim satisfaction with which in 1876 it sent to the gallows ten Molly Maguires accused of employing terrorist methods in labor struggles in the Pennsylvania coal fields.

What the astonishingly lenient treatment of the Confederates reflected was the Northern ruling class's desire to prevent a deepening of the social revolution which had begun in the South with the end of slavery.

President Johnson allowed the defeated region to hold new elections in which only whites could vote. The new state governments which resulted represented a continuity with the previous governments but were not a simple continuation. Within their personnel a noteworthy shift had taken place, as recent historical research has shown. Candidates of the old proslaveholder Southern Democratic Party, the party of secession and war, had largely gone down to defeat; the winning candidates tended to be those who had been moderate secessionists and had been inclined to favor industrial development of the region.[7]

The presidential election of 1860 had been a three-way race in the South. Lincoln was not even on the ballot in ten Southern states. The three candidates were John C. Breckinridge for the

Southern Democrats, Stephen A. Douglas for the Northern Democrats, and John Bell for an ad hoc party called the Constitutional Unionists, representing elements from the defunct Whig Party.

The Whigs had been a conservative, traditionalist, business-oriented party. It had come into existence in opposition to the Jacksonian Democrats, who with plebian demagogy had consolidated the national coalition of the slavocracy, the frontier farmers, and the city workers of the East. Whigs stood for high tariffs to help develop industry, federal subsidies for shipping and internal improvements such as canals and railroads, sound money, and a national banking system. They were mildly critical of slavery and favored compromise solutions for the conflicts between the slavocracy and Northern capitalism.

In the South, slaveowning families with aristocratic pretensions tended to identify with the Whig Party as the party of old wealth and social position; they disdained the crudity and feared the political recklessness of the upstart layer of planters who had pushed the Cotton Kingdom to the Mississippi and then beyond. More importantly, Southern capitalists connected with industry tended to be Whigs. Though Southern industry in 1860 constituted only 10 percent of the national total, it included 350 woolen mills, 180 cotton mills, and, in all, a product of $238 million worth of manufactured goods. Southern Whigs moreover reflected the political and ideological pressures exerted by developing Northern industrial capitalism.

As the road of compromise neared its dead end in the 1850s, the Whig Party split into Northern and Southern wings and then disintegrated. Northern Whigs found their way into the Republican Party, sometimes with a detour through the short-lived Know-Nothing Party. They had been for the national triumph of industrial capitalism by conciliation and pacific means; now they would have to go along with it through fire and battle.

The Southern Whig Party disintegrated in the early 1850s. Some of its members joined the short-lived Know-Nothing Party which in turn quickly fell apart, leaving the old Whig tendency with no political vehicle. The remnants of this tendency revived sufficiently in 1860 to hastily set up the Constitutional Union Party pledged to avert the inevitable by good will and vague proposals of further compromise. This Lazarus-like effort, with John Bell as its banner bearer, evoked a wide response in the South. Bell received 40 percent of the Southern vote; Douglas, the

Northern Democratic Party candidate, received 9 percent, thus leaving Breckinridge, candidate of the Southern Democrats, the party of secession, with only 51 percent.

So in the first postwar elections in the South the candidates who came out on top were those identified with the political currents which had supported Bell and Douglas just before the war. This was the new feature—the shift in personnel—but the governmental system was not new; the old state apparatus remained though the social and economic base had been pulled out from under it.

The new governments in the South acquiesced in the end of slavery, accepting the Thirteenth Amendment without too much resistance. What occupied their attention more were schemes for redeeming the bonds issued in the South during the war. The Northern capitalists had unanimously declared that the Confederate war debt should not be honored. But the new crop of Southern political leaders—many of whom held such bonds themselves—hoped that something might be wangled by speaking only of the bonds of the various states rather than the bonds of the Confederacy itself.

For political allies in the North, these new Southern leaders naturally were attracted to the Democrats, the opposition party, which was dominated by that wing of the capitalists which had been most closely connected with the Southern economy prior to the war. They were the Northerners least inclined to favor any radical social experiments in the South that would continue the postwar turmoil. Also they were the most understanding of these Southern politicians' desire to reestablish stability through the Black Code solution to the labor problem. While they renewed relations with their old business friends from below the Mason-Dixon line who had "mistakenly" gone with the Confederacy, these old friends were busily explaining to them how they had been "forced" against their will to do so. Long declarations of loyalty now flooded the White House and the Northern press as the Southern political leaders endeavored to adapt to the new circumstances.

It is important to bear in mind that, though the old Whig tendency had been a catchall for those in the South opposed to the chosen party of the slavocracy and had at first opposed or been lukewarm to secession, its leading figures had gone along with secession after the firing on Fort Sumter. Many had served in high capacities in the Confederate government and army.

Indeed, when the Southern contingent of those elected to Congress in the 1865 voting arrived in Washington to take their seats, there were among them the former vice-president of the Confederacy, six former Confederate cabinet members, fifty-eight former Confederate congressmen, four former Confederate generals and five former Confederate colonels.

4

The Rise of Radical Reconstruction

The Confederacy's surrender ended the pressure in the North for the social and political unity which had been proclaimed by the Republicans, and accepted by the masses, as a necessity for military victory. Immediately, the social and political rifts which had been suppressed or restrained reemerged, often added to or heightened by the great economic and social changes which had taken place during the titanic conflict. The masses who had been asked to sacrifice for the war now hoped to enjoy the deferred rewards for that sacrifice. There was a ferment of radicalism producing activity and agitation among the most diverse sectors of the population: the Blacks, both those newly freed in the South and the discriminated-against Blacks of the North; women; the settlers already in the West and the newcomers pouring in to claim free homesteads; the workers, both the skilled and the factory "hands"; and the Irish-Americans seeking ways to strike a blow for the freedom of Ireland.

In the conquered South the Afro-American people were demanding democratic rights, schools, and, above all, land. *Forty acres and a mule* became their central slogan. The right to vote was demanded not only by the freed slaves but by Blacks in the North, for only in a few New England states did they already have the franchise. With the incubus of slavery lifted from the country, Blacks sought full and equal citizenship rights throughout the land. Many Northern Blacks went South to aid in the struggle there.

Militant feminist organizations grew and widened their agitation. The traditional roles of women had been altered by the war. It was, for example, the first war in American history in which women had participated as nurses. Gains were also made in areas of employment and legal rights. In campaigning to rally the Northern masses behind the war effort, women had established their long-challenged right to speak at political gatherings. Many young women—Black and white—went South as teachers for the Freedmen's Bureau or church organizations. They taught Black children in daytime schools and adults in night schools.

The most important demand of women was for the right to vote. After their bitter disappointment in being left out of the Fifteenth Amendment, this remained the central demand of the women's movement.

The labor movement had begun to revive in the last two years of the war. Citywide trade councils reappeared as early as 1863, along with reorganized or new unions. By the end of the war, such councils existed in New York, Chicago, Albany, Buffalo, Troy, Philadelphia, Cincinnati, Detroit, St. Louis, Pittsburgh, and San Francisco. Seven national unions were formed by the end of the war. This figure had climbed to eighteen by August 1866, when sixteen of them sent representatives to form the National Labor Union.

Wages and hours were the two most important issues for the new unions. A wave of strikes in 1866-67 centered around the issue of wages but it also raised the demand for passage of a law establishing an eight-hour workday. This pressure resulted in legislation in a number of states, but the new laws, lacking teeth and national scope, were ineffective.

In spite of the new laws, the workday generally continued to be ten hours or a total of sixty hours per week except in the textile mills, which ran eleven to thirteen hours a day. The workers' movement took direct action in Massachusetts seeking a ten-hour day for textile workers, and in Chicago a general strike movement demanded enforcement of the state eight-hour law. In almost all cases such struggles were defeated. By 1876, these laws, undermined by Supreme Court decisions, had become meaningless.

Along with economic struggles, workers became involved in the political questions of the day. The idea of a labor party was debated, and in various cities and occasionally at a state level labor tickets appeared.

Radicalization among the American Irish took the form of the swift growth of the Fenian Brotherhood. This powerful secret movement, operating in Ireland and among the Irish in all overseas lands, was committed to freeing Ireland by armed struggle. It had supplanted the parliamentary reformist movement of the preceding generation and was bitterly opposed by the Roman Catholic hierarchy. Many Irish Americans had vainly hoped that the notoriously pro-Confederate English ruling class would embroil Britain in war with the U.S. and that after the South's defeat American troops would invade and liberate Ireland. After the war some 150 former Union army officers did, in fact, go to Ireland to aid the struggle there.

In 1866 some 800 American Irish, armed and organized by the Fenians, crossed into Canada from American soil and briefly captured Fort Erie. This and several similar military adventures by the Fenians were doomed to defeat but caused tremendous excitement in America's Irish communities and were a measure of their militancy and readiness for action.

Though the war had produced a readiness for social changes and currents of radicalism in the population as a whole, it was a different story with the capitalist class. It congratulated itself that the period of radical emergency measures was now over. The capitalists' instinctive reaction to the termination of hostilities was to bring changes to a halt and to preserve and consolidate the status quo. Social stability and a favorable climate for business were its postwar goals. Thus with the pressures of war removed the capitalists reverted to the stance they had at the very beginning of the war, one of conservative opposition to any social reforms.

Yet within two years after the war's end the majority of the capitalist class had executed a turnabout and consented to a Radical Reconstruction of the South which involved the use of federal troops to guarantee democratic rights for Afro-Americans. Why did this turnabout take place? The answer is somewhat complex.

The essential reason was that the industrial capitalists, although victorious on the battlefield and in the marketplace, had still to consolidate their political rule. The ending of the war and the expropriation of the slavocracy did not automatically abolish the anti-industrial political bloc traditionally associated with the Democratic Party. Two of its components, the small farmers and the merchants, were still in part tied to the national political machine of the now Northern-dominated Democratic Party. For reasons to be discussed further on an immediate effect of the war's end was to reinforce the Democratic Party on a national scale under the leadership of Northern commercial interests.

66 *Racism, Revolution, Reaction*

Crucial in this new dilemma for the industrial capitalists and their party, the Republicans, was how the conquered ex-Confederate states were to be ruled, especially when returned to statehood within the nation. The desire of the Republican Party politicians to remain in power, the pressure from the Black masses in the South for equality, and the popularity of their demands among Northern whites fused with industrial capitalism's need to consolidate its rule, and resulted in a new political alliance. This temporary bloc required a democratic reform in the South in the form of the establishment of new, Radical Reconstruction governments. The following is an explanation of these developments.

New Social Divisions

The termination of the war ended the imperative necessity for ruling-class unity in the North. Many war measures which had been accepted as necessary evils favored one section of the capitalists to the disadvantage of others. Rifts now developed, or more precisely reemerged, among sectors of the Northern ruling class and in the population as a whole.

The most important of these was between the farmers and the industrial and financial capitalists. The farmers of the Midwest had entered into an alliance with the industrial capitalists in opposition to the slavocracy. But now that slavery was dead their fear of the competitive expansion of slave territory was also a thing of the past.

The farmers' interests conflicted with those of the industrial capitalists on some of the most important economic questions of the postwar period. With few exceptions farmers preferred and would be benefited by a policy of low tariffs, that is, free trade. Yet high tariffs to protect American industry from British competition were a prime aim of the industrial capitalists.

With the outbreak of the war, the industrial capitalists put their high tariff policy into effect. Later, when taxes were placed on industry to help finance the war, the tariffs were again raised to allow manufacturers to pass along the cost in the form of higher prices. When the war ended and the war tax was removed, demands for lowering the tariff became quite strong. Congress passed a "reform" bill ostensibly to lower the tariff but it actually maintained the abnormally high rates.

For the farmers who had to purchase manufactured goods, the

difference in price resulting from the tariffs was enormous. Iron sold for $32 a ton in England while in the United States it cost $80. A tariff raised the price of steel to a level 100 percent higher than that prevailing in England.

Generally being debtors, the farming population opposed "hard" money. Even farmers who had done well during war inflation and were not in debt took this stand. They favored inflationary money policies, "soft" money such as the "greenbacks" that had been printed by the government and introduced during the war. Inflated currency brought about a reduction in fixed debts and mortgages relative to the prices for which they could sell their products. Naturally the creditors, primarily Eastern capitalists, would correspondingly lose, so they favored "hard" or noninflationary money policies.

Farmers made up an enormous section of the population. They could not simply be ignored. But their strength of numbers was undermined by other characteristics. They were more heterogeneous than most other social layers. A majority were petty-bourgeois owners of small family farms. Some were really agricultural workers, owning no land or having to supplement income from their small farms by hiring themselves out. Others were really agricultural capitalists. (This layer grew in numbers after the invention in the 1850s of McCormick's reaper, which facilitated large-scale farming in the prairie states and Mississippi Valley.)

The goal of the landless agricultural worker was to own a farm. The dream of the small farmer was to become a large farmer, and of the large farmer to become a capitalist. The leadership of the farming communities normally tended to gravitate to the wealthier farmers, who often had investments outside of agriculture, lessening their hostility to the Eastern capitalists.

Then again, there were farmers with special interests which strongly affected their overall views. Those who raised sheep, for example, wanted a high tariff on foreign wool. They might have preferred low tariffs on the other items but their special interest made them susceptible to high-tariff propaganda in general. The same held true of farmers producing certain other crops, such as sugar in the South.

Farmers, moreover, were widely dispersed geographically. The urban centers dominated the countryside socially, politically, and culturally. Factories were springing up in all the urban centers of the Midwest, thus planting enclaves of industrial-capitalist influence right in the midst of these agricultural states.

To achieve public expression and to effectively influence events, opinions must be filtered and funneled through some media, organizations, and/or political spokespeople. But the existing newspapers, party organizations, and politicians were all subject to the influence of big money. The opinions of hundreds of thousands of farmers did not carry the same weight as those of a handful of capitalists whose funds were used in manipulating public opinion.

Independent farmers' organizations such as the Grange make their initial appearance in this period, but it will not be until a few years later that they express themselves politically in a strong movement. Then, in the late 1870s, the Greenback Party, for example, will mushroom, only to decline precipitously in the early 1880s. With the economic downturn in agriculture in the last years of that decade, they will revive again, giving birth to the Populist or People's Party. But in the immediate post-Civil War years the farmers as yet had no such organizations.

In fact, voices attempting simply to express the interests of the farmers were largely stifled by their opponents. Newspapers tending to views unfriendly to the industrial capitalists were deprived of the legal and government advertising which in those days was crucial for financing most papers, or they were simply bought by capitalist interests in order to change their editorial line. In one celebrated case the courts simply prohibited the publication of a book exposing the monopolies and financial machinations.[1] Politicians and military heroes looked to hopefully by the farmers were frequently bought off with cash or appointments.

Historically the farmers as a class had always depended for leadership on one or another wing of the ruling class. For decades before the Civil War they had accepted the leadership of the slavocracy—agricultural capitalists—who, as fellow agriculturalists, claimed to be their protectors from the avarice of the Eastern capitalists. After the farmers' interests had come into conflict with the slavocracy, they had accepted the leadership of the industrial capitalists in the new political coalition of the Republican Party. But the destruction of the slavocracy in the Civil War had ended the great fundamental division in the American ruling class which had existed since the founding of the Republic.

The farmers could become a grave threat to the hegemony of

the industrial capitalists only if a sector of the capitalist class should find that some of the farmers' demands coincided sufficiently with its own interests to justify a political alliance with them. And among the Northern capitalists differences did exist. Moreover, though the slavocracy had been destroyed, the traditional means for a political bloc between the Midwest, the South, and Eastern commercial interests still existed in the form of the Democratic Party. And it was to the tradition of a bloc with the agricultural South that the Midwest farmers were instinctively beginning to look.

The most obvious division in the capitalist class was that between commercial interests in New England and New York and the manufacturing interests, particularly of Pennsylvania and further west.

The New York financial and commercial circles generally were associated with the Democratic Party. On the eve of the Civil War, they had been the most hesitant, fearing a decline in international trade and a default on the debts owed them by Southerners. But once the war was an established fact, these capitalists supported the federal government and helped finance the war effort. As creditors after the war they feared inflation and wanted the national debt paid in gold, "hard money." They had no sympathy with the farmers who favored payment in greenbacks.

On the issue of the tariff, however, many held the same views as the farming population. This was especially true of those capitalists engaged in international commerce. They were quite willing to hide their hard money views, even to give lip service to planks for soft money, to court the support of the farmers on the tariff question.

The industrial capitalists, on the other hand, were entrenched in the Republican Party. Most favored hard money, although some, especially in the Midwest, being in debt to bigger capitalists, were not averse to inflationary money policies. (One of the most desired goals of the hard money advocates was a resumption of payments on the government debt in gold. However, after a short economic slump in 1867 they hesitated in carrying out their full money policy lest it provoke a major economic collapse. Gold payments did not resume until 1879.) The big industrial capitalists were almost unanimous in their support of high tariffs. Both their money and tariff policies, then, were in conflict with the objective needs of the farming population.

There were certain exceptions to this commercial-industrial split over tariffs. Some industrial capitalists in New England who were in general agreement with their protariff compatriots in the rest of the country disagreed on several specific items. Iron manufacturers around Boston, for instance, favored low tariffs on iron and coal since they could import cheap coal from Nova Scotia and scrap iron from Britain.

The split between commercial and industrial capitalists partially paralleled, as has been noted, the party lineup within the ruling class. This fact multiplied the importance of these differences qualitatively. Those opposing the policies of the now dominant industrial wing of the capitalist class had political machinery and traditions to wield in the conflict, making them appear more threatening than was justified by their relative economic strength. To this fact must be added the impact of the labor question in the South. Many wealthy people in the South who favored industrial capitalist policies, "Republican policies," went over to the Democrats in national politics because of their imperative need for a stable supply of cheap labor which could be furnished by forcing Blacks into a caste. The ex-Whigs who may have been contemptuous of the Democratic Party, and were still contemptuous of it, nevertheless had to subordinate such feelings to achieving an immediate economic goal—a cheap labor supply. This was an important political factor and gave the Democratic Party nationally the full backing of the newly elected Southern governments.

It is important to note that this economic and political division, between commercial and industrial capitalists, while partially a legacy from the pre–Civil War period, was essentially unlike the previous major division in the ruling class. The slavocracy had been an extremely powerful force with independent control of a substantial sector of the country. It was based on a peculiar form of property, chattel slavery, giving its economic order a specific dynamic, narrowly orienting it around staple crops and leading to an "irrepressible conflict" with the growth of industry further north.

The post–Civil War differences between commercial and industrial capital were of a qualitatively different nature. The commercial capitalists were dwarfed by the capitalists with interests in industry and related finance. They had no separate territory or labor system. They could in no way replace the slavocracy as leaders of an anti-industrial Midwestern-South bloc. The commercial-industrial conflict was a vestige of a previous counterposing of forces, a fast-receding past stage of economic development.

This conflict would be outmoded and resolved by the rapid economic triumph of industrial production and the formation of immense concentrations of capital. The new banks that had appeared with the war were integrated into the entire economy by 1870. These banks financed all lines of business—manufacturing, commerce, and agriculture—and their interests cut across party lines. But as yet, in the post-Civil War period, the industrial capitalists were predominant. Only at the turn of the century would finance capital, representing the merger of industrial and banking capital, reign supreme over the major sectors of the capitalist economy.

With the relentless expansion of industrial capitalism, the Democratic and Republican parties outgrew their traditional roles as political instruments of different and conflicting wings of the ruling class. Within a short time, the top command of both parties came under the control of essentially the same economic interests.

But the legacy of the past, especially its reflection in the two political parties, played an important role in the immediate postwar period. The experience of the previous sixty years had made the business community well aware of the consequences if one wing or another of the ruling class succeeded in gaining the support of the farmers. In their debates over economic policies New York's commercial and Pennsylvania's industrial interests threatened one another with the specter of such a bloc with the farmers.

Democrats and Republicans

The spoils system was in full force—civil service reform being something in the future—and all government jobs were by political appointment. The Republican Party consequently was now a huge bureaucratic machine. It not only possessed the federal patronage but had established its control over the patronage in every major state of the North. This involved tens of thousands of jobs. Federal clerical workers alone numbered 54,000. Expenditures of the federal government for the first seventy-two years of the nation's history had totaled $1.7 billion. In the years 1865-1869 alone, they came to $1.6 billion. The

Republicans had consolidated their power over these jobs and funds and had no intention of letting them slip from their hands.

The Democratic Party, on the other hand, had been shattered and transformed by the Civil War. Its Northern wing, the junior partner in the pre–Civil War party, split from the slavocracy as the impending conflict drew near. The top command was taken by commercial and financial interests in the East, primarily around New York. Samuel Tilden, August Belmont, and Horatio Seymour were representative figures among the new leaders.

The Democrats survived the war as the "opposition" party. Abuses by the capitalists during the conflict, especially those directly associated with the Republican-led federal government, such as the draft, which exempted the rich, kept substantial sectors of the masses behind the Democratic Party. Its tradition of being pro-agriculture and its pro-plebian demagogy made it attractive to some farmers and permitted its machines to control many important urban centers, including the largest of all, New York.

Although weakened, the Democratic Party was still a force. Its leadership was in the hands of the most conservative wing of Northern capitalists but its voting ranks extended widely among workers and farmers. In the state elections in the North, in 1865, the Democrats polled 44 percent of the vote; in 1866, they received 45.4 percent and in 1867, a few months before Radical Reconstruction was voted by the Republican-dominated Congress, they polled 49.5 percent. This impressive electoral showing, however, was not matched by corresponding power or influence. The machinery of the Democratic Party could in no way compare with the Republican machine entrenched by the war years and fueled by the federal and state patronage and control of government spending.

The Return of the South

Taking the above factors into consideration, we can begin to understand the material import of the great debate which swept the country over the conditions for the renewal of Southern representation in the Congress and control of the Southern state governments.

Now that the slaves were freed, each would no longer be counted as three-fifths of a person but as five-fifths, giving the South even more representation in Congress and Electoral

College votes for president than it had had before the war. Thus the question of the terms of the South's return into the Union came into the center of all political struggles. What to do with the South became an element in the jockeying and maneuvering between the factions of the Northern ruling class over the issues of the tariff and monetary policy. This became a conflict not only between the two big political parties but within each party. The interests of the farmers, workers, and most of all the ex-slaves also were refracted through the prism of the struggle over the South.

Though the industrial capitalists had triumphed militarily and economically, they had not as yet fully consolidated their governmental control. The political dissatisfaction and contrariness of the huge farming population presented them with a dangerous problem. It had been an element of the problem they had faced in the years prior to the Civil War and now it seemed to have revived to haunt them.

One method of assuring their continued control of the federal government would have been, of course, to abandon the bourgeois democratic form of rule. But such an extreme measure seemed dangerous if not impossible. The ruling class had to contend not only with its own internal differences but with a population predominantly of small farmers, all of whom possessed arms and were convinced believers in the democratic rights which they had enjoyed since the first American revolution. Only as a very last resort would the industrial capitalists gamble on a solution outside the framework of bourgeois democratic rule.

Although there were many rumors of plots and impending military coups—and in some cases force was actually used—in the struggle over the South in the period prior to Radical Reconstruction, no proposal to abandon representative government was seriously considered. Instead, the industrial capitalists turned in the opposite direction—to an expansion of bourgeois democratic forms—in order to strengthen their grasp on governmental power.

Their problem was how to turn the Republican Party into a majority party. That party had never yet won a majority of the voters, i.e., white males over twenty-one, in a national election. In 1860 Lincoln had come into office as a minority president. But even if the vote split between his three opponents had been combined behind one candidate, Lincoln still would have been elected. He would have lost the election in terms of the popular vote but would have won in the Electoral College because his vote was concentrated in key Northern states. Only the subsequent secession and nonparticipation of the eleven Confederate states in national elections turned the Republican Party into a majority party in the North. But even so, the Democrats, as we have seen, were polling over 45 percent of the vote in the North right after the war.

If the former Confederate states were readmitted to the Union with only whites voting in them, a victory for the Democratic Party in the next national elections seemed not only likely, but assured.

The American industrial capitalists had triumphed in the biggest and bloodiest war of the nineteenth century, a war that had cost the North 360,000 dead and 275,000 maimed and wounded; they had control of the state with its repressive forces; they had economic hegemony. Yet they were now faced with the possibility of losing governmental power not only in the very region of the country they had just conquered but nationally as well.

A chill of fear ran through the industrial capitalist class and through the Republican Party machine as they envisioned a political bloc of Midwestern farmers, Northern Democrats, and the new state governments in the South, all dominated by Eastern commercial capitalists, winning control of Congress and then the presidency. Such a victorious coalition would erect all sorts of obstacles to further industrial development, if not an outright roadblock. It would be nothing short of a disaster for the Republican Party machine. And finally it would have sealed the complete denial of democratic rights to the Afro-American people in the South.

Andrew Johnson, a former Democratic senator from Tennessee, became president upon the assassination of Lincoln shortly after the termination of the war. Johnson had been chosen as the vice-presidential candidate by the Republican Party in 1864 in an attempt to broaden its base by including pro-Union "War Democrats." The party name was temporarily changed to the National Union Party and Johnson, the only Southern senator who had remained loyal to the Union, was added to the ticket. Shortly after assuming the presidency, Johnson revealed his sympathies for many of the positions favored by farmers and Eastern commercial interests. He opposed high tariffs and even hard money. Although formally a Republican with a Republican cabinet, Johnson threw the weight of the presidency behind the Democrats and attempted to form a bloc between the Democrats and a wing of the Republicans. This development added to the fears of the industrial capitalists and the Republican Party machine. The presidency, in their eyes, had already passed over to the opposition. The Democratic Party in turn was encouraged by Johnson's course and openly sought to revive the antebellum bloc that had permitted it to rule for almost half a century.

Horatio Seymour, a central leader of the Democratic Party and its future presidential nominee, openly argued for a commercial-farmer bloc. Speaking in New York in October 1866, he said that the tariff "will fall heavily upon the commercial and farming interests of our country. It will harm this great city. It will lengthen the hours of labor, and will scant the food and clothing of the poor; but who hears of this amid the howlings of sectional rage? . . . This question of tariffs and taxation, and not the negro question keeps our country divided. . . . The men of New York were called upon to keep out the Southern members [of Congress], because if they were admitted they would vote to uphold our commercial greatness and the interests of Western agricultural states."[2]

The fear of the industrial capitalists and the claim by Seymour that the return of the South would tip the scale for the Democrats and the interests they represented, or at least partially represented, was well founded. A comparison between the actual votes on matters such as the tariff and what the vote would have been if the South's elected representatives had been seated reveal this to be true. For instance, on the tariff bill of 1866 the vote in the House was 95 for to 52 against. If the South had been readmitted and its representatives had voted in a bloc, the tally would have been 95 for and 122 against.[3]

The desire of the industrial capitalists to stop any further social reforms in the South right after the war had boomeranged. They had permitted state structures to be set up which were not directly under their control. Blacks had not been allowed to participate in the voting, while speedily pardoned ex-Confederate leaders took leadership roles in the new governments.

At first, most industrial capitalists had assumed that the end of the war and their economic domination would easily lead to their political ascendancy. General Sheridan expressed this view explicitly in 1865 when he wrote, "There are without doubt many malcontents in the State of Louisiana and much bitterness but this bitterness is all that is left for these people, there is no power of resistance left, the country is impoverished and the probability is that in two or three years there will be almost a total transfer of landed property, the North will own every Railroad, every steamboat, every large mercantile establishment and everything which requires capital to carry it on. . . . The slave is free and the whole world cannot again enslave him, and with these facts staring us in the face we can well afford to be lenient to this last annoyance, impotent ill feeling."[4]

General Sherman likewise argued for permitting the continuation of the old governmental structures and for leniency toward Southern politicians: "The poor whites and negroes of the South have not the intelligence to fill the offices of governors, clerks, judges, etc., and for some time the machinery of State Govts must be controlled by the same class of whites as went into the Rebellion against us."[5]

These two statements typified the thinking of the majority of the big bourgeoisie at the end of the war. They felt the military victory and their economic hegemony would automatically solve any remaining problems. They thought it best not to stir up the poor people, Black or white, but to leave things alone as much a possible. They opposed any proposals that smacked of social reform. This political current became known as the Conservatives. It was to be found in both parties. Within the Republican Party it was opposed by the current which went under the name of Radicals.

The Radicals

The Radicals originated as strong advocates of decisive measures against the Confederacy during the war. Within the Radical current were elements that wanted to carry through a full bourgeois democratic revolution in the South. These bourgeois revolutionaries favored confiscation of the ex-slaveowners' property, the division of their land among the Afro-Americans and poorer whites, and the disfranchisement of Confederate leaders. They advocated full democratic rights for the ex-slaves, including the right to vote and hold office. To a certain extent, they were also responsive to appeals for social reforms from other plebian elements. But most of those who came to be known as Radicals were in only partial agreement with these revolutionary views. In particular, they balked at land reform. What they did was to accept one part of the program of the bourgeois revolutionaries in order to achieve a limited goal: political hegemony of the Republican Party.

The final Radical plan for the South dealt only with governmental reorganization; no social measures such as land reform directly affecting the economic well-being of the ex-slaves were included. The Southern governments were not to be immediately dissolved. Instead military commands were to be set up to prepare new constitutional conventions which would reorganize the governments on the basis of a new electorate consisting of all males over age twenty-one regardless of race. To hold such conventions, delegates would have to receive the votes of an absolute majority of registered voters, not just of those voting. Confederate leaders were to be disfranchised. For the new governments to be formally readmitted into the Union they would have to approve the Fourteenth Amendment and guarantee Black suffrage.

The plan was expected to assure pro-Republican governments in the South, based on the assumed support for the Republicans from the Black population. It was calculated that if even a small percentage of whites joined with the Blacks, majority governments favorable to industrial capitalist interests could be established in almost all the states. Thus, "Radical Reconstruction" was aimed at guaranteeing the industrial capitalists not only hegemony in the federal government but control of the state governments in the South.

The Radical proposals became more and more appealing to growing layers of otherwise conservative capitalists and politicians in the years 1865-66. The Republican machine politicians, now aware of the danger of an electoral victory for the Democratic Party, began throwing their support behind the plan. Former Conservatives, such as Oliver Morton of Indiana, John Sherman of Ohio (brother of the general), Lyman Trumbull of Illinois, John Andrew of Massachusetts, and General Philip Sheridan, were among those that switched over. They were important in helping to convince many hesitant capitalists to support the Radicals.

It became clear that the industrial capitalists would not lightly abandon the instrument that had carried them to victory in the war. The threat of a new agricultural-commercial alliance under the banner of the Democratic Party helped convince them to go ahead with Radical Reconstruction.

Many capitalists also had immediate interests in keeping the Republican machine in power. The giveaway of the nation's wealth was now in full swing. Enormous fortunes were being made through corruption and graft as government funds and lands were handed over to railroads and other corporations.

The land grants to railroad companies amounted to an area larger than Maine, New Hampshire, Vermont, Massachusetts, Connecticut, Rhode Island, New York, New Jersey, Pennsylvania, Delaware, and Maryland combined! If we recall the refusal of the federal government to grant a land reform for the poorest of all, the 4 million ex-slaves, which would have required only a fraction of the land that was turned over to a handful of capitalists, the injustice of their rule becomes glaringly evident. The railroad barons were also often granted funds to build their railroads, usually beyond the actual cost of construction.

If industial capitalists had strong incentives for maintaining Republican rule in Washington, D.C., they were similarly motivated in favoring the establishment of Republican rule in the South, which would thereupon become more responsive to their operations in that market.

To achieve their economic and political goals, the industrial capitalists accepted the necessity of the Black franchise in the South, though without enthusiasm. Charles Sumner, a left Radical from Massachusetts, in trying to win over the more conservative machine politicians and capitalists, made a revealing statement in the Senate in favor of enfranchising Blacks as the key to achieving political stability: "Only through him [the Black man] can you redress the balance of our political system and assure the safety of patriot citizens. . . . He is our best guarantee. Use him."[6] That is exactly what the industrial capitalists agreed to, using Blacks for their own purposes.

The Opposition to Radical Reconstruction

Opposition to Radical Reconstruction stemmed from two separate sources, old-line Democrats and Conservatives. These two forces represented different interests and had different programs.

The old-line Democrats reflected in part capitalist interests still in conflict to some extent with industrial capitalism. They were led by politicians who dreamed of a revival of the old Midwest-

South-commercial bloc. Within their ranks were to be found all kinds of individuals trying to recoup personal fortunes destroyed by the war. These included ex-slaveowners seeking to have the Southern state debts paid and Northern politicians who had opposed the war and thereby discredited themselves by the standards of postwar bourgeois politics.

The old-line Democrats won support from the discontented in many areas. Many poor workers, believing in the Democrats' demagogic support for the "people" against the rich, voted for them. Farmers opposing the tariff and mistakenly believing that the Democrats would fight for inflationary financial policies backed them. Bitter ex-Confederate leaders joined in, viewing the Democrats as their old traditional party. Among the deeply embedded Democratic Party traditions was racism. It was the "white man's" party, as it proudly proclaimed.

The Conservatives, unlike the Democrats, represented a political point of view among those who favored industrial capitalism. Most were to be found within the Republican Party ranks. Some were formally Democrats, while a few were not clearly affiliated to either party. They had no sympathy for a revival of the old farmer-commercial coalition as a weapon against industrial capitalism. And they were repelled by the Democratic Party's plebian demagogy and its anti-tariff policies. They were, however, unconvinced of the need for a social experiment of the nature of Radical Reconstruction. Many commercial capitalists had one foot in the Conservative camp and the other in the camp of the old-line Democrats. They ended up being swept along by the momentum of a straight-out old-line Democratic approach, believing this could bring an electoral victory while leaving them in the driver's seat.

Andrew Johnson attempted to bring the Conservative wing of the Republicans into a bloc with the Democratic Party by the formation of a third force or new party in 1866. The Republican Conservatives were relatively strong. If they could be united with the Democrats, whose polling strength was well known, an electoral victory could be expected. Yet this effort met complete failure. Historians find themselves at a loss to explain why what appeared to be a majority in the populace at large failed to coalesce into an effective political force. The answer is not to be found in the personal errors or lack of campaigning skill of Andrew Johnson and his supporters, as many contend. The

Conservatives and Democrats represented two different historical currents. One had its origins in the pro-industrial forces of the second American revolution; the other was a dying remnant of the past. There was no way a "new" party or political program could unite them. Forced to choose between the Republican Radicals and the old-line Democrats, most Conservatives in the East and Midwest voted Republican.

In the South, however, they made the opposite choice and supported the Democrats. The pro-industrial forces there were much weaker than in the North. With the outbreak of the war, they had been swamped. Forced to choose between their immediate economic well-being and their general support to industrial ideals and the maintenance of the Union, they opted for support of the Confederacy in most cases.

With the defeat of the Confederacy they reemerged as a political force although still a relatively weak one. The peculiar Southern labor problem, however, made them hostile to Radical Reconstruction, pushing them into the camp of the Democratic Party. Only a few crossed over to the Radicals. But this Southern bloc of Conservatives and Democrats was a temporary one stemming from the specific problems of their region. In socioeconomic terms, the Southern Conservatives were the counterparts of Northern Conservative-Republicans.

The elections of 1866 were a triumph for the Republican Party. More specifically, the outcome was a decisive triumph for the Radical wing of the Republican Party. The Radicals set out to clinch the military and economic triumph of the industrial capitalists with political control both in the South and nationally.

Until the 1866 elections, the Radicals had proposed the Fourteenth Amendment as a stopgap device to gain time and strength. This amendment specifically stated that no Confederate debt would be paid. It also provided for reducing the South's representation in Congress proportionately if Blacks in the Southern states were not allowed to vote.

Most important of all, the amendment denied Southerners who had been congressmen, state officials, or army officers before the war and who had sided with the Confederacy the right to be elected to any state or national office. Since most Southern politicians fell into these categories the Radicals assumed that the new Southern governments would never accept the Fourteenth Amendment. Yet its acceptance was required for readmission to the Union and thus for representation in Congress. In this way the Radicals gained time till after the 1866 elections, when they were able to present a more decisive program and had the strength to override President Johnson's vetoes.

The only Southern state that approved the Fourteenth Amendment was Tennessee, and that is why it reentered the Union prior to Radical Reconstruction. Unlike their counterparts in other Southern states, the Radicals in the Tennessee legislature were strong enough to ratify the amendment although they did not have sufficient numbers to assure a quorum. Their opponents prevented a vote simply by walking out. That problem in parliamentary procedure was finally overcome by arresting the necessary number of recalcitrant legislators and keeping them present while the roll call was taken and the vote recorded. The federal army commander making the arrests wired President Johnson, the commander in chief, asking his approval in advance of the operation. But Johnson never received this request, which he undoubtedly would have refused, because the War Department was the only telegraph center for the government and it was under the control of the Radicals.

In Louisiana the struggle over control of the state government took a bloody turn. During the wartime military occupation of that state a provisional government favorable to the Republican Party had been established. After the war it was replaced by an elected government dominated by old-line Democrats and Southern Conservatives. In 1866 when an attempt was made in New Orleans to hold a convention of the pro-Republican forces, which included many Blacks, the delegates were met by an armed attack by local police. Driven by gunfire into a building, they attempted to surrender. When they walked out they were massacred. This went down in history as the "New Orleans Riot." It had a great impact on public opinion in the North at the time, reinforcing the Radicals.

The Radicals were also aided by the general radicalization in the immediate postwar period, which increased support for their proposed Radical Reconstruction. There was a substantial sympathy among whites in the North for the ex-slaves. Midwestern farmers and Eastern workers who might still believe in white superiority nevertheless felt the Blacks in the South, who had sacrificed for the Union, were owed a "fair shake." This mood combined with hatred for the ex-Confederates, who had killed a brother, son, or friend of almost every family in the North. Memory of the war and its propaganda was still very much alive.

The struggle against the "traitors" and the "murderers of starving Union prisoners" was not over.

The Radical Republicans focused their campaigns on this sentiment. They did not stress tariffs or hard money but concentrated on the fear of a return to power of the Democrats, referred to as the "rebels," "Confederates," "slaveowners," etc. Atrocities committed against Blacks in the South were widely publicized throughout the North. Radical politicians such as Thaddeus Stevens and Charles Sumner, and abolitionists such as Wendell Phillips and Frederick Douglass, sincerely campaigned in the interest of the ex-slaves. Other Republican politicians, who opposed letting Blacks vote in their own states, advocated in eloquent terms the franchise for Southern Blacks.

The election to the U.S. Senate by the new Southern governments of such figures as Alexander Stephens, former vice-president of the Confederacy, helped win votes for the Radicals. The strategy of campaigning around the issues of the Civil War, of making the question appear to be whether the Blue or Gray would rule, became and remained the stock-in-trade of the Republican Party long after everything progressive had been removed from its program. This campaign technique became known as "waving the bloody shirt."

The Radicals controlled most of the Republican press and party machine, which meant most of the federal and state machinery in the North. They won the backing of the majority of the ruling class and could draw on it for funds to supplement those generated by the party machine and government sources.

In 1866 the secret ballot did not yet exist. People could watch how others voted. Capitalists would march their employees to the polls and make sure each voted Republican. Many poor people hung around the polling places waiting for monetary offers before proceeding to vote. The buying of votes was common, especially in close districts. Here again the Republicans had the clear advantage and purchased thousands of votes.

To sum up: Radical Reconstruction came into being because of the neeed of the industrial capitalists to consolidate political control. To achieve this they needed an alliance with the Afro-American people and thus extended democratic rights to them. The struggle of Afro-Americans for their social well-being and political rights, the general postwar radicalization, and the internal dynamic of a Republican machine seeking to perpetuate its rule were all contributing factors in the rise of Radical Reconstruction.

The instinctive shift to the right by the ruling class immediately after the war had been premature; they now made a tactical adjustment and gave one more final push to the revolutionary process unleashed by the war. Radical Reconstruction was the last progressive act of the American ruling class. It took this step out of its own genuine class interest, not as a concession wrung from it by opposing social forces. Since Radical Reconstruction, every gain made in the U.S. by working people, oppressed nationalities, women, and small farmers has required a struggle against the ruling class.

But Radical Reconstruction was itself a halfway measure. It called for bourgeois democratic rights for Afro-Americans juridically and electorally but opposed a land reform. Thus from the start it had a built-in contradiction. It gave Blacks legal rights without the economic basis upon which those rights could be exercised and defended. Moreover, while solving an urgent problem for the industrial capitalists—governmental power—Radical Reconstruction left the South's "labor problem" unsolved.

5

Class Struggle Under the Radical Regimes

Radical Reconstruction was a blow to racial oppression. It altered the thinking of both Blacks and whites, continuing a process begun in the Civil War.

Prior to the war, most whites in both the North and South accepted chattel slavery on the basis of belief in the natural inferiority of Blacks as a race. One can draw an analogy between these views and those held by most people in the United States today, who accept as part of the natural order of things a system that allows a few families to appropriate fabulous wealth while millions live in slums. The abolitionists in the pre-Civil War period, like the socialists of today, were a small minority who challenged the basic premises of accepted opinion. They denounced slavery as unjust, unnecessary, and detrimental to society as a whole.

Under the impact of the Civil War, the deeply imbedded racial prejudice among whites began to crack. When Blacks were first armed, many whites, especially in the North, did not believe they would fight. (The Confederates seemed to know better and declared, initially, that all captured Black soldiers would be shot.) Contrary to these expectations, Black combatants were the fiercest fighters of all because they had so much to fight for. Not only were their own lives at stake but the freedom of their people. They saw themselves as participating in a revolutionary war of liberation.

As white workers and farmers became aware of the victorious battles of ex-slave soldiers, a new respect for Blacks grew. The mounting casualty toll among Black soldiers added to this admiration and at the same time hardened the determination of Blacks to pursue the war.

Even more important was the war's effect on the self-image of Black people. It is not difficult to appreciate the effect on slaves of the arrival of all-Black units coming to liberate them. A dramatic example was the taking of Charleston, South Carolina. The Confederate troops withdrew from one end of town as the entire Twenty-first United States Colored Troops and several companies of the Fifty-fourth Massachusetts entered. The Twenty-first marched up Meeting Street led by a soldier carrying a banner with the inscription "Liberty," while the Black infantrymen of the Fifty-fourth Massachusetts were singing "John Brown's Body" to the enthusiastic cheers of the Black population, most of whom had been slaves the day before.

In 1867, the passage of the first Radical Reconstruction legislation dealt another blow to white supremacy. Although not fully conscious of the reasons for it, the masses of people then, as now, were deeply influenced by the decisions and views of the ruling class. In this case the rulers through their government had declared the ex-slave a full citizen with an equal right to vote and hold public office, and therefore more worthy in a sense than the many leading Southern whites who were disenfranchised by the same legislation.

Radical Reconstruction was more than simply a juridical change. It profoundly altered the relationship between classes in the South and set forces into motion that could not be easily stopped.

By the time the new registration process mandated by the Reconstruction Acts of 1867 was completed, about 10 percent of the whites had lost their right to vote. The total number registered was 660,181 whites and 703,459 Blacks in the ex-Confederate states, not counting Tennessee. These figures break down as follows for each state:[1]

State	Black	White	% Blacks	% Blacks in population
S. Carolina	76	48	61	59
Mississippi	17	83	17	55
Louisiana	49	49	50	50
Alabama	18	90	17	45
Florida	18	27	40	45
Georgia	33	137	19	44
N. Carolina	15	118	11	37
Virginia	25	80	24	35
Texas	9	81	10	30
Arkansas	8	58	12	26

The following figures give a breakdown of the representation at the state constitutional conventions:

State	Registration Black	Registration White	% Blacks	% Blacks in population
S. Carolina	80,550	46,882	63	59
Mississippi	77,328	62,362	55	55
Louisiana	84,436	45,218	65	50
Alabama	104,518	61,295	63	45
Florida	16,089	11,914	57	45
Georgia	95,168	96,333	50	44
N. Carolina	72,932	106,721	41	37
Virginia	105,832	120,101	47	35
Texas	49,497	59,633	45	30
Arkansas	17,109	49,722	26	26

This new majority of Black voters in the South was registered prior to the adoption of the Fifteenth Amendment and prior to the winning of the right to vote by Blacks in many states of the North. W.E.B. Du Bois estimated that of the approximately one million Black males over age twenty-one in the South, only 10 to 20 percent were literate and only about 25,000, including Black immigrants from the North, could be said to be educated.[2]

When the ruling class found it advisable to give Blacks the right to vote, they received it forthwith, without any to-do about educational requirements. This should be compared with ruling class policies 100 years later, when Black people had to fight for decades to regain the franchise, suffering deaths, imprisonments, beatings, and other injustices. During the civil rights struggles of the 1950s and 60s, the national Democratic and Republican parties both hypocritically claimed to be completely behind the Fifteenth Amendment and the right of Blacks to vote!

In 1867 Blacks held a majority of almost two to one in both the electorate and population in South Carolina. In Mississippi, the only other state where Blacks were a majority of the population, they were also a majority of the voters. In Alabama, Florida, and Louisiana they had electoral majorities but were slightly less than 50 percent of the population. In Georgia they were just under half of the electorate.

However, after elections were held the number of Black officeholders, both elected and appointed, did not come close to reflecting the relative voting strength of the Black population. Whites were a majority in all the governments under Radical Reconstruction except in South Carolina, where Blacks were a majority in the lower house. The senate in South Carolina was predominantly white and the governorship was always white, although some statewide offices were held by Blacks.

Elections were held for constitutional conventions to establish new state governments. The most determined opponents of Radical Reconstruction called for a boycott of these elections. Although many whites heeded the call, sufficient numbers voted to make the boycott a political failure. As a countermeasure to the attempted boycott, Congress dropped the provision that delegates had to receive the votes of a majority of all those registered, requiring instead only a majority of those voting.

The New Radical Coalition

The new governments that emerged from this process were based on the Black electorate, with a fraction of the whites supporting them. Overall it is estimated that about 20 percent of the whites voted for the Radical tickets. But this vote was concentrated in certain areas such as Tennessee, Mississippi, and North Carolina, and in many states the percentage of whites supporting the Radicals was much less.[3]

Whites who joined with the Black voters break down into three categories. First, there were poor whites who were hostile to the rich planters. Second, some wealthy Southern whites of Whig background joined with rich Northern-born whites to lead the Radical coalition. Finally, Northern whites of middle-class background who had come South as teachers or preachers joined in.

Northern Blacks who came South to help the cause of their people also played a leadership role within the Radical coalition and the Black community.

In class terms the new governments represented a coalition of industrial capitalists and Black labor, with a thin layer of poor white farmers also involved. The top command of the coalition was in the hands of the industrial bourgeoisie. Although some very wealthy individuals participated, and many smaller capitalists and store owners also joined the Radicals, the rule of the industrial capitalists was not direct or personal but through representatives reflecting their interests.

The ranks were composed overwhelmingly of propertyless Black laborers. A few Blacks were to be found in the lower and middle sections of the party hierarchy but only rare individuals further up—usually those who by chance had gotten an education. Many in the middle echelons were middle-class whites—ex-Union officers, preachers, and teachers. The top commands involved some local rich but the entire structure depended on the power that created it, the Republican machine in the North, which was directly led by the industrial capitalists.

The most "radical" aspect of Radical Reconstruction was the opening it provided for Black labor to wage struggles in its own behalf. Blacks, who had been slaves only a few years earlier and who had not even had the right to vote the day before, were now registering, voting, and sitting as delegates to write their state constitutions. Later they would take seats as legislators in their state capitals and even in Washington, D.C.

In all, fourteen Blacks would go to Washington as congressmen from six different Southern states, and two from Mississippi would enter the Senate. Several others were elected to Congress but were refused their seats on one pretext or another. Most of these representatives were ex-slaves. On the other hand, there was not a single Black from the North in the House until the 1920s and none in the Senate until 1966.

It is difficult to grasp the full revolutionary implications of this Black representation. No parallel exists in the United States today, there not being a single worker, much less a socialist, in the House or Senate. The election of Black legislators was testimony to the depth of the revolutionary changes unleashed by the Civil War. Even though some of them maintained moderate political positions they were, regardless of the rhetoric used, above all representatives of the oppressed nationality of Afro-Americans, a nationality composed almost entirely of laboring people.

The voice they raised in the halls of Congress was anomalous among the paid representatives of the Robber Barons. They spoke up for the Cherokees and other dispossessed Indians and for the hounded Chinese laborers in the West. They sought to increase the rights of women and argued for federal support to education, a concept that would not be accepted for another generation.

In the South the pressure and influence of Black officeholders resulted in a series of progressive reforms. Most important, of course, was the elimination of the Black Codes and the guaranteeing of juridical rights for Afro-Americans, including the right to serve on juries, hold office, speak, organize, and serve in the police and militias.

Other important reforms were also achieved. An enormous demand went up from the Afro-American people for schools. There was more interest in education among the ex-slaves than among the poor whites, who were not caught up in such a profound social transformation as was the Black population.

General Pope, referring to his military district, which included Georgia, Florida, Alabama, and Mississippi, wrote in 1867: "It may be safely said that the marvelous progress made in the education of these people, aided by the noble charitable contributions of Northern societies and individuals, *finds no parallel in the history of mankind*. If continued, it must be by the same means, and if the masses of the white people exhibit the same indisposition to be educated that they do now, *five years will have transferred* intelligence and education, so far as the masses are concerned, to the colored people of this District."[4]

By 1869 there were 9,000 teachers in the South instructing the children of ex-slaves. By the next year there were 4,300 schools with close to 250,000 Black children in attendance. Apparently these students learned fast, as the following student-teacher exchange indicates.

Teacher: Now children, you don't think white people are any better than you because they have straight hair and white faces?
Students: No, sir.
Teacher: No, they are no better, but they are different, they possess great power, they formed this great government, they control this vast country.... Now what makes them different from you?
Students: MONEY. (Unanimous shout)
Teacher: Yes, but what enabled them to obtain it? *How* did they get money?
Students: Got it off us, stole it off we all![5]

The first statewide free public schools in the South were established during Radical Reconstruction. The Black lawmakers sought schools for both Blacks and whites and preferred integrated schools. Integration for all schools was established by law in Louisiana and at the university level in other states. In most cases separate schools were established because most whites insisted on all-white schools before they would allow their children to attend. When schools of higher learning were integrated many whites withdrew.

New rights were granted to women during Reconstruction. The first divorce and property rights laws for women were passed. Better facilities for the care of the sick, blind, and insane were established. The judicial system and penitentiaries were modernized.

Albion W. Tourgee, a Union soldier who settled in North Carolina after the war and wrote *A Fool's Errand,* the best-known historical novel in defense of Radical Reconstruction, summarized the achievements of those governments as follows: "They instituted a public school system in a realm where public schools had been unknown. They opened the ballot box and jury box to thousands of white men who had been debarred from them by a lack of earthly possessions. They introduced home rule in the South. They abolished the whipping post, and branding iron, the stocks and other barbarous forms of punishment which had up to that time prevailed. They reduced capital felonies from about twenty to two or three. In an age of extravagance they were extravagant in the sums appropriated for public works. In all that time no man's rights of person were invaded under the forms of laws."[6]

The governments under Radical Reconstruction were in many ways the most democratic the South has ever had up to the present day.

Economic Struggle Prior to Reconstruction

Radical Reconstruction, while representing the apex of democratic achievement in the second American revolution, was already being undermined by adverse economic factors when it came into existence.

The greatest revolutionary opportunity had come as the war ended in 1864-65. Then even Andrew Johnson shouted that "traitors must be punished and impoverished." And by this he meant, "Their plantations must be seized, and divided into small farms. . . . The day for protecting the lands and Negroes of these authors of the rebellion is past."[7]

In the last years of the war, Blacks had got some land one way or another. Forty thousand had settled on the Southeastern coast in all-Black communities. At Davis Bend in Mississippi the enormous plantations of Jefferson Davis's family were taken over and administered by the slaves, resulting in enormous profits for them.

During the war confiscated property was sometimes sold for unpaid taxes or turned over to the government. The Freedmen's Bureau acquired 800,000 acres of land through confiscation. Blacks were allowed to rent land from the bureau with the result that in the first year, Blacks financed the entire cost of the bureau, totaling some $400,000. When public lands in Alabama, Mississippi, Missouri, Arkansas, and Florida were opened to settlers some 4,000 Blacks succeeded in becoming property owners. The number was so small because of obstacles put directly in their path to prevent them from acquiring land and because of their own lack of access to the necessary credit, stock, and farm implements.

Most Blacks got no land. And for those who did, the tide turned as early as the end of 1865 and they began to lose it. The federal government under Andrew Johnson sought to pardon the owners and return to them land on the South Carolina coast settled by 40,000 Blacks. This return of property extended to Freedmen's Bureau land, so that by 1868 the bureau had only 139,000 of its original 800,000 acres left. It was at the beginning of Radical Reconstruction that the Davis family was pardoned and their land "returned," that is, expropriated from the ex-slaves. The return of lands continued under Radical rule.

The class struggle unleashed by the end of the war developed both on a general political level and on a day-to-day basis over working conditions on the land. Conventions of Blacks organized to protest their treatment and to demand democratic rights swept across the South. In 1865 such conventions were held in Jackson, Raleigh, Richmond, Nashville, Alexandria, Vicksburg, Petersburg, and Norfolk.

The first concern of the ex-slaves at that time was, of course, to establish their freedom in actuality. The test of freedom was to be able to walk away from their ex-owner. This was immediately put into effect by large numbers of slaves. Frequently the first to go were the house slaves, both male and female, whose "selfless dedication" to the slaveowners is still depicted in films and novels. That commitment apparently vanished upon their learning that they had been emancipated.

This newly won freedom immediately posed a new question for the ex-slaves: under what terms would they labor? A complicated struggle broke out around this question. Ex-slaves were hesitant to come to terms with landowners because they hoped that land would soon become available, and they were not interested in signing contracts until that question was clarified. Also, the longer they held back while planting was still possible, the more desperate were the landowners to sign contracts and the better the terms offered. Often in this period the ex-slaves refused to work or sign contracts but remained on the land to see if they could occupy and hold it.

Unfortunately most historians writing on these matters have based themselves on the records, memoirs, and diaries of literate and wealthy whites. This is the main source of the "history" to be found in our school books about the ex-slaves believing freedom meant they didn't have to work, or how they wandered aimlessly through the countryside refusing to work. The more openly racist books cite this as evidence of the ex-slaves' laziness.

William Heyward, one of these landowning whites who left memoirs, wrote at the time, "If the reality ever comes on me that I must labor, I am sure I cannot do it, I must then lie down and die."[8] It is from such memoirists as William Heyward that historians have drawn their information on "Black laziness."

The refusal to work at the beginning of the farming season mysteriously reappeared the next year and the year after that. What was clearly involved was a spontaneous strike-type action aimed at forcing better working conditions. The ex-slaves tended to band together, at least at the plantation level, and bargain with the landowners as a collective body. With the general shortage of labor prevailing, Black laborers would walk off the plantation of an exceptionally vicious employer and establish a general boycott. Then all Blacks would refuse to work for that landowner.

Another tactic used to gain better contracts was arson. If a landlord refused to grant a minimally decent agreement, his barn might burn down the next day. This age-old peasant form of sabotage parallels the tactic Northern workers—particularly construction workers—later used in organizing their unions. Bosses who wouldn't sign with the union found their half-built structures mysteriously blown up by dynamite.

The landowners responded to this struggle with their own traditional methods, including terrorism. They attempted to fire militant leaders and sometimes had them assassinated. They also demanded help from the government. First they wanted war-confiscated plantations returned to the previous owners so that

Blacks' hopes for getting land would be dashed. They understood that such a rollback would demoralize Blacks and weaken their bargaining position. Most confiscated lands were returned. Then the landowners demanded that the Union army help enforce their contracts or evict ex-slaves occupying the land. This was also acceded to. The Union army and the Freedmen's Bureau officials in a few cases employed physical torture on recalcitrant Blacks, such as whippings and hanging by the thumbs.

The widespread use of terrorism by landowners caused Blacks to seek to arm themselves. At times Union troops met armed resistance when they came to throw Blacks off the land they were occupying.

In the two-year period between 1865 and Radical Reconstruction, Blacks were losing out in their efforts to obtain land. On contract agreements with landowners, they were at least stalemated. They were not gaining and in some areas ground they started losing ground. Radical Reconstruction altered the existing relationship of forces, unleashing a new wave of struggles under different conditions.

Land and Wages

With the granting of democratic rights to Blacks, the possibilities for resisting the landowners increased, taking on a new dimension. Sheriffs, judges, and legislators elected by Blacks were generally responsive to Black labor, making organization easier. The Union or Loyal Leagues, the basic political expression of the Radical rank and file, grew into mass organizations. By 1868, for instance, the Loyal League of Louisiana had some 50,000 members. It is estimated that the Leagues had 500,000 members throughout the South. In some areas, at least for a period, substantial numbers of whites also joined.

The struggle for the land was resumed. Blacks in their overwhelming majority favored outright expropriation without compensation. The ex-slaves argued cogently that they had produced the wealth of the planters and that therefore their demand for land was only asking for what they had created.

In South Carolina and Mississippi this meant that a majority of the population favored expropriation of the major existing form of private property. Many poor whites were also for redistribution of the land, giving such a measure majority support in probably three other states at least—Alabama,

Louisiana, and Florida—where Black majority electorates existed—and possibly in Georgia as well.

This is one of the few times in American history when the majority of the people, at least in one region, consciously favored confiscating the property of the rich and dividing it in some more democratic manner. But the bourgeois wing of the Radical Reconstruction coalition would not permit any such step. As pointed out previously, although they represented but a small number of people, their interests dominated the coalition and they succeeded in blocking any direct expropriation of land, even with compensation.

To get around the obstacles put up by the bourgeois Radicals, Black representatives attempted to achieve land reform indirectly. Without questioning the "right of private property," they sought to have the land taxed in such a way as to force its public sale. For instance, they proposed that a heavy tax be levied on the enormous tracts of unused lands. If the landowners refused or failed to pay the tax, the government could then legally confiscate the land and sell it. The Black representatives hoped that such land would be sold in small parcels to ex-slaves or poor whites. Since these purchasers would work their land, a different, much lower, tax would then apply. Moreover, in several states, acts were passed prohibiting the expropriation of small family homesteads for tax delinquency.

The bourgeois elements in the coalition approved this plan for their own reasons. However, they sucessfully blocked proposals by Blacks to set a limit on how much land any one person could purchase.

In South Carolina, Blacks also pushed for using state funds to buy land and then provide reasonable terms for its purchase by the landless. A Land Commission was established for this purpose, and it parceled out 100,000 acres to 4,000 Black families. Similar proposals were made in other states, but in almost all cases were defeated.

Tied to the struggle for land was the struggle over the conditions of labor on the land. Right after the Civil War, Blacks generally wanted to rent land in preference to working for wages. They feared that wage labor would mean working in gangs with white overseers as in the days of slavery. Since most landowners had little cash for paying wages, they generally preferred a rental-type agreement also.

These agreements were not of a kind that gave Blacks any

independence, however. The rent was to be paid by turning over a share of the crop, and the landowners retained the right to oversee the farming to guarantee that their rent would come into existence. This arrangement became known as sharecropping. Since most ex-slaves had few farm implements or none at all, and no money to maintain themselves, they had to borrow these from the landowner. Thus, hidden behind the sharecropping arrangements was debt peonage to one degree or another (being bound to labor for payment of debt).

Under Radical Reconstruction, Blacks took advantage of their right to organize by struggling for a status as close as possible to that of free landowners. Short of acquiring land, this meant renting land only on reasonable cash terms. In some parts of Mississippi, for example, the Loyal Leagues organized the ex-slaves to pledge themselves not to work as laborers and not to pay more than $1.50 per acre rent. But the resistance of the landowners to such demands was unbreakable, especially when they were aware that the Blacks' own Republican Party would not back them up.

The argument that the landowners owed ex-slaves back pay was raised by a Black representative from Dallas County, Alabama (where Selma is located). He proposed that former slaveowners be required to pay ex-slaves at least $10 a month for every month after the Emancipation Proclamation of January 1, 1863, to May 20, 1865. Such an ordinance was adopted 53 to 31.[9]

For the overwhelming majority who were landless, the Black legislators also sought to establish a sort of minimum wage scale. Most contracts involved a sharecropping arrangement, and the legislators attempted to set 50 percent as the tenants' minimum legal share. Previously the prevailing share had been 33 percent. In the lower courts, because of the influence of Radical judges, some of whom were Black, laborers now stood a chance of having complaints against landlord abuses upheld.

But the tragedy of Radical Reconstruction was reflected in the actual contracts signed by the ex-slaves. For the absolute opposition of the ruling industrial capitalists to distribution of the land was undermining the Blacks' ability to fight effectively, even with their newly won rights, for a decent life for their families.

The greatest weapon in the hands of the landowners was hunger. Most Blacks had only a few days' supply of food at any one time. They were forced more and more to agree to peonage-type contracts to feed their families.

Some of these contracts even required performance of labor in addition to a share of the crop, an arrangement that had prevailed in feudal Europe and in more recent times among the Indian peasants in Peru. Called the "two-day system" because it required two days free labor on the owner's land in return for use of a plot, it appeared alongside many other arrangements. A ten-hour day became the norm, which was only a small improvement over slavery's sunup-to-sundown workday. A struggle for a five-day week was generally lost although in some places Black tenants were able to take Saturday afternoon off.

Some contracts included limitations on the workers' personal freedom. These included bans on alcohol, pets, and talking in the fields, and silence after 9 P.M. No sick leaves were permitted.

More and more Black tenants found themselves at the end of a year's work owing the landowner money. Penniless, without farm equipment or seed for the next year, without the possibility of getting credit for fertilizer, and above all, with no land to work, the Black tenant came under the harsh economic control of the landowners. Starting first in the most isolated rural areas and spreading towards the cities, Radical Reconstruction was being undermined by the survival of the plantation system.

Poor White Farmers

The discussion so far has concentrated on Black labor because most poor whites owned their own land and thus found themselves in a totally different situation.

Poor whites had mixed feelings regarding Radical Reconstruction. Had a full revolutionary transformation, including the division of the land, been embarked upon, they would have been rapidly attracted. They had the worst lands, generally in the upcountry or mountain areas. For years they had hated the slavocracy, which had driven them off the better lands. Representatives from among the poorer whites joined with Blacks in proposing confiscation of the plantations, and other measures aimed at dividing the land. Countering the attractive force of Radical Reconstruction on poor whites were the advantages of a continuation of racism to maintain them in a privileged position relative to the Blacks.

Although Radical Reconstruction had conferred upon poor whites all kinds of rights denied them by the slavocracy, the appeal by the plantation owners for race solidarity against Black labor met a strong response. This was especially true after it became clear that a genuine land reform was ruled out. Who would control the best jobs in the cities? At what wages would Black farm laborers work for small white farmers? These questions combined with another development to push the small white farmers towards racism: the moneyed interests were penetrating the farming markets with excessive interest on loans, excessive taxes on the land, and excessive charges for railroad transportation. These economic policies were associated with the Radical Reconstruction regimes and made the small farmer susceptible to appeals for their overthrow.

The possibility of an alliance between the poor whites and Blacks for a division of the land, although not realized, sent tremors through the ruling class. After the workers' uprising in the Paris Commune of 1871, the wealthy in this country began to suspect that Radical Reconstruction might open the door to similar events. The June 21, 1871, issue of the *New York Tribune* printed the opinion of a Northern Republican of the poor illiterate Southern whites and his warning that "if to them were added the whole bulk of the Negro population, so vast a mass of ignorance would be found that, if combined for any political purpose it would sweep away all opposition the intelligent class might make. Many thoughtful men are apprehensive that the ignorant voters will, in the future, form a party by themselves as dangerous to the interests of society as the communists of France."

Similar thoughts had been expressed even earlier. The provisional governor of South Carolina, realizing Blacks were to get the vote, said, "I greatly fear there are many white persons in South Carolina who will vote for a [Radical Reconstruction] convention. . . . This class may influence the Negro vote to unite with them, and then, in return, they can unite with the Negro in parcelling out the lands of the State. One step leads to another. . . ."[10] Unfortunately such an alliance was never formed.

Struggle Within the Ruling Class

The establishment of the Radical Reconstruction governments acted as a catalyst to speed up the process begun with the triumph of the Northern armies in the South. Control over the economy was shifting from landowning to banking and industrial interests. Northern capitalists were penetrating the South, obtaining the most profitable enterprises and much of the land.

Prior to the Civil War, the landowners had dominated the local governments. Thus taxes on land had been low. State taxes as well had generally been minimal, since the slavocracy had opposed using tax money to promote industrial development.

Under Radical Reconstruction, taxes began to go up as school systems were established and other reforms were initiated. Land was now much more heavily taxed. This led to large tracts being sold to pay the taxes, thus facilitating a rapid shift in ownership. The amount of land that changed hands was rather large. In South Carolina alone, 270,000 acres acquired through tax confiscation were sold in 1873 and 500,000 acres in 1874.

This shift brought to the fore new, powerful, often absentee owners. Members of the old slaveowning aristocracy who remained on the land were generally reduced to the status of medium or small farmers. Although no detailed study has been made of what happened to the slavocracy after the Civil War, and the land ownership statistics for this period are faulty, historians of all viewpoints confirm this trend.

Roger W. Shugg, author of *Origins of the Class Struggle in Louisiana*, in his chapter on the survival of the plantation system notes this change. "Scores of families in Tensas [Parish] could be mentioned—the Andrews, Buckners, Harrisons, Lynches, Montgomerys, and Penns—who had once operated large plantations with handsome profit but now managed simply to hang on to them for a comfortable livelihood." He continues, "Many properties, especially in East Carroll, had passed into the hands of partnerships or companies which administered them through the agency of managers and overseers. New families with names strange to the region were to be found everywhere."[11]

Shugg was describing the change in Louisiana, but the same was true for the other states. Francis Simkins, in his book *The Tillman Movement in South Carolina*, notes, "It is a common observation that many of the landholdings of the older families have passed into the hands of men with new names and traditions." He describes the transformation that took place in the following way: "In the towns arose a new class of merchant-farmers, who made small fortunes out of the credit system of financing many farmers, who were forced to borrow after the War. The members of this new class often invested their surplus incomes in agricultural lands. Today, as the wealthiest citizens of many South Carolina communities, they have in some respects taken the places of leadership once held by the ante-bellum planters."[12]

This shift from landowner to merchant-moneylender as the dominant economic layer in the South was consolidated under Radical Reconstruction. Many storekeepers became money lenders to the credit-hungry landowners. Loans were made at high interest rates, well above the legal limit of 7 percent. Behind the storekeeper's or merchant's loan was credit provided by the city banks, which in turn depended on credit from Northern banks, particularly in New York. A portion of the usurious interest charged by the merchant was often reinvested in land.

What railroads existed in the South were bought up by Northern corporations. This process was facilitated by the new Radical regimes to such a point that it may be more accurate to say that the railroads were *given* to Northern corporations. Also much of the new tax money collected by the Radical regimes was used to help Northern interests finance new railroads.

As previously noted, the old prewar Democrats, with their pro-agriculture, anti-industrial development policies, lost out in the South with the rise of Radical Reconstruction. It was not they but the Conservatives who became dominant within the opposition camp. These Conservative leaders went along with most of the goals of the industrial capitalists nationally and even regionally except for the status given Black labor and many of the reforms strengthening its position.

Recognizing the relationship of forces within the ruling class revealed by the Radical triumph in the 1866 elections and the initiation of Radical Reconstruction, the Southern Conservatives split over what policy to pursue. Some chose to join the Republican Party in the South and work within it to moderate the new regimes. Others organized an opposition to the Radicals, usually calling themselves Conservatives, but occasionally using the name Reform Republican or some variant. Many hoped for a turn of events that would strengthen the Democratic Party nationally and replace Radical Reconstruction with a "Conservative Reconstruction" based on the subjugation of Black labor.

The complete eclipse of the Southern Democrats in this period has not been given adequate attention by most historians, nor has its significance been correctly appreciated. Since, as we shall see, the term Democrat will later reappear, most historians have not bothered with even informing their readers that the party dominant in Southern politics for decades collapsed and all but disappeared between 1865 and 1869. Others use the terms Conservative and Democrat interchangeably. Designations themselves are not the crux of the matter. At the time, the word Democrat undoubtedly was still used, especially by Radicals, to describe and discredit the Conservative opposition. But beneath the two party labels there were different socioeconomic currents whose recognition is essential to an understanding of how and why Radical Reconstruction appeared and later collapsed.

The Richmond *Enquirer and Examiner*, annoyed by references in the Northern press to Democrats in Virginia during this period, wrote, "There has been no such party in this state for eight years, and its very bones have rotted and now crumble at the very touch."[13] Similarly the *Appeal-Avalanche* noted that in not one Southern state had the opposition to Radical Reconstruction rallied under the name "Democrat."[14] Historian David Donald, writing on the role of the ex-Whigs after the Civil War, notes that "the Democratic party itself was virtually defunct, and . . . influential southern newspapers were urging a dissolution of that party."[15]

Often, friendly relations existed between the very top levels of the Radical and Conservative camps. This is not surprising if we keep in mind that both wings were led by capitalists representing essentially the same interests. As capitalist elements among the Radicals, including Northerners, acquired lands, the explanation of the "Negro problem" by their well-to-do Conservative friends seemed to make more sense.

Feuds between major industrial capitalist interests, especially railroads, often found their expression in the Radical-Conservative divisions in the South. If one capitalist group found a rival group entrenched among the Radicals, it might turn to the Conservatives for support, or vice versa. Thus in Alabama, the Louisville and Nashville and the Alabama and Chattanooga railroads, both owned by rich Northerners, battled it out as Radical versus Conservative.

Much of the notorious state debts that were a legacy of Radical Reconstruction represented money given to railroads. This corruption stirred the indignation of historians for decades. It is true that looting of state treasuries was at an unusually high level throughout the country during the late 1860s and the 1870s, and in the South this involved both Conservatives and Radicals.

This was a natural byproduct of the penetration of capital in the new order established by the Civil War.

But graft was substantially larger in the North during this period than in the South. The money stolen by the Democratic Party Tweed Ring in New York City alone was probably greater than all the corrupt giveaways in the entire South during the Radical regimes.

Though Northern capital penetrated the South after the Civil War, there was very little genuine industrial development. Most capital flowed westward rather than southward. Few new industries were begun and even the infrastructure of the economy was left generally backward. The major changes Radical Reconstruction brought were the transfer of economic power from the landlords to the merchants, banks, and railroads and the political ascendancy of forces favorable to Northern industrial interests.

Class Struggle Within the Radical Camp

Right from the start the Black labor-industrial capitalist coalition was unstable. We have already described conflicts that arose over land and wages. The differing class interests continued to reappear in various forms. Personal and political feuds over patronage, for example, could easily come to reflect the underlying class antagonism. In Mississippi the underrepresentation of Blacks in office became the issue around which this conflict expressed itself. In Louisiana the conflict arose from the moment the constitutional convention assembled and various committees presented majority and minority reports divided according to race, each reflecting a different class view.

Lerone Bennett, Jr., in his book on Radical Reconstruction entitled *Black Power U.S.A.*, refers to a wing within the Louisiana Radicals, called the "Pure Radicals," that advocated a full bourgeois democratic revolution and implied positions that went even further. "They demanded 'an entire renovation of the political element' and 'a truly democratic system of labor,'" Bennett writes, and cites them further as declaring, "'we cannot expect complete and perfect freedom for the working men, as long as they remain the tools of capital, and are deprived of the legitimate product of the sweat of their brow.'"[16]

In the last period of Radical Reconstruction this class conflict within the Radical camp became more acute. It revolved around the question of armed defense of democratic rights—whether a state militia would be organized and used and whether federal troops would be called in to defend civil and legal rights. Although these struggles tended to take the form of racial conflicts, occasionally a few whites were to be found on the side of the Blacks. These were usually middle-class Radical elements from the North, such as teachers who had come South with the aim of aiding the newly freed slaves.

Traditions from Slavery

Though slavery was abolished, the hundred and one ways in which slavery had affected Southern society could not be eliminated overnight. The economic one-sidedness and backwardness of the South blocked the development of industry and consequently of an industrial working class. The general ignorance of the population, of both Blacks and whites, as compared with the North was a direct heritage of slavery.

The most important element was the deep penetration of racism among whites. The belief that Blacks were inferior, though weakened by both the Civil War and Radical Reconstruction, still pervaded the country but to a qualitatively stronger degree in the South. The landowners especially struggled to keep racism alive. It was essential for their economic well-being. It brought the pressure of the entire white community to bear against Black labor. It helped block any alliance between Black agricultural labor and the poor white farmers against the larger plantation owners. It limited the bargaining power of Black laborers, whether agricultural workers in the fields or artisans in the city.

Blacks under Radical Reconstruction fought to end segregation in so far as it meant degradation for Blacks. They sought equal treatment on public transportation and at hotels, parks, resorts, etc. The property-owning whites were able to frustrate the Blacks through their power based on ownership. Thus the hotels refused to admit Blacks, or the railroads forced Blacks into segregated cars. The bourgeois wing of the Radical coalition refused to counter these racist practices effectively, though many of them violated laws enacted by the state governments.

The heritage of backwardness from slavery, especially that of racism, offered the newly triumphant industrial ruling class a powerful weapon for strengthening its domination. During the Civil War, racist ideology had hampered its advance; in fact, for the industrial capitalists it had become a question of life or death to counter racism and call upon the oppressed Afro-American people to aid in the desperate struggle against the slavocracy. After the war the industrial capitalists turned to the Afro-American people again to assure their rule nationally by consolidating their power in the South through Radical Reconstruction.

But the more Radical Reconstruction succeeded, the less necessary was the alliance with Blacks. The industrial capitalists wanted both governmental power and effective economic exploitation. The first aim required that the Afro-Americans be raised up, temporarily; the second that they be rechained. As the political threat of a West-South agricultural bloc waned, the thinking of the industrial capitalists and their political representatives underwent a change.

The rise of Radical Reconstruction had made of the South a great stage on which the major events were acted out according to a script written in the North. So too with the end of Radical Reconstruction.

6

The Industrial Capitalists Consolidate Their Victory

The Radical sweep in the elections of 1866 brought new power and prestige to the Republican Party. But the Radicals were far from homogeneous and the fruits of victory were not spread evenly among them. The three following currents can be distinguished:

1) A genuine bourgeois revolutionary current composed mostly of those who had participated in, or been strongly influenced by, the abolitionist movement. Among Northern whites, that movement had been preponderantly middle class. It had spread from the New England and Middle Atlantic states to the Midwest as the conflict with the slavocracy over the new territories grew. The newer adherents to abolitionism in the Midwest, unlike the Easterners, often had a touch of agrarian radicalism about them.

Many hard-core abolitionists held back when the Republican Party was formed because its program went no further than opposing the spread of slavery into the western territories. But others, and sympathizers of the movement in particular, joined the new party right off or gave it critical support. With the coming of the war, and then with the transformation of the war into a war against slavery, almost all abolitionists went into the Republican Party.

2) A second current consisted of former Whigs. The old Whig Party in the North had been preeminently the party of business and industrial development. After its demise many ruling class elements with manufacturing interests joined in the founding of the Republican Party. More followed as the party registered electoral successes. It was this current among the Radicals which most directly expressed the views of the industrial capitalists.

3) A very important third current consisted of machine politicians created by the growth of the Republican Party itself.

With the rapid expansion of federal power during the war and the centralization of the government apparatus for greater efficiency, a new layer of officials came into existence. By the end of the war this bureaucracy, appointed and controlled by the party, numbered more than 100,000. It constituted a powerful party machine in every Northern state.

Many individual Radicals were responsive to more than one of the above currents. Some switched their loyalties in the course of time. But the events following the Radical victory of 1866 revealed the persistence of these currents even though it may not be easy to pinpoint the position in them of each political figure throughout the period.

The idealistic, revolutionary current was led by such men as the Pennsylvania ironmaster and congressman Thaddeus Stevens, Midwestern congressman George W. Julian, Massachusetts senator Charles Sumner, and the famous abolitionists Wendell Phillips and Frederick Douglass. Others, like the 1848 German revolutionary Carl Schurz, Ohio senator Benjamin Wade, and General Rufus B. Saxton, military commander in South Carolina, should probably also be placed in this current.

The machine politicians are somewhat easier to categorize. Each state machine by its very nature had to create a top boss, an arbiter, to settle disputes within the bureaucracy. These machine bosses often had themselves sent to Congress, usually to the Senate, where they also functioned as part of a caucus in controlling the federal government. Outstanding among these were Roscoe Conkling, New York; Oliver Morton, Indiana; Simon Cameron, Pennsylvania; Zachariah Chandler, Michigan; John A. Logan, Illinois; and Matthew Carpenter, Wisconsin.

The ex-Whig current, which later acquired the name Halfbreeds, was the most responsive to the general needs of the capitalist class. These were the more moderate Republicans, though as their power grew in the second half of the 1870s, machine politicians and new "reform" politicians joined their ranks. In the 1860s William Seward and Salmon P. Chase, both of Whig background and former members of Lincoln's cabinet, were of this current. The young James A. Garfield and the older ex-Whig Rutherford B. Hayes, both to be future presidents, can be added to their number. Senator John Sherman of Ohio, who played a leading role in government finance during and after Reconstruction, also belongs in this category.

Senator James G. Blaine, a very influential figure, was a power in himself as head of Maine's Republican machine; at the same time he was responsive to the overall interests of the ruling class. Blaine was one of the first Republican politicians to envisage a future imperialist empire for the United States. His power was curtailed by the assassination of Garfield in 1881, over whom he had great influence, and his public reputation was clouded by rumors of corruption. As the Republican presidential candidate in 1884, he lost by a very narrow margin.

Lyman Trumbull, senator from Illinois, is difficult to place. He exhibited the idealism of the bourgeois revolutionaries and at the same time a "statesmanlike" attitude about stability in government. At times he was considered a moderate, at other times a Radical.

Almost every one of the above figures was, formally speaking, a Radical in 1866. But the Radical victory, which was a defeat for the most conservative "Lincoln Republicans," was really the victory of the machine politicians. The idealists occupied the front of the stage in the struggle for Radical Reconstruction, but they were not in command of the party. Soon they either had to adapt to the machine politicians or be pushed out of their positions of influence precisely at the moment when it seemed their program was beginning to triumph. The fact was, as we have seen, that the failure to institute land reform in the South had really limited the program of Radical Reconstruction to the consolidation of national political control by the industrial capitalists through the Republican Party. The machine had triumphed, not the revolutionaries or their policy.

Bureaucrats and Capitalists

The relationship between the industrial capitalists and their political arm, the Republican Party, evolved. The industrial capitalists had helped initiate and promote the Republican Party by taking a substantial part of the old Whig Party into the new formation. During the war they had supported its growth out of necessity, but were also quite pleased with the results. The Republican Party had led them to victory over the slavocracy, opened the West, set high tariffs, provided a national banking system, granted millions in dollars and land for railroads and other projects, and protected them from any and all enemies, ranging from English industrial might to the agrarian masses and industrial workers.

But capitalists and politicians, or government bureaucrats, are not one and the same. The master and the servant do not always have identical interests and can at times come into conflict. Capitalists depend on profit-making capital to maintain their power and privileges. Bureaucrats depend on their jobs or positions. Thus, they do not necessarily see eye to eye as to the purpose and course of government. To capitalists the government's task is to administer society so as to make it possible for them to engage in profitable business activity with a minimum of problems. This does not require any "illegal" conduct in most cases. On the contrary, part of the function of "law" is to create conditions that are conducive to profit-making, i.e., reduce to a minimum interference or obstruction due to turmoil or "lawlessness."

Capitalist privilege is protected by the repressive agencies of the state—the police, army, courts, and prisons—through their defense of private property. An individual capitalist can't be "fired" from his privileges while he retains his capital.

Bureaucrats, on the other hand, *can* be fired from their jobs and lose their privileged status. If removed from their positions, they may lose everything. Needless to say, bureaucrats seek to make sure their jobs are safe. Their first loyalty is to whoever can assure their continuity in office. In the 1860s and 1870s, election day could bring a complete turnover of jobs at the city, state, or federal level. The loyalty of the 100,000-strong bureaucratic army was to the political machine that assured their jobs, the Republican Party.

The second American revolution had created its political instrument to lead the struggle, the Republican machine. That instrument had to be given great power and thus considerable independence from direct control by the class it served. Its relative autonomy was strengthened after the Civil War by the self-financing of its campaigns.

Radical Reconstruction further reinforced its power. To Thaddeus Stevens and many other revolutionaries, as well as to the machine politicians, the ascendancy of the party was seen as a necessity. In arguing for Radical Reconstruction, Stevens had been completely frank: "*It would assure the ascendancy of the Union [Republican] party.* Do you avow the party purpose? exclaims some horror-stricken demagogue. I do. For I believe, on my conscience, that on the continued ascendancy of that party depends the safety of this great nation."[1]

After the victory of 1866, the Republican Radicals proceeded to impeach and try President Andrew Johnson, but failed to remove him from office by one vote. The Republican Party was so strong that it took the votes of all the Democrats plus seven defecting Republicans to save Johnson by that thin margin from the necessary two-thirds to convict in the Senate.

Again, the more idealistic Radicals had fought alongside the machine politicians in the impeachment of Johnson. But even at this early date, some leading capitalists were beginning to have second thoughts about the growing power of the Republican politicians. There was less enthusiasm for the removal of Johnson among capitalists than among party figures. This hesitancy was partly explained by the radicalism of Benjamin Wade, who, as president of the Senate, would have replaced Johnson if the latter were removed from office. Wade had favored land for Blacks and the right of women to vote and had expressed sympathy for workers and farmers. Capitalists like Jay Cooke and Hamilton Fish, solid Republicans, saw no reason to convict and dump Johnson only a few months before the presidential election, which would undoubtedly replace him anyway.

Much has been made of the fact that Senator Edmund Ross from Kansas cast the decisive vote. Ross, a strong Radical and a new arrival in the Senate, had been expected to vote for conviction. It is of more interest to note the failure of men like Lyman Trumbull of Illinois and William P. Fessenden of Maine to vote for conviction. Fessenden, an ex-Whig of high bourgeois standing, could be said to have been Senator Blaine's teacher. He stood against the pressure of the machine because he was more conservative and farsighted in protecting the interests of his class. Trumbull had some of the same perspicacity. In fact it was not in the interest of the ruling class to carry through the impeachment and conviction of Andrew Johnson. At the time, these backsliders on the vote were considered traitors to the party. But as the more conservative views of the ruling class came to prevail, they were gradually transformed into heroes.

The election of 1868 brought General Ulysses S. Grant to the presidency on the Republican ticket. Though a Democrat before the war, he ran in support of Radical Reconstruction. He had held a conservative position in 1865 regarding the South. And he had worked with President Johnson to some extent, even serving in his cabinet. His popularity as the victorious general in the war made him an excellent prospective candidate for either party, and both parties sought him as their standard-bearer.

Grant's advisors, consciously seeking to make him president, had him switch over to the Radicals when it became clear they were the vehicle for entering the White House.

Though a man of remarkable military talent and strength of character, as a politician Grant was pliable, ambitious, without a fixed ideology but of conservative inclination. He was a candidate suited to the needs of the machine. His electoral victory brought the influence of politicians like Morton, Conkling, Cameron, and Chandler into the White House.

The revolutionary elements fell by the wayside. Thaddeus Stevens died a few months before the 1868 elections. His last instructions were that he be buried in a Black cemetery so that in death, as in life, he could protest against racist discrimination. The fiery Radical Benjamin Wade was denied renomination for the Senate at the end of his term. Charles Sumner was pushed aside in party councils, eventually being relieved of his control of the influential Senate Foreign Relations Committee. Others, such as George W. Julian and Carl Schurz, found themselves on the outs with the machine politicians.

Conflict Over Division of the Spoils

Corruption in government, which had reached unprecedented heights during the war, continued and increased through the 1860s and 70s. Conflicts soon developed over division of the spoils. It was one thing when the Republican machine joined with the industrial capitalists to hand over the public lands of the West to the railroads, with the politicians cutting themselves in for a share. That was all right. When fortunes had been made during the war at the expense of working people and with the full backing of the government, or when officials took bribes to carry out certain requests of the new aristocracy of capital, that was understandable. But the machine became so powerful that it simply began to absorb too much government revenue for itself and began levying its own extralegal tax on the capitalists. This excessive corruption grew intolerable.

Everything had its price. Legal papers for shipping and importing, business licenses, and proposed legislation were placed on the auction block. Even elective posts, including judgeships and congressional seats, were up for sale. A head tax for the machine was placed on all government officials, usually a set percentage of their salaries. Many government functionaries had little time for their official jobs because the machine assigned them to party tasks.

It was in this period of history that politicians began to have the ill repute that has become a constant feature of American thinking. The price of a judgeship was set at $15,000. Interestingly enough, this was more expensive than a Congressional seat, which usually went for $4,000, while state legislature seats sold for only $1,500. In South Carolina, John J. Patterson, a Pennsylvania industrialist friendly with Thomas Scott, Lincoln's railroad czar, purchased a senatorial seat for $40,000.

At city and state levels, public works projects resulted in enormous losses owing to corruption, creating large municipal and state debts. Sometimes out-and-out counterfeiting of bonds led to large losses by capitalist investors.

It is estimated that approximately one-third to two-thirds of all federal tax revenue was lost through inefficiency and graft.[2]

Corruption verged on extortion from some capitalists. One example was the case of Phelps, Dodge and Company, which attempted to import $1.75 million worth of goods through the port of New York. The port was under the control of Chester A. Arthur, a machine politician who rose from the ranks and later would be president of the United States. Using a legal technicality, Arthur had the entire shipment held up until the company settled out of court. The end result was that the capitalists were forced to fork over $135,000 to the machine. Roscoe Conkling and Ben Butler collected $50,000 for "legal services" in the affair.

All this corruption led to governmental inefficiency and complications, often entailing outright losses to the capitalists. The Republican Party machine, a valuable tool of the revolution, had become a malignant growth endangering the class which led the revolution. It was necessary to bring it under control, to reduce it from an independently financed apparatus to a controlled and subordinate bureaucracy whose election campaigns would depend on contributions—made voluntarily—by the capitalists. It was necessary to increase the efficiency of government by cutting down the excessive corruption and separating the ranks of the governmental bureaucracy from the direct control of the political parties through a civil service reform.

These goals gradually became more and more popular among

members of the ruling class. Radical Reconstruction was identified with the Republican Party machine. Both seemed to bring endless turmoil and complications for the normal course of business. For reasons to be discussed further on, the original need for Radical Reconstruction in the eyes of the industrial capitalists began to fade. The struggle to tame the Republican machine became connected with the search for social stability, especially in the South.

Reform Campaign

Well before the majority of the industrial capitalists were prepared to take any decisive measures to bring the Republican Party machine under control, a reform movement developed. As is to be expected, the intelligentsia provided many of the first campaigners for reform. The middle-class abolitionists had anticipated the long-range requirements of rising industrial capitalism before the industrial capitalists had even dared to consider the idea that abolition of slavery would be in their own interests. Now a new reform movement arose that again was a forerunner of the needs of industrial capitalism.

This movement, however, was not associated with an oppressed layer of the population as abolitionism had been. The demand of the new reformers was not part of any social program for Blacks, workers, or farmers. It was a call for stability, tranquillity, and efficiency in the interest of capital. It sought to reorient America to make industrial capitalism work more efficiently and to end turmoil (i.e., class struggle) in the South.

This shift on the part of the middle-class intelligentsia reflected a more fundamental turn being made by the ruling class. The industrial bourgeoisie, regardless of its vacillations, cowardice, corruption, or criminal disregard for the lower classes, had nonetheless promoted social progress during the revolutionary upheaval. They had finally freed the slaves and made land in the Midwest available to white farmers. This had constituted an expansion of the bourgeois-democratic revolution. But now their aim was solely to consolidate their power. They sought no new alliance with the lower classes but wanted instead to rule more effectively over them and extract profits from their labor with as little social disturbance as possible.

The ruling class was turning against the ideals of its own revolution. The intelligentsia, like the topmost leaves of a tree, were the first to move in response to the new breeze beginning to blow.

These new reformers had various origins. An amazingly large number were former abolitionists. At a reform meeting in Cooper Institute in New York in the spring of 1872, observers noted that the audience was composed of the same "sober, thoughtful middle class" types that had gathered in the same rooms in earlier years to hear the abolitionists.[3] The rebellion within the Republican Party that this movement presaged is most closely associated with Carl Schurz. Schurz was a German who fought bravely in the Revolution of 1848 until the last barricades fell. His fame really grew afterwards when he reentered Germany clandestinely to break into jail and liberate his old professor and teacher of revolutionary ideals.

Coming to the United States in the 1850s, Schurz joined the antislavery struggle. He became associated with Lincoln during the 1860s and undertook various important governmental assignments. In 1865 he was asked by President Johnson to report on conditions in the South. Johnson was unaware that Schurz was already working for the Radicals, his trip being secretly financed by them.

Schurz became one of the period's most outspoken ideological radicals. He favored land reform in the South and at one point called not merely for the impeachment of Johnson but for his hanging. But as early as 1868, repelled by the corruption surrounding all Republican Party activity, he began to change. Speaking out against the corruption, he soon found himself isolated by the party machine. As his anger against the machine politicians grew, his interest in and support for Blacks in the South waned. He became sensitive to the complaints of the Southern Conservatives about the "excesses" of corruption and Republican Party abuses in general.

Schurz had been elected U.S. senator from Missouri in 1869 as a Radical. But he soon joined hands with another reform-minded Radical, B. Gratz Brown, to organize a split in the state's Republican ranks, creating a "Liberal" wing. With Schurz's support, Brown ran for governor in 1870 on a platform calling for civil service reform and for "pacification" and "stability" in the South. But both remained Republicans in their overall economic policies. The Conservatives in Missouri immediately noted the similarity of the Schurz-Brown program to their own and threw their weight behind the new movement. Brown defeated the

Radical Republican candidate by 40,000 votes, and with that election Radical Reconstruction ended in Missouri.

Joining Schurz and Brown in the Liberal Republican rebellion was Indiana's George W. Julian, who had possibly been the most radical member of Congress during the war. Julian had fought relentlessly for land for Blacks. He had proposed a Southern homestead act not only in the early 1860s but in 1866. He fought for the eight-hour day, women's suffrage, and better treatment of Indians.

An even better-known figure from the Senate's abolitionist ranks was Charles Sumner of Massachusetts. Sumner was more hesitant to make the break, his dedication to the Afro-American people being more genuine than that of most defenders of Radical Reconstruction. But after he was gradually pushed out of power by the Republican machine bosses he switched his support to the Liberals.

The influence of the Liberals grew and people joined the movement on a national scale in response to a call by Schurz issued in Nashville in 1871. The famous abolitionist editor Theodore Tilton, along with the more moderate editor of the *New York Tribune,* Horace Greeley, joined in New York. Charles Francis Adams and Henry Adams, the sons of Lincoln's ambassador to England, volunteered their journalistic talents, along with Whitelaw Reid, Horace White, Henry Watterson of the influential *Louisville Courier,* George William Curtis, editor of *Harper's Weekly,* and Murat Halstead of the *Cincinnati Commercial.* The poet-editor William Cullen Bryant and the progressive young president of Harvard University, Charles W. Eliot, also took up the cause.

The Massachusetts Bird Club, so called after its original organizer, Frank W. Bird, a small select circle of powerful Radicals, passed over to the Liberal camp en bloc. Members included Senators Sumner and Wilson along with Governor John A. Andrew and many wealthy personalities.

As the ranks grew, one of "the most striking features was the large number of free-soilers and founders of the Republican party among the bolters. . . ."[4] But the movement did not include all of the old abolitionists. Some, whose commitment to the ex-slaves was deeper, quickly saw the true nature of this trend and its social meaning for Blacks. The Liberal reform movement led, in effect, to a split in the ranks of the now unorganized remnants of the abolitionists. The American Anti-Slavery Society was formally dissolved in 1870, most members having become convinced that the passage of the Fifteenth Amendment guaranteeing the freedmen the right to vote had ended their task. This amendment, they declared in a resolution, was "the capstone and completion of our movement; the fulfillment of our pledge to the Negro race; since it secures to them equal political rights with the white race, or, if any single right be still doubtful, places them in such circumstances that they can easily achieve it."[5]

Such were the illusions in the magical power of the ballot entertained by the abolitionists. Even Wendell Phillips, who supported the Paris Commune a year later, joined Theodore Tilton in declaring that the Fifteenth Amendment would take the "Negro question" out of politics.

Soon after the Liberal reform movement began, however, Phillips, along with the grand old man of abolitionism, William Lloyd Garrison, protested against the turn of many of their former comrades away from the original commitment of support to the Afro-American people. Black abolitionists (the term having meaning only in an organizational sense, since all Blacks were abolitionists) had little trouble discerning the real nature of the Liberals. They chose to back the regular Republicans, the Stalwarts. Many were shocked to see abolitionist leaders with whom they had worked in the past and whom they admired, such as Charles Sumner, join the Liberal camp. Discussions on the new development took place throughout the Black community and a fairly solid consensus against the Liberals was established. Abolitionists like Wendell Phillips and Frederick Douglass and many Black leaders hated the corruption of the Republican machine and had little respect for Grant, but they regarded the Liberal development as a threat to the rights of Blacks.

Although the Liberal movement drew its main strength from the middle classes, leading capitalists supported it from the start. These included a fair number of rich men involved in international commerce, many of whom were not Republicans and thus were the most vulnerable to the demands of corrupt officials. As time passed, their ranks were swelled by a steady influx of converts from among the industrial capitalists as well.

As David Montgomery amply demonstrates in his treatment of the Liberals in *Beyond Equality*, "this new reform current regarded the lower orders of society with scorn and anxiety and sought its support from the top of the social ladder. It was, in a word, elitist."⁶ Among the new reformers were not only those against the Republican machine and Radical Reconstruction but some who opposed extension of the franchise to women and even argued that the universal male franchise was wrong and needed to be restricted by some sort of tax or property qualification.⁷

The Liberal movement also had many sympathizers who refused to break from the regular Republican ranks when a full split developed in 1871-1872. Henry Adams, George William Curtis, E.L. Godkin, Robert C. Winthrop, and others who sympathized with the Liberals nonetheless voted for Grant in 1872. Well-known politicians such as Garfield remained regular Republicans but sympathized with civil service reform. In this layer we have the beginnings of the current that became known as the Half-breeds, the name implying a foot in each camp, Stalwart and Liberal.

The Reform of the Democratic Party

Industrial capitalism was fast consolidating its dominion throughout the nation. While the reorganization of the governmental apparatus and the shift of economic power were going on in the South, dramatic changes were also taking place in the agricultural Midwest.

In Ohio and Michigan, for example, the value of manufactured products had by 1870 well exceeded that of agricultural commodities. In Wisconsin industrial production had almost caught up with agriculture. Railroads and banks dominated the region's economy and politics. Even some large-scale farming was beginning to appear alongside the small family-owned farm. Similar developments were unfolding in the Far West.

The Democratic Party, obviously, could not help but be affected by all of these developments. It too entered into a period of metamorphosis, casting off vestiges of the pre–Civil War days to adjust to the new era of industrial capitalism.

As we have seen, the rapid turn towards conservatism at the end of the war created a short-lived illusion that the South would return to the Union with its political structure essentially unchanged. Andrew Johnson's entry into the White House had reinforced this view. The Confederate leaders, irretrievably crippled by the war, turned to political remnants of the past to salvage what they could. The Eastern import-export capitalists, having conflicts with the industrial bourgeoisie, likewise turned to their traditional political vehicle, the Democratic Party. Reinforced by the farmers' fear of Eastern money, the old South-West-commercial alliance seemed to be a potential victor in the national elections.

The defeats of 1866 and 1868 shook the Democrats. The rise of Radical Reconstruction reflected—and reinforced—the real relationship of forces in the country. It was clear that Democratic Party politicians could not succeed if they continued to lean on the past—a past which had brought them power because it had given political expression to social forces which then had been dominant or at least on a par with industrial capitalism.

Internally the Democratic Party was racked by this and other contradictions. The appearance in its ranks of ex-Confederates making "Rebel" speeches served to strengthen its image of being against the new order and lessened the possibility of winning the support of capitalists or popular support in the North. The machine element in the party, the party politicians, instinctively wanted to rid themselves of the party's past image. As early as 1867 Charles A. Dana, editor of the *New York Sun,* a Republican who became a Democrat, called for a "new look." More importantly, the commercial capitalists of the East and the small but influential fraction of industrial capitalists who considered themselves Democrats had misgivings about that party's plebian, pro-agriculture and anti-industrial image.

It should be kept in mind that on the crucial question of money policies the commercial and industrial capitalists were in agreement against the farmers. In 1868 the capitalist-farmer economic conflict manifested itself inside the Democratic Party in a sharp struggle between the Western and Eastern wings. The Midwest politicians favored a soft money policy to appeal to the farm vote. The Eastern wing opposed them. A typically American political compromise was struck. The platform would include a call for soft money to garner votes, while the presidential candidate would be Horatio Seymour, a 100 percent hard-money advocate. What appeared to put the Democratic Party on record as a soft money party, in actuality placed party power against such a policy.

After the defeat in the 1868 elections a campaign began within the Democratic Party under the name "New Departure." Its goal was once and for all to make it clear that the party was no longer the same old Democratic Party. By 1871 even Clement L. Vallandigham, the best-known Northern "Copperhead" (a wartime epithet for Northerners who favored or were soft on the Confederacy), helped promote the New Departure. Resolutions declaring complete acceptance of the results of the war were adopted and widely publicized. Facilitating this turn was the growth of industrial capitalist influence in the top command of the party.

It is important to recall that the Eastern commercial and financial circles, which had inherited control of the party at the end of the war, had never been impelled into an "irrepressible conflict" with industrial capitalism such as that which destroyed the slavocracy. A tendency towards interlocking interests, investments, and influence developed between the two branches of capitalism. The general domination of industrial capitalism rapidly became an accepted fact in moneyed circles throughout the country. Capital from all sources poured into railroads and other enterprises offering a high return. Lines of differing economic interests within the ruling class became blurred and intertwined. Events moved rapidly to end the old division.

Most Republicans of conservative inclinations were persuaded to support the Radicals in the 1866 elections, but not all. Some moderates refused and instead went over to the Democrats. Among those "Lincoln Republicans" who went over to the Democratic Party with the rise of Radical Reconstruction were Chief Justice Salmon P. Chase and Senator James R. Doolittle of Wisconsin.

For many, the New Departure was not by itself convincing enough. But it gradually became clearer and clearer that on most crucial issues the Democrats were no longer essentially different from the Republicans or, more precisely, that their differences were more and more of a strictly tactical character. The Democratic Party was becoming an alternate expression of the same class interests as the Republicans.

The Southern allies of the Northern Democrats, the opponents of Radical Reconstruction, were also carefully explaining that they favored the growth of industry. Most of them avoided calling for soft money or an end to tariffs. What they really wanted was to bring industry south. They envisioned a "New South" as opposed to the "Old" strictly agricultural South. To achieve this they thought Radical Reconstruction should be ended so they would be able effectively to exploit the Black labor force.

While this process was unfolding within the Democratic Party, the ruling class effort to undercut the independence of the

Republican machine was also in progress. The two struggles intensified and became closely interrelated after two important events: in 1872 the Republicans suffered an important split, and in 1873 the country entered a depression.

The 1872 Elections

The Liberal rebellion rapidly turned into a political party on a national scale, splitting the Republicans. Though it had many famous and popular figures at the top, there was little if any organization at the precinct level. Nevertheless, in the 1872 elections the new party challenged the Stalwarts—who had renominated President Grant—with the famous editor Horace Greeley as its candidate. For vice-president the Liberals ran B. Gratz Brown, the ex-Radical governor of Missouri.

Their program called for "amnesty" for all ex-Confederates who were still prevented from voting and holding office. Most Confederates had already been pardoned, so the main role of the amnesty demand was to demonstrate their opposition to Radical Reconstruction in a veiled, defensive manner. The platform also called for civil service reform, hard money policies, and high tariffs. There was talk of possibly scaling down some of the excessive tariffs, but the Liberals remained solidly in the protariff camp. Though supporters of free trade had their hopes raised by the new movement, their policy was rejected.

In essence, the Liberals called for stability through efficient, honest government and ending the turmoil caused by Radical Reconstruction in the South. Occasionally their reform spirit cut deeper as when they proposed limiting the continued giveaways of land grants to the railroads.

Their opposition to Radical Reconstruction expanded into an anti-Black stance. For example, Schurz and Trumbull joined in efforts to block civil rights legislation—in order, as they explained, to further the campaign for amnesty.

The one-time abolitionist Horace Greeley toured the South in 1871 speaking in favor of industrialization and reconciliation. In the North he called for a better understanding of the South, the word "South" meaning, of course, Southern whites—mainly rich, conservative whites. Phrases like "home rule" for the South were now used more and more. These terms—"amnesty," "home rule," and "conciliation"—were code words for support to a Conservative triumph in the South.

Greeley blamed the poverty Blacks were suffering on themselves: "Had [Blacks] saved the money they have since 1865 spent in drink, tobacco, balls, gambling, and other dissipations they might have bought therewith at least Ten Million acres of soil in their respective states. . . ."[8]

Schurz revealed even more clearly the growing racism that accompanied the Liberals' movement against Radical Reconstruction. In the Senate he argued on the basis of social Darwinism that people from tropical lands were simply not assimilable into American society.

George W. Julian visited the South and was won over by the gracious manners of the leading Conservative whites. He wrote home that he was "in love with the South" and "more and more pleased with the refinement of the upper ten here, and the perfect ease and gracefulness with which they do everything in the department of social life."[9]

Just a few years earlier Greeley, Schurz, and Julian had been in the forefront of the struggles on behalf of Afro-Americans. During the war they had pressed for emancipation, then for Blacks' right to vote, even for land. Now the bourgeois revolutionary current was ebbing, its exponents were turning colors, a counterrevolution was in the air.

The New Departure campaign among the Democrats coincided with the rise of the Liberal Republicans. The Democratic Party tried to present itself as opposing the "excesses" of the revolution, Radical Reconstruction, and Republican corruption, but as loyal to the basic accomplishments of the new order under the slogan: "acceptance of the results of the war."

However, many ruling class figures and rank-and-file Republicans who were sympathetic towards the new reform campaign were on the whole still too suspicious of the Democrats to turn to them. The latter took two steps to try to deal with this problem.

The Democratic Party had corrupt machines within its own structure, the most notorious being Tammany's Tweed Ring in New York City. Joining in with the growing reform current, some of the richest (mainly Republican) capitalists in New York, such as William Astor, William E. Dodge, and Moses Taylor, got behind Democratic Party leader Samuel J. Tilden to smash Boss Tweed and his ring, even though Tilden himself had previously been on good terms with the Tweed machine. The fight raged through 1871 and 1872 until the Tweed Ring was finally broken. A few years later New York City was again under

Democratic Party machine rule. But the flagrant abuses associated with the Tweed Ring were ended. Of more importance, it made Tilden and the Democrats appear sincere in their call for reform.

Secondly, the Democrats decided not to enter the presidential race of 1872 but to throw their support to the Liberal Republican candidates. This decision has too often been passed off by historians as simply a tricky maneuver to improve the Democrats' own political fortunes. But this is an oversimplification. The split in the Republican ranks undoubtedly raised the electoral hopes of ambitious Democratic politicians, but something more fundamental was involved. The Liberals made it clear that in important respects they were still Republicans, in other words that they favored those socioeconomic policies that broadly differentiated all Republicans from those associated with the old-line Democrats. On economic matters the Liberal Republicans stood by traditional Republican pro-industrial policies. For the Democratic Party to endorse such a campaign shows how far it had evolved and the direction in which its leaders were driving it.

A small wing of the Democratic Party broke ranks and tried to run a straight out "Democratic" party ticket. The failure of the campaign to get off the ground further confirms the strength of the change that was going on. Bourgeois politics in America was being reduced to factions contending within the socioeconomic program of Republicanism.

Charles Sumner half apologetically explained his support of a ticket backed by the Democrats by noting their support of Republican policies. He argued, "The Democrats have accepted absolutely a Republican platform, with a life time Abolitionist candidate. This is a revolution; and my hope is to obtain from it a final settlement of all the issues of the war."[10]

The regular Republicans, the Stalwarts, were not readily going to allow the Liberal splitaway, backed by the Democrats, to break their hold on the government. They campaigned vigorously on the same old platform, accusing the Democrats of being "rebel Confederates in disguise." Horace Greeley, George W. Julian, Lyman Trumbull, and Charles Sumner were labeled traitors in the service of the ex-slaveowners who hoped that the war lost on the battlefield could now be won through the ballot box.

These machine politicians had their own reasons for supporting Radical Reconstruction. It not only permitted them the spoils of posts in the South and some graft—although the poverty of the region limited this—but it also helped them retain their power in Washington. While they had no sympathy for the idealistic or progressive aspects of Radical Reconstruction, they realized that the triumph of the Conservatives in the South would mean a weakening of their own position nationally. At least this was their view in the period 1867-1873.

While the Stalwarts were waving the "bloody shirt" and calling for protection of Blacks in the South, they were already bending to the pressures for "stability" exerted by the reform movement and its supporters in the ruling class. They tried to head off the civil service reform movement by proposing their own set of reforms. They even went so far as to set up a committee to investigate corruption—of course they stacked the committee so as to prevent any serious results.

More importantly they began to concede on Radical Reconstruction in indirect ways. To counteract the amnesty campaign, they proposed and passed their own amnesty bill during the 1872 election campaign. Charles Sumner, who in spite of his support of the Liberals was still genuinely concerned about the interests of Blacks in the South, tried to attach a civil rights rider to this amnesty bill. But Stalwarts and Liberals joined to defeat the civil rights amendment while passing the amnesty bill.

Much more crucial than the amnesty bill was the fate of legislation called the Ku Klux Act. In 1871 an act had been passed to give the necessary teeth to measures for the protection of Blacks against terrorist attacks. The section which permitted the effective use of force against the terrorists expired in 1872. The Stalwarts refused to renew it. While waving the "bloody shirt" with one hand, they were capitulating on Radical Reconstruction with the other. While they wanted the votes of Blacks in the South, they did not want to lose the support of ruling class elements in the North who were developing second thoughts about Radical Reconstruction. Thus they began the policy of vacillation which so weakened the Radical Reconstruction governments.

Some historians have discovered in the personal correspondence of several Stalwarts expressions of racial hate at the same time that they were proclaiming themselves for the defense of Blacks in campaign speeches. In a letter to his wife, for example, Benjamin Wade urged her to remove the Black servants and hire whites because he was "sick of Niggers."[11] Senator Howe from Wisconsin recalled that the war was not "fought for the nigger." Another wrote after the 1872 campaign, "Hard times and heavy taxes will make them wish the nigger—the everlasting nigger—were in hell or Africa."[12]

122   *Racism, Revolution, Reaction*

The Stalwarts had a strong slogan in 1872, directed primarily to the ruling class. It was simply "Let well enough alone." The country was enjoying prosperity, business was good and profits were high. Why experiment?

Most capitalists who were sympathetic to civil service reform or were beginning to question or oppose Radical Reconstruction still felt hesitant about making any major change. The desire not to disturb the current prosperity proved to be a critical factor in the 1872 election campaign. That consideration, combined with the uneasiness over the heavily intellectual, middle-class composition of the Liberal Republicans' top command, served to keep most capitalists behind the Stalwarts.

The result was a resounding victory for Grant, who garnered 3,597,000 votes to 2,833,000 for Greeley, who died shortly after the election. Having suffered what was generally considered a devastating defeat, the Liberal Republicans collapsed as an organized national party. The battle was lost, but most Liberals were unaware of how much progress they had made in winning the war for "reform."

The Liberals now either went back to working within the Republican Party, where a new current—the Half-breeds—was growing in response to the reform campaign, or, more commonly, joined the Democrats.

The latter had a party structure down to the grass roots level, precisely what the Liberal Republicans had lacked. With the defeat of Greeley, the Democrats appeared to be a much more realistic vehicle for the struggle against the Republican machine. Thus the Liberals served as a bridge for a sizable passage of Republicans into the Democratic Party. These included George W. Julian and Lyman Trumbull.

The Panic of 1873

The years 1865 to 1873 had seen a general condition of prosperity. In 1873 the United States entered a depression, which lasted until 1879. The House of Jay Cooke, the banker-financier of the Civil War and a supporter of the Stalwarts, collapsed, dragging hundreds of others down with it. Five thousand businesses failed in the last three months of 1873. Unemployment grew sharply. Workers' pay dropped, over 37 percent according to one estimate. Prices for farm products plummeted, leaving millions of small farmers in severe economic straits.

Farmers had already begun to protest excessive railroad

charges. They had organized associations in the late 1860s which now grew into a sizable movement. By 1873 the farmers were ready to rebel politically, but could find no vehicle since neither major party offered them an alternative.

The anti-agriculture policies of the New Departure had lessened the Democrats' appeal to farmers. At the same time, farmers who had become staunch supporters of the Republican Party grew more and more disenchanted with its policies. The Homestead Act, which was supposed to give the poor farmer a chance, was being abused by corrupt politicians. Rich speculators, along with the railroads, were taking the best land. The statistics of 1890 would reveal the final results. Forty-eight million acres had gone to homesteads, only one-third of what was given to the railroads.

After the collapse of the Liberal Republican Party following the 1872 elections, a somewhat similar current of third partyism began to appear in the Midwest, arising from a combination of farmer unrest and sentiment for civil service reform. The groups making up this current were primarily oriented to local elections in 1873; by 1874 some ran candidates for statewide office. They called themselves the Reform Independent or Anti-Monopoly parties.

These parties were half Liberal Republican and half agricultural-populist in character. Their programs included sections of the 1872 Liberal program and also farmers' demands. Thus, they would run on a program calling for civil service reform but also placing great emphasis on limiting land grants to railroads as well as other restrictions. The question of hard vs. soft money was not easily resolved. Those most influenced by the Liberal Republican reform forces favored hard money, while many of the farm forces favored soft money.

Because of wide farmer support, these formations registered rather surprising successes in the elections at the county and occasionally at the state level. In areas where the Republicans were deeply entrenched or where the local Democrats were under farmer influence and had become somewhat disillusioned with their own national organization, the Democratic Party backed these third party candidates. Thus the challenge of 1872 was being repeated with more success at the local level in the Midwest.

But the two components, Liberal reformers and farmers, though they had some points in common, really represented two conflicting class interests that could not long coexist. Consequently, these hybrid formations soon entered a crisis, with the farmers splitting away to support the soft money "Greenbackers" and, in the process, creating the first strictly populist-farmer party. The rise of such a party is in itself proof of the Democrats' turn away from their pro-agricultural past.

The Greenback Party in 1876 fielded its first presidential candidate, Peter Cooper, the social reformer and philanthropist, who received a little more than 80,000 votes. But in 1878, under the impulse of the depression, over a million votes were cast for Greenback candidates, fourteen of whom were elected to Congress. With the return of prosperity in 1879 the party's fortunes declined rapidly, leading to its dissolution in 1884.

In the cities, the working class faced a grim situation. The standard of living had risen after the war but then went into a decline. Strikes began to spread until the wave of militant struggles in 1877, led by the railroad workers, swept the country. The militia and other armed units were used to put down the workers' uprisings, which in some places verged on insurrection. Federal troops were sent to West Virginia, Maryland, Pennsylvania, and Illinois. In a number of areas the forces of law and order lost control of cities. The militancy of the workers so terrified the ruling rich that directly afterward they embarked on a program of building armories, fortress-like structures which are still an architectural feature of American cities. Carl Schurz now added to his program of conciliation with the South the need of a large standing army to crush strikes.

In the South during this period, Black labor continued to use its democratic rights wherever it could to fight for better conditions.

The rulers were now beset by struggles on many fronts: the strikes of workers in the Northern cities, the farmers' political actions in the Midwest, the guerrilla warfare of the Native Americans in the Far West, and the political and economic struggle of Blacks in the South. Restoration of stability became the central aim of the ruling class.

By this time industrial capitalism's old fear of the Democratic Party had been allayed. It no longer saw in the Democrats the pre–Civil War opponent it had once fought. Moreover, thanks to Radical Reconstruction, there was no longer anything to fear politically in the South. The Southern Conservatives, as well as the Radicals, were behind industrial capitalism, but Conservative rule held out the promise of social and political stability.

As Kenneth Stampp explains in his *Era of Reconstruction*, "since southern conservatives were being converted to the gospel of a 'New South' which would emphasize commerce and industry, they could now be relied upon to give northern businessmen a friendly welcome. Radical reconstruction was then not only not essential, it was a nuisance."[13]

Under these conditions the toleration of the capitalist class for further abuses by the politicians rapidly eroded. Whereas in 1872 only some of the capitalists had been persuaded to support the Liberal Republicans, a steady stream now joined the campaign for civil service reform and the ending of Radical Reconstruction.

Early in the depression, the boards of trade (the forerunners of today's chambers of commerce) in Chicago, Detroit, Philadelphia, New York, Cincinnati, Kansas City, and Burlington, Iowa, urged an end to the "troubles" disturbing commerce. Those calling for "conciliation" with the Southern Conservatives now included hardcore Republican capitalists such as William E. Dodge, Theodore Roosevelt, Sr., and John Jacob Astor, as well as the banking firms of Brown Brothers and Company; Drexel, Morgan and Company; and J. & W. Seligman in New York. In Philadelphia, businessman John Wanamaker, banker Anthony J. Drexel, and publisher Henry C. Lea joined with their fellow capitalists in New York as well as others throughout the land in supporting this call.

By the elections of 1876 the trend was firmly established. Famous Republicans like John Jay, the former abolitionist; Merchants' Bank president Jacob M. Vermilye; and United States Trust Company president John A. Stewart sponsored a meeting of bankers on Wall Street that urged civil service reform and conciliating the "South."

By 1880 the process encompassed the top figures of the ruling class. Those favoring strong civil service reforms now included in their ranks Jay Gould, who controlled the Union Pacific Railroad; Chauncey Depew, manager of the Vanderbilt family's New York Central Railroad; John D. and William Rockefeller of Standard Oil; and Levi P. Morton, reputedly the richest banker next to Morgan.

Demands for bringing the machine under control were widely raised in the wake of the Credit Mobilier exposures in 1872, one of the greatest political corruption scandals in U.S. history. This front corporation had been set up by those in control of the Union Pacific Railroad to siphon off the 20 million acres of land and $60 million in funds that Congress had voted the UP for railroad construction. To approve the steps in the swindle and coverup, judges and congressmen had been bribed wholesale with Credit

Mobilier stock. Among those implicated were the outgoing vice-president, Schuyler Colfax; the incoming vice-president, Henry Wilson; and Speaker of the House James G. Blaine. Though the Republican machine was able to protect its members from serious penalties, the scandal had an important effect on the struggle between the capitalist class and its runaway political machine. More and more Republican politicians now found it expedient to desert the machine and campaign for reform. In return they received support from ruling class elements. Leading politicians touched by the brush of scandal, among them Garfield and Blaine, moved in this direction.

The Whiskey Ring, which had diverted huge sums from tax revenue to the Republican Party, was broken in 1875. Secretary of War Belknap resigned in 1876 one jump ahead of impeachment. Exposure of corruption reached so high that Grant's cabinet presented a dizzying spectacle of resignations and appointments, with only Secretary of State Hamilton Fish remaining permanently untouched by scandal. Eventually the Republican state machines were challenged and even New York's leading Stalwart, Roscoe Conkling, was defeated.

In 1880 a heated battle for control of the Republican Party revolved around selection of the presidential nominee. The defeat of Grant's bid for a comeback nomination and a third term, and the choice of James A. Garfield instead, confirmed the triumph of the Half-breeds over the Stalwarts. In an effort to restore party harmony the winners gave the vice-presidential nomination to Chester A. Arthur. As Collector of the Port of New York, Arthur was the party's key patronage dispenser and a vassal of the corrupt Conkling machine.

A few months after Garfield's inauguration a crazed party rank-and-filer, who had been denied a federal job by the Half-breed reformers, approached Garfield in a train station and shot him. The assassin cried out: "I am a Stalwart and Arthur is president now."

But the assassin's bullet could not change the relationship of forces that had developed. Arthur proceeded to carry out the reformers' program, even helping to imprison some of his former fellow grafters.

The struggle inside the Republican Party raged from 1873 until 1884, when the machine was broken and the party's self-financing ended, forcing it to depend thenceforth on capitalist contributions.

With each passing year after 1873 more and more capitalists went over to the Democrats as an alternative to the Republican machine. By 1876, most historians agree, there was no essential difference between the two parties. Stampp writes, "Samuel J. Tilden, the Democratic presidential candidate in 1876, was a wealthy, conservative New York corporation lawyer, thoroughly 'sound' on monetary, banking, and fiscal policy, in no respect unfriendly to business interests. Which ever way the presidential election of 1876 had gone, these interests could hardly have lost."[14] Ironically, during the 1876 elections George W. Julian and Carl Schurz, both with the same program and having been bedfellows in the Liberal movement of 1872, were contending for the same post. Each hoped to be appointed secretary of the interior—Julian as a Democrat, Schurz as a Republican. But the Democrats did not gain the support of the majority of the capitalist class as an alternative until 1884. After that date capitalists went back and forth between the two parties, frequently giving financial aid to both.

It had been in 1874 that, riding the wave of discontent caused by the depression, the Democrats for the first time since the Civil War won a majority in the House of Representatives. Added to the increased strength of the Democrats was the growing wing within the Republican Party that favored terminating Radical Reconstruction. By this time only the Stalwarts—for strictly machine interests—stood as defenders of Radical Reconstruction within the government.

The masses presented a somewhat different picture. There was still broad sympathy for the rights of Southern Blacks. That is proven by the effectiveness of the Republican campaign technique of waving the bloody shirt. It was used successfully to win elections well into the 1880s, after Radical Reconstruction had ended. The success of the bloody shirt tells us a great deal about the real mood among the masses.

Just as Stalwarts who waved the bloody shirt and defended Radical Reconstruction for party ends cared little about the fate of Blacks, so the Half-breed reformers who opposed Radical Reconstruction would also turn to the bloody shirt in order to get elected. Garfield, a Half-breed writing privately about another Half-breed, Ohio senator John Sherman, said, "I have never been more disgusted with Sherman than during this short session. He is very conservative for five years and then fiercely radical for one. This is his radical year which always comes before the

Senatorial election. No man in the Senate has talked with so much fierceness as Sherman."[15] But Garfield himself resorted to the same duplicity in order to win elections.

As we have seen, the ruling class in the period between 1868 and 1872 began to have doubts about Radical Reconstruction. After 1873 a decisive turn took place against the continuation of the Radical regimes in the South. Fundamental to this change was the conviction within the Northern ruling class that the Southern Conservatives did not represent the pre–Civil War Southern ruling class but rather the selfsame socioeconomic forces as itself. This conclusion was based not only on Southern statements and claims but on concrete evidence. Events in the state of Virginia served as a test case.

The history of Reconstruction is complicated in that each Southern state went along its own particular path of evolution. The case of Virginia is of special interest because it telescoped into one year a process which took up to ten in other states.

The first elections in Virginia under Radical Reconstruction brought victory to the Conservatives. The Republicans had split into Radicals and moderates. The moderates then formed a bloc with the Conservatives which resulted in the election in 1869 of Gilbert C. Walker, a carpetbagger Republican banker, as Conservative governor. The new Virginia government was accepted back into the Union in 1870 by Congress, although many Republican politicians were displeased by the results.

Virginia's Conservatives were controlled by the railroad interests. The state government proceeded to sell the state-owned railroad lines to Northern railroads at give-away prices. The capitalists in the North could find no complaint with this Conservative government, although it supported the Democratic Party nationally. It certainly did not manifest the antebellum political opposition to the economic needs of industrial capitalism.

The Virginia Conservatives at first were cautious with Blacks because of the mood existing in the country as a whole. Blacks were permitted many formal rights until pressure from the North was eased and an openly repressive stance could be taken.

Thus, Virginia, along with border states such as Missouri, Kentucky, and Tennessee, played an important role in helping to convince the Northern capitalists that it was not contrary to their economic interests to allow the Conservative faction in the South to exercise governmental power.

The Civil War became a war for liberation as Blacks were armed. In this 1863 battle a former slave captured his master.

Blacks registering to vote in Richmond, Virginia, after the war.

RADICAL REPUBLICANS. Top row: Frederick Douglass, abolitionist leader; Thaddeus Stevens, Pennsylvania manufacturer and leading revolutionary in Congress. Bottom row: Mississippi Senator Blanche K. Bruce, only Black elected to a full term (1875-81) until 1966; Charles Sumner, leader of Radicals in the Senate.

Top: Blacks of all ages and both sexes learning to read in Vicksburg, Mississippi. Their teacher is one of the many Northern women who helped start public education in the South under Radical rule.
Bottom: White terrorists burning down a Freedmen's Bureau school in Memphis, Tennessee, in 1866.

Top and middle: Roscoe Conkling, Zachariah Chandler, Oliver P. Morton, and Benjamin Butler were Radicals who rose to power in the Republican machine. Bottom: Carl Schurz and George W. Julian were extreme Radicals, then Liberals, then Democrats.

Top: Radical members of the South Carolina legislature. Bottom: Pinckney B.S. Pinchback of Louisiana, only Black ever to serve as governor; Julia Hayden, Black teacher murdered by White League in Tennessee.

A GRAND MASS MEETING

SIXTH WARD

THE WORKINGMEN SAVED THE COUNTRY IN WAR, THEY WILL RULE IT IN PEACE.

OF THE
UNITED LABOR PARTY!

WILL BE HELD

ON FRIDAY EVENING, OCT. 19, 1877

AT THE

COR. of FOURTH AND BRANCH STS.

Rise in your might, irrespective of the former Parties, and throw off the shackles of bondage! Rally in defence of your Rights! Come from your work-shops, hand in hand, and overthrow the non-producing class that now govern you. Earnestly labor for your whole Ticket, without money or price, and thereby place your fellow-workmen in the Councils of the Nation.

Above: A sample of the upsurge in labor struggles in 1877.

Facing page: PRESIDENTIAL POLITICIANS.
Top row: Andrew Johnson tried to unite Conservatives and old-line Democrats against Radicals; Horatio Seymour, last of the old-line Democrats, ran in 1868; Ulysses S. Grant brought Stalwart machine to power in 1868 and 1872.
Middle row: Horace Greeley led attack on Stalwarts, Radicals as 1872 Liberal candidate; Rutherford B. Hayes, "Half-breed" reformer, allowed last Radical regimes to fall; he opposed Samuel J. Tilden, first "New Departure" Democrat, in 1876.
Bottom row: Half-breed James A. Garfield was assassinated by a crazed Stalwart; Chester A. Arthur, a Stalwart himself, carried out reformers' program; General Winfield Scott Hancock, who presided over massacres of workers and Indians, won Democratic nomination in 1880.

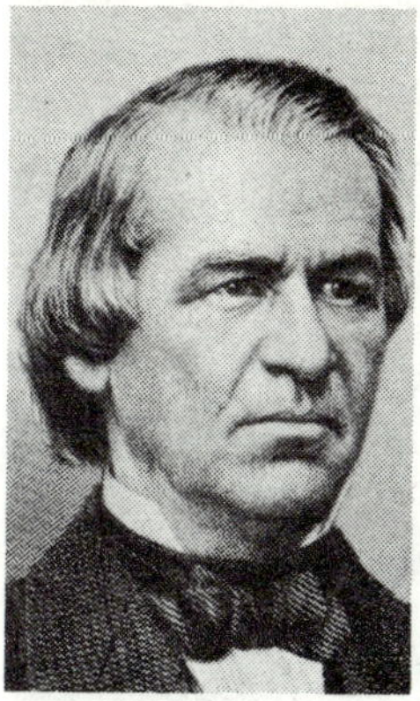
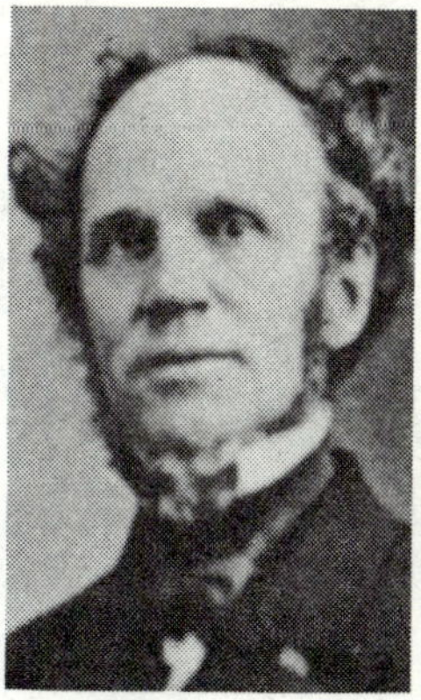
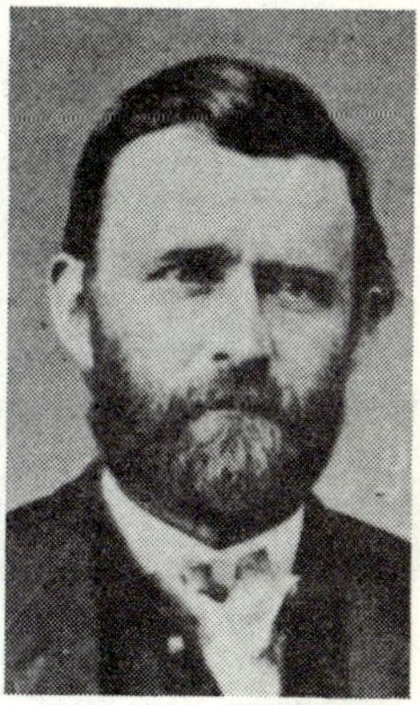
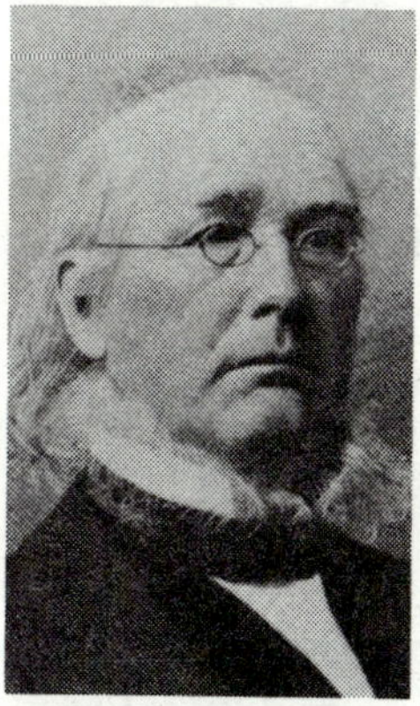
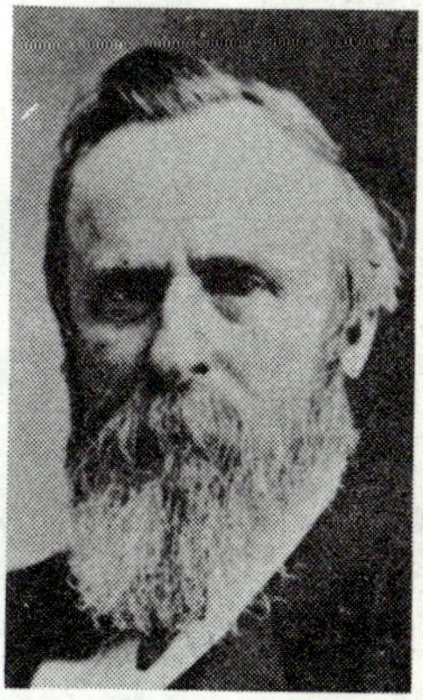
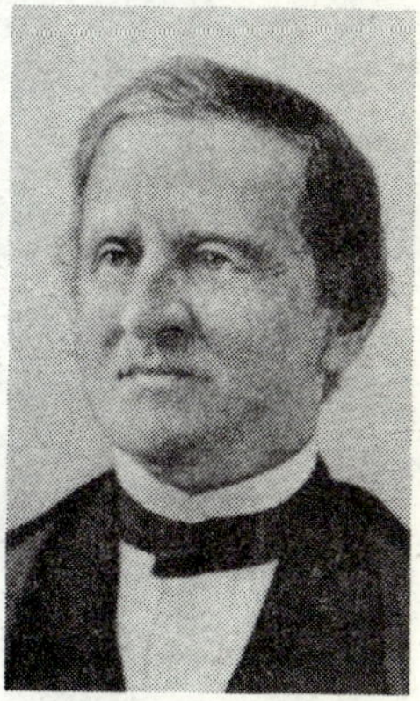
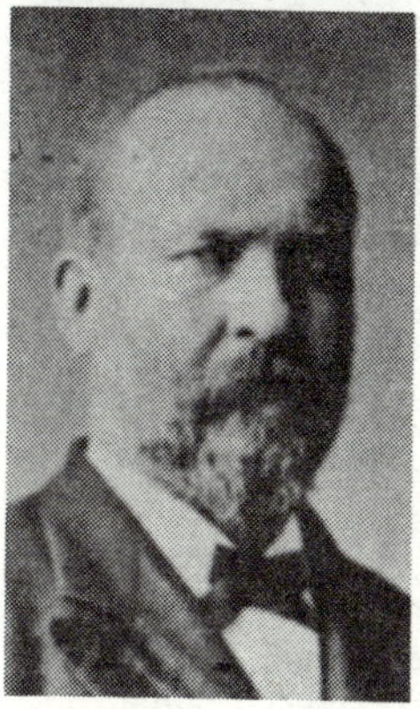
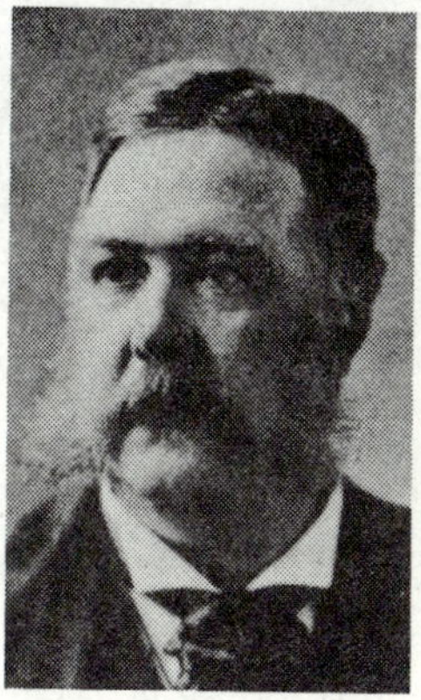
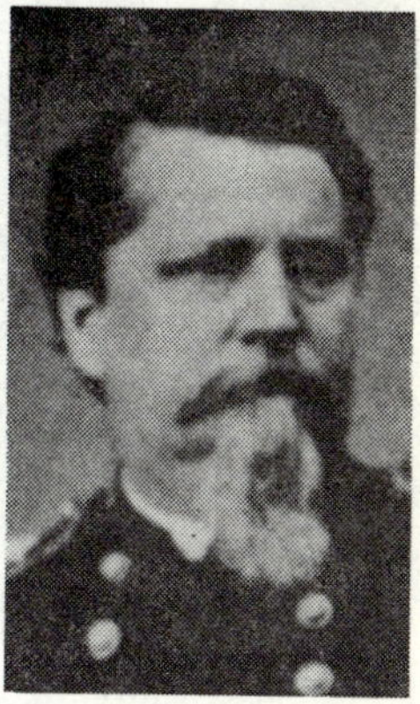

CONSERVATIVES. John B. Gordon of Georgia; Wade Hampton of South Carolina; John C. Brown of Tennessee; L.Q.C. Lamar of Mississippi.

White League army parades triumphantly in Lafayette Square, New Orleans, January 1877, as federal forces prepare to abandon Radical government of Louisiana.

SOUTHERN RADICALS. John R. Lynch, Adelbert Ames of Mississippi; R.H. Cain, Robert K. Scott of South Carolina.

7

Counterrevolution— the Mississippi Model

The turn of the Northern ruling class away from Radical Reconstruction had an immediate and deep impact in the South. The Republican Party split in every state where the Radicals were still in power. The splits reflected the conflicting class interests within the Radical coalition: on one side stood Black labor and on the other Northern industrial capitalism.

From the very start, Southern Conservatives had tried to work with moderate Republicans, hoping to convince the bourgeois wing of the Radical coalition to modify—if not eventually to end—Radical Reconstruction. After 1872 such cooperation increased, while some wealthy Radicals passed over to the Conservatives.

Even before 1872, the divisions in the Republican ranks and white terrorism had brought about the downfall of Radical Reconstruction in such states as Georgia and Tennessee. However, the states that were crucial for the Afro-American people were those where their strength was so great that it would be extremely difficult to end Radical Reconstruction. In Mississippi, South Carolina, Louisiana, and Florida, for example, Blacks either were an absolute majority of voters or could be assured of a majority with only a small fraction of the whites supporting them.

But the change in mood in the Northern ruling class had repercussions even in these states, as well as the others. In Louisiana, the Radical governor, Henry C. Warmoth, supported the Liberal Republicans and started working with the Conservatives. In Mississippi, Governor James L. Alcorn did the same. In South Carolina, a more complex set of circumstances led to the same result with Governor Daniel H. Chamberlain collaborating with local Conservative forces. In each case, under the impact of events in the North, top leadership elements of the Radical governments either went over to the "reform" pro-Conservative forces or began collaborating with them.

As in the other states, there was a deep division in the Republican organization in Florida. Here, however, the rift had existed from the start, and the moderate wing of the Republicans was able to remain dominant with the backing of the local federal commander and local men of wealth.

Throughout the camp of the opposition, the Northern political events of 1872 and after brought nothing but jubilation. The Conservatives sensed immediately that the tide was turning and they now began to campaign not to modify Radical Reconstruction but to overthrow it. Under the slogans of "home rule" and "white supremacy," the Conservative opposition to Radical Reconstruction now sought to actively mobilize the white population to smash the Radical regimes. The counterrevolution constituted a new class alliance: industrial capitalists and white farmers against Black labor.

The slogan of "white supremacy" was clearly directed at racist sentiments stemming from slavery days; the demand for "home rule" was a demagogic appeal which may be compared to the anticapitalist and antimonopoly slogans raised in this century by fascists to dupe and mobilize the lower middle classes. In the end the fascists turned out to be in the service of the very interests they denounced. So it was largely with the Southern counterrevolution. It was aimed not at ending the power of Northern industrial capitalism over the South but at changing the manner of its rule. Yet the poor whites thought their struggle was going to "free" the South of Northern domination.

The Northern industrial ruling class had turned against Radical Reconstruction and now wanted a change. This was not so easy to bring about, however. It is difficult to reverse political developments that have set masses of people into motion. Radical Reconstruction had done precisely this. A whole governmental apparatus had come into existence that was based on keeping the Radicals in power. Blacks had organized and, in spite of all difficulties, represented a powerful defense of the Radical regimes, a defense that seemed unbreachable in Mississippi and South Carolina.

The New Democrats

With the new impulse given for the overthrow of Radical Reconstruction, the name "Democrat," which had been seriously tarnished, began to be revived. While the Democratic Party had been socially undermined and weakened organizationally as the old planter influence declined, some of its traditions nevertheless still exerted great influence in the Conservative camp.

Some party structure doubtlessly survived and many individuals continued to regard themselves as Democrats. Under the Radical regimes, however, they became part of the general Conservative opposition to Radical Reconstruction. Within this bloc the title "Democrat" became associated with the most hardened opponents of Radical Reconstruction, those elements willing to take decisive steps. Generally it was applied to those who wanted to engage in a direct struggle rather than to collaborate with the moderate Republicans, and to those most vehemently for "white supremacy."

As the campaign for the overthrow of the Radical regimes built up steam, the traditions associated with the Democrats took on increasing importance. The "rebel yell," racism, and plebian demagoguery to mobilize the counterrevolution, in particular the poorer whites, came back into prominence. But they were now being employed in the service of industrial capitalism, of policies diametrically opposed to those of the antebellum Democrats.

While the name "Democrat" was reviving, its original meaning was being buried deeper than ever in the transformation sweeping the nation. From one coast to the other, from the Northern Democratic Party to the controlling interests of the anti-Radical camp in the South, the days of the old pro-agricultural Democrats were gone with the wind and the new era of industrial capitalism was triumphant.

But the illusions of the poorer whites were an important factor in their mobilization. They were convinced that the old Democrats were rising once again. It is no coincidence that the years 1872 to 1877 saw the development of some sort of third, profarmer party in every Midwestern state but that there was little support in the South for such formations until Radical Reconstruction ended. The Southern small farmers were caught up in the Democrats' struggle for "home rule" against the Republican "carpetbaggers," while many of their Midwest counterparts were rapidly recognizing that both major parties were essentially the same.

The more sophisticated counterrevolutionaries called themselves Redeemers. They were "redeeming" their states from Northern carpetbag misrule, returning to normalcy, to "home rule."

Although the organizations that overthrew Reconstruction were often officially named Conservative, the demagogic value of the term Democrat was such that it eventually came to prevail. Another factor favoring this was the existence of the Democratic Party in the North. In Alabama for thirty years after the end of Radical Reconstruction the official name of the Redeemers' party was "Conservative and Democratic."

The course of the counterrevolution was quite different in each state. Mississippi's history provides a good example of the dynamic of the class struggle which led to the fall of Radical Reconstruction.

With the passage of the Radical Reconstruction acts, a moderate military commander unsympathetic to the Radical legislation was sent to Mississippi to put it into effect. The result was that the first attempt to enact a new state constitution failed to gain the approval of the voters. A more radical commander, Adelbert Ames, son of a New England abolitionist family and son-in-law of Massachusetts Stalwart senator Ben Butler, was then sent in. New elections were held and a slightly modified version of the constitution was adopted overwhelmingly.

Two slates were entered in the ensuing elections for the state government. That of the Radicals was headed by James L. Alcorn, the candidate for governor. Alcorn was a former slaveowner of wealth. He had owned over a hundred slaves and an estate worth $250,000. A Whig, he had opposed secession. Once the war began, however, he offered his services to the Confederacy and served in the army as a brigadier general. At the end of the war, he supported the first state government set up in 1865 under President Andrew Johnson's reconstruction plan and was sent by it to the United States Senate. But like the other Southern representatives and senators at that time, he was not seated. With the advent of Radical Reconstruction, he joined the Republican Party and advocated accepting the results of the war.

The Conservatives, the opponents of Radical Reconstruction, ran a slate under the designation of National Union Republican.

Their candidate for governor was a Northern carpetbagger, Judge Louis Dent, President Grant's brother-in-law.

Here we see the legend of the struggle between carpetbaggers and ex-slaveowners in reverse. An ex-slaveowner and Confederate general leads the Radicals while a carpetbag Republican leads the Conservatives.

Mississippi was not the only state in which an ex-Confederate led the Radicals. We have already noted that in Virginia a carpetbag Northern banker led the Conservative forces to victory. In fact, the Radical Congress in Washington, D.C., had to pass several acts of amnesty in 1868 in order to make eligible for office a thousand ex-Confederates who, as ex-Whigs or new converts, were ready to help build the new order. These included the first Reconstruction governor of North Carolina, W.W. Holden; a Radical governor of South Carolina, Franklin J. Moses; the Radical Reconstruction governor of Georgia, R.B. Bullock; also Joseph Brown, Georgia's wartime governor.

Leading advocates of the new industrial capitalist order were to be found in both the Radical and Conservative camps. As Alcorn himself said, "The 'old master,' gentlemen, has passed from fact to poetry."[1]

Alcorn, pardoned in time, swept the elections by winning 90 percent of the Black voters, a majority by themselves, and 15 to 20 percent of the whites. But no sooner were the Radicals in office than the different orientations of the wealthy whites, who dominated the party, and the Blacks, who made up the overwhelming majority of the rank and file, revealed themselves. Underlying the conflict were the land and labor questions, but the concrete form it took was a fight for control of posts. Alcorn consciously limited the number of positions held by Blacks. Blacks were not allowed a majority on any city council although they made up the majority in many cities. In the boards of aldermen of only two towns, Coffeeville and Greenville, were there Black majorities. In all of Mississippi only one Black mayor, Robert H. Wood of Natchez, was placed in office by the Radicals under Alcorn.

After the split within the Northern Republican Party in 1872, a parallel process developed in the Mississippi party. In 1873 Alcorn led a faction that split the Republicans. This group included many upper class whites who supported the "reform" movement. This "reform" faction became a bridge for the crossing over of bourgeois elements and some poorer whites from the Radicals to the Conservative opposition.

The Radical military commander, now U.S. senator from Mississippi, Adelbert Ames, took up the fight against Alcorn within the Republican Party. Ames's overall economic views were not essentially different from those of Alcorn, but as a politician closer to the Stalwarts he continued to support Radical Reconstruction. The Conservative opposition to the Radicals now regrouped behind Alcorn under the official designation of the Republican Party of Mississippi. In 1873 Alcorn ran for governor against Ames but was decisively beaten. The number of Black officeholders now increased somewhat, but not to anywhere near their proportion of the population.

The passage of Alcorn and his supporters to the Conservative camp had a fundamental sociopolitical significance: the Radical coalition of the industrial capitalists and Black labor had come to an end. This outcome in Mississippi was the end product of the developments in the North. The 1873 depression had begun and the national campaign for stability was gaining momentum. However, governmental power in Mississippi was still in the hands of the political apparatus created by Radical Reconstruction.

The Black population—the majority—and a small group of white supporters, some of whom like Ames were associated with the Republican machine in the North, still upheld Radical Reconstruction, meaning democratic juridical rights for Blacks. But the relationship of class forces was now becoming unfavorable. The Conservatives, sensing the change in the North, became bolder. Terrorism began to revive as the more determined elements in the Conservative camp, the "Democrats," came to the fore.

Forms of Terrorism

Violence of a terrorist nature against Blacks existed from the end of the war and throughout Radical Reconstruction. But its different phases and forms have not often been adequately noted. Yet the changing forms of violent opposition to the rights of Blacks are important in revealing the nature and class basis of the final overthrow of Radical Reconstruction.

Under slavery, whites had been organized by districts into "patrols" to maintain a continuous vigilance against the slave population. With the end of the Civil War and the disbanding of the Confederate army the landowners instinctively turned to patrol-type organizations to fight Black labor, now emancipated. The most famous terrorist group, the Ku Klux Klan, arose in 1865. It spread throughout the South using the methods carried over from slavery.

The goal of these first organizations was to force Blacks into a labor caste, somewhere between chattel slaves and free but propertyless laborers. In essence, it was an attempt to establish a peonage system. The Black Codes written by the first Southern governments established in 1865 recognized the end of chattel slavery, the direct ownership and buying and selling of Black labor, but established guidelines for a caste labor system.

The initial postwar terrorism aimed at enforcing the official Southern governments' Black Code policies. But the effects of the war and emancipation were too deep-going for this form of terrorism to triumph easily. There was resistance from the Afro-American people backed up by federal occupation troops. With the rise of Radical Reconstruction, the terrorist groups acted out of desperation, seeking to hold to a minimum the rights won by Blacks under the new regimes and to prevent the new governments from consolidating their power. This phase of terrorist activity met success or failure in direct proportion to the efforts made to crush it by the local Radical governments or the federal forces.

In Arkansas, Radical governor Powell Clayton organized a militia of Blacks and whites, established martial law and crushed the terrorists by 1869. It was only after the defection of Carl Schurz and B. Gratz Brown from the Radicals and the resulting victory of the Liberal Republicans in neighboring Missouri in 1871 that terrorist activity revived in Arkansas. It was the rise of the Liberal Republicans and the splitting of the Arkansas Radicals into warring factions which led, through a complex process, to the collapse of Radical Reconstruction in that state in 1874.

In Georgia, on the other hand, terrorist activity in support of an early collaboration between moderate Republicans and Conservatives was able to overturn Radical Reconstruction by 1871.

Events in Mississippi and South Carolina followed a different and more typical pattern of development. In these states terrorism became relatively widespread with the beginnings of Radical Reconstruction. It declined in 1871-72 and then reemerged on an expanded scale after the political turn in the North. In neither Mississippi nor South Carolina was the militia used for effective counterterrorist action, as had been the case in Arkansas in 1869. In both states the bourgeois elements in the Radical coalition were fearful of arming the Blacks.

But in spite of hesitations the question of forming Black militias was posed because of the widespread terrorism. This terrorism took many forms. The homes of Black militants would be burned down or raided by bands of hooded whites. Militants would be flogged. Radical leaders often were assassinated from ambush. The victims included Black preachers and state senators and also white Radicals. Teachers, both Black and white, who taught Black children were special targets of the terrorists.

Between 1867 and 1871 it is estimated that no less than 20,000 murders took place.[2] This is roughly the same ratio of deaths to the Southern population as the entire United States suffered during the Second World War.

Meridian Example

The character of terrorist activity was revealed in events in Meridian, Mississippi, in 1871. Blacks and some Radical whites fleeing from terrorist intimidation in Sumter and Greene counties, Alabama, had crossed into Mississippi and gone to the city of Meridian for safety. Among them was Daniel Price, a white Radical. In Meridian he became a school teacher and continued to work with Blacks as he had done in Alabama.

Alabama plantation owners for whom the fleeing Blacks had worked, now desperate for laborers, sent kidnap squads over to Meridian to bring back their workers. The Blacks organized to resist. In one of the ensuing fights, two Black county commissioners were killed. After a Black was beaten up by other Blacks for helping the Alabama landowners, charges were brought against Daniel Price by whites in Meridian, accusing him of responsibility in that incident.

The Alabamians considered Price the leader of the armed resistance and wanted him removed. Local propertied whites joined in recommending that Price leave Meridian as the best solution to the existing turmoil. But the Black community and the mayor rejected the proposal. Fear of a confrontation between armed whites and Blacks caused local officials to vacillate in carrying out the law either by protecting Blacks or by bringing Price to trial.

Conservative whites then turned to Mississippi governor Alcorn. They warned of the imminent danger of race war and called for the removal of Price and the local mayor, William Sturgis, who backed him. Blacks also went to Alcorn, demanding protection from terrorist activities. Alcorn vacillated, taking no steps to protect the rights of the citizens of Meridian, including the mayor.

Seeing the hesitations of the governor and having the support of the Alabamians, the local Conservatives decided to attempt to take control of Meridian. They ordered the mayor to leave town and prepared for an armed confrontation.

Three Black leaders who had been arrested on an earlier charge stemming from these events were suddenly brought to trial. The Conservatives apparently had decided to use the trial as the occasion for the showdown. While the court was in session, shots were fired, general pandemonium ensued, and the white Republican judge and two Blacks were killed. Outside, over 300 armed whites, most of whom were Alabamians, had gathered. One of the Black leaders attempting to escape through a window was caught and killed. The white mob then took over Meridian and proceeded to search for other Black leaders and for weapons. Four Blacks were lynched that day, a Black church was burned, and the home of a white Radical, who was fortunate enough to escape, was also put to flame. In the days that followed other Black leaders were killed.

These events were important because they played a role in bringing about federal action, since it appeared that the state militias, such as they were, were unable to cope with the terrorist campaign. The weakness of the existing militias stemmed from the adamant opposition of property owners, both Republican and Conservative, to any policies which would permit the formation of powerful armed units of Blacks that could act in defense of Black labor.

In Alabama the Radical governor refused to permit the formation of a militia even though that meant his own political demise. In Mississippi a primarily Black militia was established by legislation in 1870, but that militia was never really activated.

In South Carolina a militia was organized in 1869. While it was never brought up to its authorized strength, it did involve thousands of Blacks. By 1870 it officially numbered 90,000 men.

The bourgeois elements in the Radical coalition rapidly became aware what a "monster" a Black militia could be. While the top commanders in South Carolina were the safe and trusted friends of the governor and saw the militia primarily as another source for graft and corruption, the lower commanders, the captains of local companies, often were Blacks, with a different viewpoint. Joel Williamson, a historian of South Carolina's Radical Reconstruction, gives us an insight as to why the militias created fear among Radical bourgeois elements. Williamson wrote of the Black commanders and their companies, "Almost invariably, they were strong characters in the Negro community, sometimes noted for their prudence, often for their bellicosity. Demanding and, frequently, enjoying the complete loyalty of their men, they often failed to accord the same measure of loyalty to their nominal commanders. Some of them used their men badly, deliberately maneuvering them in ways menacing to the whites or calling out their companies to settle personal grudges."[3]

We must take Williamson's interpretation with a grain of salt, noting his value judgment that the militia was "badly" used because it menaced whites or was used to "settle personal grudges." Whether this was true or not is irrelevant. In the context of the ongoing class struggle in South Carolina the very existence of a force of armed Blacks had revolutionary implications.

The racist terrorists naturally made the militia leaders special targets for assassination. Charles Caldwell of Clinton, Mississippi; Joseph Crews of Laurens, South Carolina; Jim Williams of York, South Carolina; Captain A.J. Haynes of Marion, Arkansas; and Colonel Sheppard of Jones County, North Carolina, are just a few of those murdered for being militia leaders.

Conservative whites also began demanding that the militias be disbanded or at least disarmed. In South Carolina the Radical governor negotiated an agreement with the Conservatives that if they would hold back the terrorists he would disarm the militia. This led to the disarming of militia units in Newberry, York, Chester, Union, and Spartanburg counties. On March 13, 1871, the South Carolina governor met with a delegation of Conservatives and agreed to the further disarming of the militia.

Only where the Radical militias had been predominantly white—in Arkansas and for a period in Tennessee—were they used with any sort of determination. Instead of relying on local armed defense, the bourgeois wing of the Radical coalition in Mississippi and other states appealed to the federal government to take steps to halt terrorist activity. In doing this they sought to avoid the growth and consolidation of Black militia units.

The bloody events in Meridian came at the same time Congress was debating anti-Black terrorism in 1871. They spurred passage by Congress of the Ku Klux Act, which included special measures strengthening legislation passed in 1870 for the suppression of terrorist activities.

When the federal government initiated even lukewarm measures to fight the terrorists, it had an immediate, marked impact. Federal arrests of just a few nightriders tended to quiet things down sharply. This was the case in Mississippi, though few of the many terrorists arrested were ever brought to trial and fewer were convicted. In South Carolina, the terrorist resistance also collapsed with federal intervention.

These facts reveal the underlying weakness of the terrorist campaigns. So long as no determined force was brought to bear against terrorism the local property owners simply carried it over from slavery as another weapon in the day-to-day class struggle. But even a slight threat by an opposing force brought a sharp decline in this activity.

The decisive problem in the struggle against terrorism was the lack of sustained will in the ruling class nationally to take stern and sustained steps against it. Unfortunately the federal government's insufficient determination in this field was even further undermined by the events of 1872 and 1873. This gave the Conservative opposition in the South good reason to believe that Washington would not intervene again. The failure of Congress in 1872 to renew those sections of the legislation permitting effective enforcement of the 1871 Ku Klux Act, for example, was taken as a message that terrorism could be resumed.

The Conservative opposition, sensing the emerging relationship of forces, opened up a campaign in 1873-74 for the direct overthrow of the Radical regimes that still existed in the South. Vernon Lane Wharton, the most popular historian of Mississippi's Radical Reconstruction period, writes, "Given the assurance [by 1874] that the national government would not intervene, most of these conservatives were then ready to join the mass of white Democrats in any methods they might use to drive the Negroes from power."[4] Of course, Blacks did not have the "power"; that was part of the problem. But such imprecise formulations are typical of the writings of bourgeois historians, even those of the modern revisionist school such as Wharton.

Wharton wrote that slavery was a civilizing institution and thought that the smashing of Radical Reconstruction was probably best for all involved. Nevertheless, his work is of value as a source of information. Regardless of his personal opinions, Wharton—while not noting the implication—depicts the situation in Mississippi as a direct outgrowth of events in the North. He writes, "The great financial depression of 1873 was reflected in the state by increased unpleasantness in political and social relations, and in the nation by a decline of interest in affairs of the South. Furthermore this financial collapse, along with the discovery of scandals in the Federal government, served greatly to weaken the power of the Republican party in the nation. There were predictions of a Democratic president in 1876. When these predictions were strengthened by the great Democratic victories which gained control of the House of Representatives in 1874, conservative leaders in Mississippi at last agreed to abandon their caution. The word went out that the time for revolution was at hand. . . ."[5]

The claimed "decline of interest in the South" is only half true and will be discussed later. The above citation, however, makes quite clear what was happening. National events had created a shift in the North politically. As we have seen, the Stalwart Republicans had been weakened as the capitalist class turned towards stability and away from Radical Reconstruction. The whiplash effect of this turn on the Southern class struggle was to unleash a mass counterrevolutionary movement.

The New Terrorism

This new movement was different in many respects from the earlier terrorism. The KKK, which became the symbol of anti-Black terror, had consisted of small groups of hooded men carrying out hit-and-run terrorist actions. These groups disintegrated in 1871-72 with the federal intervention. The KKK as an organization disappeared. (An organization with the same name reappeared in 1915.) New organizations with new names arose after 1872 on a different basis. Although some secret actions continued to be carried out, these new groups functioned more and more openly. They involved thousands, if not tens of thousands, in state after state, growing into mass movements organized under names such as White Line, White Leagues, People's Club, Red Shirts, and Modocs.

These groups were the military arm of a political movement: the Conservative and Democratic counterrevolution. This movement, in terms of its real program and leadership, was the expression of the new coalition described above of industrial capitalism and the white farmers of the South against Black labor. After its victory this coalition will fall apart as the poorer whites come to realize that no basic change in economic policies resulted: the same prorailroad, probanking interests remained in power. The result will be a gradual rise of dissatisfaction among farmers, culminating in the Populist mass rebellion of the 1890s.

These events of 1872-74 had a logic of their own. Once the new terrorist groups began to act and met little resistance, they expanded rapidly. Ruling class whites now passed over en masse to the counterrevolution and within the Conservative bloc the more extreme positions became predominant. Defensive formulations were dropped and open calls were made for the violent overthrow of the legally elected governments in all the remaining states under Radical regimes.

The armed counterrevolutionary organizations reached enormous strength. In Louisiana a figure of 14,000 members is one estimate. The 2,000-strong White League of New Orleans had excellent arms, including several cannon; two-thirds of its members had Belgian muskets purchased in New York; almost all had pistols.

A Mississippi newspaper boasted that 1,700 mounted horsemen could be put into action in one county alone. One outfit was said to include infantry, cavalry, and artillery units equipped with shotguns, needle guns (very advanced rifles for the time, with needle-shaped firing pins) and a six-pounder cannon. A Senate committee later estimated that in Mississippi almost one-half of the white voters were organized into the counterrevolutionary bands.

The racist forces aimed at taking power while using the electoral process for cover. They counted on intimidating sufficient numbers of Black voters by means of mass terror to become the "winners" at the polls. This campaign met with initial success in 1874 in the rural areas of Mississippi. The counterrevolutionaries then set their sights on taking over the state government in the 1875 election.

They began with a concerted effort to demoralize and break up the Radical Republican Party, aiming at preventing Blacks from effectively using their majority in the elections. Although they felt confident that the federal government would not intervene, they still needed the cover of having "won" the elections lest they arouse popular opinion in the North.

The methods used to carry the elections in Mississippi were subsequently outlined in the Boutwell Report (named after Senator George S. Boutwell, a Stalwart from Massachusetts) to the U.S. Senate. The following information taken from the report has been confirmed by other sources.

The armed military organization began organizing attacks on Republican meetings in Mississippi. In majority Republican counties such as Warren, Hinds, Lowndes, Monroe, Copiah, and Holmes, the Radical meetings were broken up. Weeks before the election, the Republicans had to abandon attempts to meet.

Where resistance was met, organized pogroms against Blacks took place. On July 5, 1875, one such attack occurred in Vicksburg, where between forty and eighty Black militants were murdered. There was another attack in Clinton on September 4, 1875. Referring to the Clinton attack, the Boutwell Report states, "for the next two days [the countryside] was scoured by detachments from these democratic military organizations over a circuit of many miles, and a large number of unoffending persons were killed. The number has never been ascertained correctly, but it may be estimated fairly as between thirty and fifty. . . ."[6]

The terror in Clinton was described by the wife of one of the most militant Black leaders, state senator Charles Caldwell. She was trying to care for two attack victims when the terrorists entered her home. They left pledging to kill her husband when they found him and then "they went to a house where there was an old black man, a feeble old man, named Bob Beasly, and they shot him all to pieces. And they went to Mr. Willis's and took out a man, named Gamaliel Brown, and shot him all to pieces . . . and they goes out to Sam Jackson's, president of the [Republican] club, and they shot him all to pieces . . . and they went out to Alfred Hastings . . . and they shot Alfred Hastings all to pieces . . . every man they found they killed that morning. . . ."[7]

From the scene of the massacre, the leader of the triumphant terrorist unit wired his commander in chief, James Z. George, "campaign manager" and chairman of the Democratic State Committee, as follows:

"There can be no peace in Hinds County while the radical leaders are at large. We are fully prepared to meet the issue and accept no terms which do not assure their surrender or removal from the county. We do not recognize the Ames government but will have no conflict with the Federal authorities."[8]

In Yazoo County a white Republican was killed, the sheriff forced to flee, and a systematic killing of Black leaders took place. An eyewitness described the counterrevolutionary forces in these words, "They were as well armed and under as perfect discipline, apparently, as any troops in our late armies were. Including the cavalry company from the county, there were not less than three hundred. . . . Their weapons were Winchester rifles, needle guns, double-barrel shotguns and pistols."[9]

Radical candidates were threatened with death unless they withdrew. Many did. On election day in some areas large contingents of armed counterrevolutionary whites paraded in front of the polling places. In one place a cannon was aimed at the voting booth. One or more of such acts of terrorist intimidation were found to have occurred in Alcorn, Amite, Chickasaw, Claiborne, Clay, Copiah, De Soto, Grenada, Hinds, Holmes, Kemper, Lee, Lowndes, Madison, Marshall, Monroe, Noxubee, Rankin, Scott, Warren, Washington, and Yazoo counties.

The pressure on Blacks was not confined to direct physical violence. White employers tried to force their laborers to vote the Democratic ticket or face being fired and blacklisted. Political intimidation was at times written into the work contract laborers had to sign to get a job. Kenneth Stampp quotes a section of such a contract in Alabama: "That said Laborers shall not attach themselves, belong to or in any way perform any of the obligations required of what is known as the 'Loyal League Society' or attend elections or political meetings without the consent of the employer."[10]

Wharton points out that throughout Mississippi the Democratic Party announced that no Black who voted Republican would find employment the following year. In some cases doctors announced they would no longer treat Blacks who did not vote Democratic. Checkers were stationed at each polling place. After the election, lists of Blacks to be discharged and refused employment were published in the daily papers. Along with these names were lists of Blacks who had voted Democratic and were recommended for employment or those who had refrained from voting. Blacks who supported the Democrats were given badges to wear which they were told would protect them from possible beatings by Democratic Party detachments.

Crucial to the success of this campaign was the default of the organizations which claimed to support the rights of Black citizens, the Radical Party in Mississippi and the Republican Party in Washington. The available evidence indicates not only their hypocritical capitulation but actual complicity in the triumph of the counterrevolution.

Governor Ames, representing the more militant wing of the capitalist allies of the Afro-American laborers, permitted this campaign to spread across Mississippi without taking any decisive measures. Finally, in 1875, he asked President Grant for federal troops to stop the advancing counterrevolution.

Grant wired back through his attorney general: "The whole public are tired out with these autumnal outbreaks in the South, and the great majority are ready now to condemn any interference on the part of the Government."[11] With this curt answer, Grant appeared to dismiss the whole matter, at least before the public. Nevertheless, he had his attorney general send a representative, George K. Chase, down to Mississippi to investigate the situation and see how best to handle it.

Meanwhile, the federal troops stationed in Mississippi were actually collaborating with the counterrevolutionaries. One federal officer had turned over a cannon to a terrorist unit.[12] After the Clinton massacre, the triumphant Democratic armed organization held a banquet and received the officers of the federal troops stationed nearby. This affair was preceded by an agreement between the federal officers and the Democratic leaders: in return for ending the killings, the officers would permit a Democratic takeover of the county.[13]

In Jackson, the state capital, Governor Ames issued a proclamation declaring that the legal governments of Yazoo and Hinds counties had been overthrown by extralegal armed groups and ordering these groups to immediately disband. Representatives of the Conservative-Democratic press present responded to the governor's declaration with derisive laughter.

Subsequently, Ames in desperation considered activating the state militia. The previous legislature had appropriated $60,000 to organize the militia, but little had been done. However, fearing that he might start a "race war," Ames could not make up his mind. He continued to vacillate, turning down desperate appeals for arms from Radicals throughout the state.

Finally, he permitted the formation of a few small units. Although officially the militia was led by ex-Confederate brigadier general William F. Fitzgerald, it was Charles Caldwell, the Black leader from Clinton whose wife described the massacre in Hinds County, who stepped forward to take command. Hundreds of Blacks began volunteering and there was now the possibility of beginning an earnest resistance.

The Democrats immediately got a judge to rule that state funds could not be used for the militia. But more importantly President Grant's representative got to work. He arranged a meeting with Governor Ames and the Democratic leader, James Z. George, to discuss how to settle the whole matter. The resulting agreement was for Ames to disband and disarm the Black militias in return for George's promise to permit a peaceful election. To make sure the agreement was carried out, Grant's representative, Chase, further insisted that the militia's arms be turned over to the federal troops stationed in Jackson.

Ames capitulated; betrayed by Grant, he turned and betrayed his own followers. The militia was disbanded October 12, 1875, while the counterrevolutionary forces continued in full battle array.

Part of the reason for the agreement was the fear of Democrat George and Republican Chase that a direct conflict between the White League counterrevolutionary troops and the state militia would draw widespread national attention to Mississippi, possibly forcing Grant to act. So long as the steady consolidation of the counterrevolution could be presented to the Northern public as "outbreaks" and "race riots," it would not cause any major political problems. It is noteworthy that most of the massacres and pogroms in that period were reported in the press as "riots."

How deep Ames's illusions were in the agreement—or to what extent he consciously participated in permitting the final triumph of the counterrevolution—is still unclear. Writing to the U.S. attorney general, he said of the agreement with the Democratic leaders: "I have full faith in their honor, and implicit confidence that they can accomplish all they undertake. Consequently, I believe that we shall have peace, order, and a fair election."[14]

Later, as reports poured in of the "breaking" of the agreement,

Ames wrote Chase, "I wish you would go to see them [J.Z. George and other Democrats], and get this thing fixed, and see what it means, and let us have quiet anyhow; no matter if they are going to carry the State, let them carry it, and let us be at peace and have no more killing."[15]

In these words we can discern the real mood permeating ruling class circles: Stability and peace can be established in the South by ending Radical Reconstruction, peacefully, if possible, but in any case let us be done with it.

The 1875 Vote

The Mississippi election results were reported as 96,000 for the Democrats to 66,000 for the Republicans. The terrorist campaign was victorious. In Yazoo County, there had been 2,500 Republican votes in 1873, but there were only 7 in 1875. In Coahoma County, where there had been 1,300 Republican voters two years earlier, now only 230 voted Republican. In some counties, Republicans were still able to vote without intimidation. Republican representatives, including some Blacks, were still elected. The end result, however, was the passage of control of the state governmental apparatus to the counterrevolution. The new legislature impeached the lieutenant governor and arranged for Ames's resignation.

The Boutwell Report, after naming the counties where intimidation was most flagrant, concluded, "if in the counties named there had been a free election, republican candidates would have been chosen, and the character of the legislature so changed that there would have been 66 republicans to 50 democrats in the house, and 26 republicans to 11 democrats in the senate. . . ."[16]

The counterrevolutionary forces continued their persecution of Radical leaders after the election. Charles Caldwell, the militant Black leader of Clinton and leader in the Black militias, was lured into a cellar for a drink by a white "friend" on Christmas day, 1875, where by prearrangement an assassin shot him. Still alive, he was taken outside and shot several more times until dead.

In Issaquena County an armed unit set out December 5, 1875, to kill Black leaders. That day they dragged seven Blacks from their homes and killed them. The following day the terrorists published a list of fourteen who they declared were banned from the county and they forced five leaders to sign a statement taking responsibility for the satisfactory behavior of the Black community on pain of facing similiar treatment.

But the triumphant Democrats generally were more cautious. They still feared possible federal intervention. Therefore they tried to make it appear that legal rights were not being infringed on and in a few places they even put up Black candidates or appointed Black officials. With the passage of time they dropped such pretenses. In 1890, when a new state constitution and laws directly abrogating the constitutional rights of Blacks were written (with the help of Alcorn), Judge Chrisman confessed publicly what all knew but had been unable to say in 1875 for fear of public opinion in the North. Chrisman stated: "Sir, it is no secret that there has not been a full vote and a fair count in Mississippi since 1875, that we have been preserving the ascendency of the white people by revolutionary methods. In other words we have been stuffing ballot boxes, committing perjury, and here and there in the state carrying the elections by fraud and violence. The public conscience revolted, thoughtful men everywhere foresaw that there was disaster somewhere along the line of such a policy as certainly as there is a righteous judgment for nations as well as men. No man can be in favor of perpetuating the election methods which have prevailed in Mississippi since 1875 who is not a moral idiot."[17]

Conclusion: Deny Blacks the right to vote and hold "clean" elections. That is how the "honest" judge and the rest of the convention proceeded to "reform" Mississippi politics.

8

The Final Defeat

The victory of the counterrevolution in Mississippi immediately inspired the Conservative opposition to the Radical regimes in the remaining three "unredeemed" states—Louisiana, South Carolina, and Florida—to attempt to apply the Mississippi plan.

South Carolina was the fortress of Radical Reconstruction. It was the state where Blacks had the greatest influence. They were a majority in the lower house of the legislature. They controlled the Republican Party's powerful state executive committee. They held an almost two-to-one voting majority over the white population. There was no way they could be dislodged in an honest election.

Events in South Carolina paralleled those in Mississippi in many ways. A division similar to that in Mississippi between Alcorn and Ames had occurred in South Carolina's Republican Party in 1872. Since this took place earlier—before the "reform" campaign had built up its full national momentum and prior to the depression of 1873—the lines were not as sharply drawn as in Mississippi's Republican Party.

As in Mississippi, the fight was partially over the treatment of Blacks and the small proportion of posts given to them compared with their role in the party and percentage of the population. In the 1872 gubernatorial election, the Republican ranks split between the more moderate Robert K. Scott, the incumbent, and the Radical speaker of the house, Franklin J. Moses, an ex-Confederate supported by the Blacks. Moses won and became the governor.

By the time the 1874 elections neared, the national "reform" movement had picked up momentum, making itself felt in South Carolina. Moses, a Stalwart, had provided ammunition for this movement because of his deep involvement in the graft which characterized the Republican machine throughout the country. Many of the leading Black politicians, genuinely concerned with the needs of their people, sought to eliminate corruption. But they also saw the anti-Black implications of this reform campaign. They attempted to adopt some features of the anticorruption program of the "reformers" while at the same time trying to prevent it from being turned into a campaign against Radical Reconstruction.

It was in this context that moderate Daniel H. Chamberlain presented himself to the Republican nominating convention as a candidate for governor. Chamberlain was opposed by a wing of the party which lined up behind the candidacy of John T. Green. With some hesitation and concern the Black leaders decided to try to work with Chamberlain. The Conservatives threw their support to Green.

Chamberlain won the nomination and election, but once in office he began to collaborate with the Conservatives. Many Conservative upper-class businessmen of Charleston felt they could work with him and gave him discreet support. However, it wasn't long before the campaign for reform began to come into conflict with the Republican machine. The Conservative forces working with Chamberlain pushed at each stage for more concessions. Soon the fight against the machine threatened the position of Blacks. The Conservatives pressed Chamberlain to appoint people from their camp to judgeships and other positions of power and influence. But Blacks regarded these people not so much as anticorruption as anti-Black. By 1875 Blacks in the Republican ranks began to break with Chamberlain.

From the start Chamberlain continued the policy of Governor Scott, who in the pre-1873 period had disarmed Black militia units in return for a promise by the Conservatives to discourage terrorist activities. In the first year of his term, for example, Chamberlain asked both sides to disarm. But after the defeat of the Radicals in Mississippi in 1875 and as the elections of 1876 approached, the situation took a decided turn. The Conservatives now believed that they could seize control by the use of force. The "Democrats" came to the fore. Serious preparations for a violent overthrow of the Radical regime began, possibly on a broader scale than in Mississippi.

The Democrats chose Wade Hampton, a former Confederate cavalry commander and owner of large plantations in South

Carolina and Mississippi, as their candidate for governor. He had gone to Mississippi after the war and had not been involved in South Carolina politics. Hampton had the advantage of seeming to represent a return to the "Old South," while holding Conservative socioeconomic views. He became the spokesman for the dominant capitalists around Charleston who had the decisive say and power in the South Carolina of 1876.

Martin W. Gary, also an ex-Confederate commander, was put in charge of organizing the "election campaign," which was to be modeled on the Mississippi victory. Gary sent out the following instructions to all Democratic Party organizations:

> 1. That every Democrat in the Townships must be put upon the Roll of the Democratic Clubs. Nolens volens [willing or not].
> 2. That a Roster must be made of every white and of every Negro in the Townships and returned immediately to the County Executive Committee.
> 3. That the Democratic Military Clubs are to be armed with rifles and pistols and such other arms as they may command. They are to be divided into two companies, one of the old men, the other of the young men; an experienced captain or commander to be placed over each of them. That each company is to have a 1st and 2nd Lieutenant. That the number of ten privates is to be the unit of organization. That each Captain is to see that his men are well armed and provided with at least thirty rounds of ammunition. That the Captain of the young men is to provide a Baggage wagon, in which three days rations for the men are to be stored on the day before the election in order that they may be prepared at a moment's notice to move to any point in the County when ordered by the Chairman of the Executive committee. . . .
> 12. Every Democrat must feel honor bound to control the vote of at least one Negro, by intimidation, purchase, keeping him away or as each individual may determine, how he may best accomplish it.
> 13. We must attend every Radical meeting that we hear of whether they meet at night or in the day time. Democrats must go in as large numbers as they can get together, and well armed, behave at first with great courtesy and assure the ignorant Negroes that you mean them no harm and so soon as their leaders or speakers begin to speak and make false statements of facts, tell them then and there to their faces, that they are liars, thieves and rascals, and are only trying to mislead the ignorant Negroes and if you get a chance get upon the platform and address the Negroes.
> 14. In speeches to Negroes you must remember that argument has no effect upon them: they can only be influenced by their fears, superstitions and cupidity. Do not attempt to flatter and persuade

them. Tell them plainly of our wrongs and grievances, perpetrated upon us by their rascally leaders. Prove to them that we can carry the election without them and if they co-operate with us, it will benefit them more than it will us. Treat them so as to show them, you are the superior race, and that their natural position is that of subordination to the white man.

15. Let it be generally known that if any blood is shed, houses burnt, votes repeated, ballot boxes stuffed, false counting of votes, or any acts on their part that are in violation of Law and Order! that we will hold the leaders of the Radical Party personally responsible, whether they were present at the time of the commission of the offense or crime or not; beginning first with the white men, second with the mulatto men and third with the black leaders. This should be proclaimed from one end of the county to the other, so that every Radical may know it, as the certain, fixed and unalterable determination of every Democrat in this county.

16. Never threaten a man individually. If he deserves to be threatened, the necessities of the times require that he should die. A dead Radical is very harmless—a threatened Radical or one driven off by threats from the scene of his operations is often very troublesome, sometimes dangerous, always vindictive. . . .

21. In the month of September we ought to begin to organize Negro clubs, or pretend that we have organized them and write letters from different parts of the County giving the facts of organization but from prudential reasons, the names of the Negroes are to be withheld. Those who join us are to be taken on probation and are not to be taken into full fellowship, until they have proven their sincerity by voting our ticket. . . .

29. Every club must be uniformed in a red shirt and they must be sure and wear it upon all public meetings and particularly on the day of election.[1]

The Hamburg Massacre

The armed Red Shirts were America's equivalent to Hitler's Brown Shirts in more than one way. (The idea of wearing red shirts was also copied from the Mississippi experience.) In July of 1876 an important clash took place between the Red Shirts and a Black militia unit in the town of Hamburg. The conflict was precipitated when local counterrevolutionary forces led by General Matthew C. Butler and called the Sweetwater Sabre Club tried to disarm the militia. The pretext was a claim by two young men that they had been insulted by Adams, the commander of the Black militia, on July 4 when they had tried to pass through the unit as it drilled.

Charges were brought against Adams, and Butler demanded of Prince Rivers, the judge and leading citizen of Hamburg, that Adams be made to apologize and that the militia be disarmed.

Judge Rivers had fought as a sergeant with the all-Black First South Carolina Regiment during the war. He had been the original organizer of the militia in 1870 in Hamburg, an almost all-Black town of only 500 people. Its militia had been dissolved earlier, but due to the pressing situation in 1876 it had been reorganized by Adams and included some eighty men armed with Winchester rifles. Judge Rivers was still a major general of the state militia, and he refused to accede to Butler's demands.

At this point, on July 8, a well coordinated plan went into effect. The goal seemed to be to give a bloody example to Blacks in South Carolina of what awaited them if they resisted the Democrats. Red Shirt units from the countryside suddenly appeared, obviously having been mobilized well before Butler's ultimatum. These counterrevolutionary forces crossed over to Georgia, Hamburg being on the state border, and brought back a cannon, as well as armed units from Georgia.

Some of the Black militia members retired to their armory, where they were surrounded by the counterrevolutionary troops. Firing began at 7:30 that evening. Thirty minutes later the first casualty fell, a counterrevolutionary hit in the head. The Red Shirts then brought up the cannon and fired through the walls of the armory, forcing the defenders to retreat to the cellar.

Completely surrounded and at the mercy of the artillery fire, some militiamen attempted to escape. The first was shot down as he fled. Then a first lieutenant surrendered, only to be shot while Butler questioned him. Finally the armory was stormed and the rest of the militiamen surrendered. The Red Shirts then sacked the town, taking twenty-nine prisoners. The prisoners were marched off at 1 A.M. Four leaders were singled out and told to run. They then were shot "trying to escape." Some of the whites from Georgia objected to the cold-blooded killing. The South Carolinians permitted them to depart, taking some of the Blacks to a Georgia prison. The rest were killed by the Red Shirts.

It should be kept in mind that the militia was a legal unit of the state government while the Red Shirts were an extralegal organization. The reaction to the massacre in the Northern press was outrage. This can best be understood if we recall that it took place in the middle of a presidential campaign in which the

The Final Defeat 163

Republican Stalwarts were busy waving the bloody shirt to round up votes.

The Conservative press condemned the use of "violence" but insisted the whole matter was a Radical trick to gain favorable publicity.

Governor Chamberlain called upon Grant to send troops to enforce the law in South Carolina. This time, under the pressure of the approaching elections, Grant acceded, and federal troops were soon stationed in South Carolina until after the elections. "The coming of the troops, however, and the retaliation of the Negroes did not deter the whites," wrote one observer. ". . . they loudly welcomed the troops and entertained the officers in their homes. . . ."[2]

About eighty of the participants in the Hamburg massacre, including General Butler, were brought to trial. None of the guilty were ever punished, however. With the federal troops around, the Red Shirts did tend to become more cautious in their actions. But the troops took no steps to disband them.

At most the federal military presence worked to prevent further major conflicts. For instance, an attack by 800 armed whites against a group of 100 entrenched Blacks near the town of Silverton was halted. Killings continued, but only in small-scale incidents.

The reaction in the Black community after the massacre at Hamburg was one of outrage and desperation. On July 10 in Charleston a mass meeting of Blacks declared: "The late unwarrantable slaughter of our brethren at Hamburg, by the order of Gen. M. C. Butler, of Edgefield County, was an unmitigated and foul murder, premeditated and predetermined, and a sought-for opportunity by a band of lawless men in the county known as Regulators, who are the enemies of the colored race in that county, composed of ex-Confederate soldiers, banded together for the purpose of intimidating the colored laborers and voters at elections, and keeping the 'negroes in their place,' as they say."[3]

Other protest meetings were held where Blacks expressed their willingness to fight back. Demands were made on Governor Chamberlain to prosecute Butler and his men. Some Blacks urged a break with Chamberlain, who was now running for reelection, if he failed to stand by the Afro-American people.

R. H. Cain, a Black leader, declared in Charleston, "There are 80,000 black men in the State who can use Winchesters and

200,000 black women who can light a torch and use a knife."[4] The mention of Black women in this comment is important. Most books on the history of Radical Reconstruction rarely mention the role of women. But several authors refer to the willingness of women to fight back during the later struggles in defense of Radical Reconstruction. For example, reports on the fall of South Carolina in 1876 speak of Black women "carrying axes or hatchets in their hands hanging down at their sides, their aprons or dresses half-concealing the weapons."[5]

The records show Black women in the South to have been politically active and quite radical from the beginning of Reconstruction till its end. Thus in the spring of 1869 we find a prominent Black woman from Charleston, Louisa Rollin, addressing the House of Representatives in Columbia on the demand for women's suffrage. And in the period of the overthrow of the Radical regimes the role of rank-and-file Black women is indicated by the following complaint of the wife of a counterrevolutionary leader: "The women are the head and fount of the opposition, some going to the polls to see the men voted right, threatening them with assassination if they did not vote as they wished. . . ."[6]

Frances E.W. Harper, a free Black woman, was born in Baltimore and was active in the antislavery movement before the Civil War. She spent several years lecturing and working in the South during Reconstruction and wrote the following poem portraying the role of women in support of the Radicals.

Deliverance

And if any man should ask me
If I would sell my vote,
I'd tell him I was not the one
To change and turn my coat. . . .

But when John Thomas Reder brought
His wife some flour and meat,
And told her he had sold his vote,
For something good to eat,

You ought to see Aunt Kitty raise,
And heard her blaze away;
She gave the meat and flour a toss,
And said they should not stay. . . .

You'd laughed to seen Lucinda Grange
Upon her husband's track

> When he sold his vote for rations
> She made him take 'em back.
>
> Day after day did Milly Green
> Just follow after Joe,
> And told him if he voted wrong
> To take his rags and go.
>
> I think that Curnel Johnson said
> His side had won the day,
> Had not we women radicals
> Just got right in the way. . . .[7]

The role of women, especially Black women, in the struggle to defend Radical Reconstruction is still unknown. As Gerda Lerner, editor of *Black Women in White America*, explains, "History, in the past largely written by white male historians, has simply failed to ask those questions which would elicit information about the female contribution, the female point of view. . . . Black women have been doubly victimized by scholarly neglect and racist assumptions."[8]

Despite such calls as R. H. Cain's for armed resistance, the Blacks' bourgeois allies in the Radical coalition went precisely in the opposite direction. On September 5, 1876, Governor Chamberlain ordered the Black militia disarmed.

Out of deep frustration the Black population of Charleston exploded in a desperate uprising the next day. It began as outraged Blacks attacked a group of Democrats, leaving one dead and several wounded. The *New York Times* described the scene: "The rioters held King Street, the main thoroughfare, from midnight until sunrise, breaking windows, robbing stores, and attacking and beating indiscriminately every white man who showed his face."[9]

For several days, in defiance of all government authority, Blacks continued to vent their frustration and outrage, but now only in their own districts. On election day another outbreak occurred, with one Black and one white killed in Charleston.

Chamberlain succeeded in disarming the forces that could have defended his candidacy, but it was different when in October he tried to disband the Red Shirts, the supporters of his opponent, Wade Hampton. Just as the Mississippi counterrevolutionaries had laughed at Ames's proclamation, so the South Carolina counterrevolutionaries scoffed at Chamberlain.

An important feature in South Carolina, however, which was

not present in Mississippi, was the 1876 electoral pressure on Grant. He felt compelled to issue a presidential proclamation on October 17 giving the Red Shirts three days to disband. The response to Grant's order was more cautious than the derisive answer given Governor Chamberlain. The Red Shirts formally complied and announced their disbanding. But, winked at by federal officials, they reconstituted themselves under such names as "First Baptist Church Sewing Circle," "The Hampton and Tilden Musical Club," and "The Allendale Mounted Baseball Club."[10]

The results of Governor Chamberlain's policy of capitulation were quickly evident in the shift in the real relationship of forces in South Carolina that evolved during the campaign. The governor himself was unable, for instance, to speak in Edgefield, where hostile whites silenced him by jeering and crowding the speakers' platform. In Abbeville 1,000 mounted whites rode up to a meeting being addressed by the governor. When they became displeased by his references to the Hamburg events they crowded up around the platform and cocked their guns. Republicans began to give up even trying to hold meetings.

Hampton's campaign tour, in contrast, turned into a victory procession. One South Carolinian described his campaign stops in the following terms. "They were preceded by processions of the rifle clubs, mounted and on foot, miles in length, marching amidst the strains of music and the booming of cannon; at night there were torchlight processions equally imposing. The speakers aroused in thousands the memories of old, and called on their hearers to redeem the grand old State and restore it to its ancient place of honor in the republic. The wildest cheering followed. The enthusiasm, as Confederate veterans pressed forward to wring their old general's hand, was indescribable. Large columns of mounted men escorted the canvassers from place to place while off the railroad. . . ."[11]

The counterrevolutionary forces tried to create the impression that large numbers of Blacks were passing over to support of the Democrats. This policy was a conscious fraud aimed at demoralizing the Black community, though in both Mississippi and South Carolina a small number of Blacks did join the Democrats. The open capitulation by the Republican Party to the counterrevolution led some Blacks to conclude that it was best to try and make peace with the Democrats so as to prevent bloodshed and the victimization of Black leaders.

Unfortunately no study exists of the positions taken by Black political leaders at that time. These varied from calls for armed struggle to acceptance of defeat under the best possible terms. Illusions about the Republican Party were quite strong among Black leaders, as they were among the Black masses. Members of the Black community had seen slavery ended and rights gained under the banner of the Republican Party, and they saw no other ally among the white population. Yet it was precisely the Republican Party which was following a policy of betrayal in the face of the rising tide of reaction.

Blacks who crossed over to the Democrats were few in number. A significant percentage of Blacks, in spite of massive intimidation, continued to try to vote Republican even after that party's defeat was definitive. Eventually Blacks stopped voting in large numbers, either because of physical danger or because of a growing awareness that their votes were not being counted and that the Republican Party in the North had no intention of protecting them from the lawlessness of the Democratic victors.

After the votes were cast in 1876 in South Carolina, both sides claimed victory. In some counties the vote was greater than the population. In Edgefield, for instance, the population was 7,122 while the vote was 9,289. Statewide, apparently 6,782 more whites than the white electorate voted, while 6,980 fewer Blacks voted than the Black electorate.[12] Both sides were involved in ballot-box stuffing and other irregularities. But there is no doubt that if the electorate of South Carolina had had a free choice the result would have been a pro-Republican majority.

Invalidating returns from the two counties—Edgefield and Laurens—where fraud had been most rampant, the Republicans claimed victory by just over 3,000 votes, 86,216 for Chamberlain to 83,071 for Hampton. The Democratic-Conservative side counted Hampton at 92,261 and Chamberlain at 91,127, thus claiming victory by just over 1,000 votes. The disputed count was thrown into the hands of Washington as two separate state governments established themselves in South Carolina. Each legislature met and named someone to fill the U.S. Senate seat that was up for election. This situation continued for four months. During this period ruling class support to Hampton's Democratic Party government was obvious: property owners paid their taxes voluntarily only to his government, leaving Chamberlain's Republican government without funds.

The final outcome in favor of the Democrats in South Carolina was ensured by the decision of the new Republican president, Rutherford B. Hayes, to withdraw the federal troops from defense of the Radicals in the state capital and to recognize the Hampton regime. The Red Shirts became the state militia. Usually this was done with a legal cover, the Red Shirt unit first formally dissolving and then each of the men volunteering to join the state militia.

Fear of opposition from the North was still quite strong, and so for a period Blacks were still permitted formal rights. Even a few Black militia units were retained for appearances' sake. In overwhelmingly Black districts, some Republicans were still elected. Professor William A. Dunning, founder of the school of historian-apologists for the Southern counterrevolution, notes that "the fact remained that in many localities the negroes so greatly outnumbered the whites as to render the political ascendency of the latter impossible, except through some radical changes in the laws touching the suffrage and the elections; and in respect to these two points the sensitiveness of Northern feeling rendered open and decided action highly inexpedient."[13]

Wade Hampton, South Carolina's new governor, went out of his way in widely publicized statements to assure President Hayes that the rights of Blacks would be fully protected. But before long it became obvious what the aims of the new regime were. The Afro-American people were to be denied the status of wage labor and forced into a caste system and the counterrevolutionary terror was to be institutionalized as the "Southern way of life." In 1877, the last Radical Republican regimes fell. The revolution was in full retreat. The emancipation of Black labor was thrown back. The new industrial capitalist order had taken one more step in consolidating its rule throughout the nation.

9

The Republican Party's Betrayal

In 1867-68, the Republican Party, with the support of most industrial capitalists, was determined to establish the right of Blacks to vote in the South. But it began to waver when the ramifications of this decision came to light in the day-to-day class struggle between Black labor and white landowners and other employers. While being for Black (male) suffrage, the Republican Party also stood for bourgeois property rights. The conflict between these two considerations was the underlying cause of the federal government's vacillating policy from the beginning of Radical Reconstruction until the ruling class's turn against it in 1872-73.

The violent encounters provoked by the landowners' terrorism thus elicited contradictory responses from the federal government. Insofar as the terrorism was part of a political struggle to break the Radical Republican regimes, Washington often felt obligated to intervene. But such interventions were strictly limited lest they result in a qualitative strengthening of the power of Black labor in its struggles with the employers.

Even in the early period of the Radical regimes, between 1868 and 1871, the federal government was hesitant to act. And when it did so it took only halfway measures in defense of the democratic rights of the Black population. In some states terrorist methods employed in the day-to-day struggles against Blacks were extended to the campaign to defeat Radical Reconstruction politically. But such political overturns could succeed only when the federal government refused to intervene.

In 1870-71 the pressure to defend the Republican-based regimes had been sufficient to bring about passage of the Ku Klux Klan control acts. Then the split in the Republican Party in 1872 and the depression of 1873 increased the vacillation in Washington, but with a discernible direction emerging. Now federal responses not only grew weaker but betrayed an uncertainty about defending the continued existence of the Radical regimes themselves.

In 1874 three Radical regimes were overthrown—those in Arkansas, Alabama, and Texas.

In Arkansas the split between Liberal and Regular Republicans had led to violence in 1874 which ended with Grant backing the Regulars. But the whole base of Radical Reconstruction in the state was so enfeebled by the split that the regime fell soon after.

In Alabama the counterrevolution had been held off by a partial victory in 1872 of the Radicals, who then had support from Washington. However, the Radical regime was unable to hold on when it was abandoned by Grant and betrayed by its own leadership—as we have seen, Alabama's Radical governor blocked the formation of a Black militia—and it fell in 1874.

In Texas, appeals by the Radical governor, E.J. Davis, for federal aid were refused. Instead he was advised "to yield to the verdict of the people."

Federal troops were on the scene in both Alabama and Arkansas when the counterrevolution triumphed. Their role in the events is well described in a passing observation of William A. Dunning, the leading historian of an openly racist interpretation of Radical Reconstruction: "Alabama, Arkansas and Texas emerged from the turmoil in 1874 with the whites triumphant; and the federal troops, after performing useful service in keeping the factions from serious bloodshed, ceased to figure in politics."[1]

One may paraphrase and amplify Dunning's statement as follows: The federal troops played the role of pacifiers until the triumphant counterrevolution was in the saddle; then they withdrew. As arbiters between the legally established forces of the state, from local sheriff to state militia, and the illegal bands of racist counterrevolutionaries, the federal army stepped in to keep the peace while allowing the armed bands and their backers to seize power.

The Battle of New Orleans

In Louisiana the Radical Reconstruction regime headed by Governor William P. Kellogg was nearly overthrown in 1874 by the counterrevolutionary White League's armed brigades. This episode, which played an important role in determining the form the struggle would later take in Mississippi and South Carolina, strikingly reveals the federal government's vacillations.

The counterrevolutionary forces had been rapidly growing in the post-1873 period. Shipments of arms, including Belgian weapons sent from the North, were arriving in New Orleans for the outfitting of Louisiana's White Leagues, the predecessor of South Carolina's Red Shirts. In September 1874, the local police moved to confiscate several arms shipments. This led to a massive protest by the local counterrevolutionary forces. This protest mobilization soon developed into a violent attempt to overthrow the Radical regime, since in view of the local relationship of forces the counterrevolutionaries calculated that they could take power.

But the attempted overthrow lacked the defensive cover of "winning" an election. Instead, the claim was made that a candidate in an election two years before had really won and should be placed in office. In view of majority sentiment nationally, this was hardly a credible enough justification for a violent coup. Nevertheless, the White Leagues went into action with possibly as many as several thousand armed men.

Defending the Radical regime were only about 500 men. They had a few artillery pieces including two 12-pounder cannons. The Radical forces consisted of Black militia units led by the famous ex-Confederate general and defender of Radical Reconstruction James A. Longstreet and the local police led by General A.S. Badger.

At 4:15 P.M. on September 14, firing began on both sides. The White Leaguers combined a flanking movement with a frontal assault, advancing with the wartime rebel yell. The attack succeeded; by morning both the police and the Black militia surrendered. The White Leagues lost sixteen killed and forty-five wounded, while the defending troops suffered eleven killed and sixty wounded. General Badger was hit three times, necessitating amputation of his leg; General Longstreet was also wounded.

For a brief time it looked as if the Conservative forces would remain in power following their successful coup d'etat. But the local commander of federal troops, who had sat back watching the violent overthrow of the Radical regime, now received orders from Washington to intervene. The overthrow was much too crude for public opinion in the North. If it were condoned, the damage to the Republican Party's popular image would be too costly. Consequently President Grant felt compelled to act in this case whereas he had stood idly by in the takeovers of Arkansas, Alabama, and Texas.

Grant ordered the "turbulent and disorderly persons" in Louisiana to "disperse and retire peaceably to their respective abodes within five days." Additional troops and three naval vessels were dispatched to New Orleans. The counterrevolutionary forces bowed to the superior federal might and withdrew to prepare for another attempt under more favorable political circumstances—which came with the 1876 election campaign.

It is important to note the mild treatment accorded the counterrevolutionary forces that had succeeded in destroying the Radical regimes in Arkansas, Alabama, and Texas in 1874. No one was put before a federal firing squad or sentenced to a long term of imprisonment. Even in the very act of curtailing the triumph of the counterrevolutionaries in Louisiana the federal government by its leniency encouraged them to try again. Two years later, these very same forces will virtually be handed control of Louisiana by Washington.

The kid-glove treatment of these illegal terrorist organizations stands in sharp contrast to the savage attacks on workers in the North by the federal government only a few months after the complete end of Radical Reconstruction. A massive strike wave swept the North in the summer of 1877. The walkouts began spontaneously among railroad workers protesting a series of pay cuts and then spread in Chicago, St. Louis, and elsewhere into broader, almost general, strikes. The immediate response of several state governments was to call out the militia to put down the unarmed protests of the workers. Many militia units refused to fire on the workers. The ruling class then turned to the U.S. government, demanding federal troops. These were quickly sent against the strikers in city after city. They were ordered to fire point-blank into unarmed crowds, killing and wounding workers in large numbers.

In 1876, when the downfall of the last Radical regimes was imminent, the number of federal troops in the South had been drastically cut, allegedly because they were needed to fight the Sioux Indians in the West. After all, 1876 was the year of Custer's last stand at the Little Big Horn. In the fall of 1876 the Southern garrison was left with only 2,500 troops.

Yet when the workers rose up in the summer strikes of 1877, troops were called back from the war in the Idaho Territory and ordered to march on Chicago. Federal forces numbering 10,000, with artillery units, converged on various cities. In Pennsylvania,

General W.S. Hancock, the Civil War hero who would be the Democratic presidential candidate three years later, personally led a massacre of workers.

The contrast between the harsh treatment of workers and the leniency towards Southern terrorists reveals the true feelings of the ruling class. Even Grant's mild treatment of the counterrevolutionaries in Louisiana in 1874 brought some protests in the North as being too harsh. Those favoring the end of Radical Reconstruction were angered by any action that hindered the triumph of the Conservatives.

In the North a propaganda campaign against "military supported" governments was intensified after the New Orleans battle of 1874. This pressure influenced Grant a year later when he refused to intervene in Mississippi. There the counterrevolutionaries were careful to center their campaign on an election. They were even cautious enough to make promises and sign "agreements" guaranteeing that the elections would be fair. This made it easier for Grant to give backhanded support to the overthrow of Radical Reconstruction in Mississippi.

A typical example of Republican duplicity was the report by Senator Boutwell on the events in Mississippi. To placate Northern opinion, the Senate had authorized the investigation and report and Republican leaders pretended to be shocked by its findings. The Massachusetts senator's report documented "acts of violence, fraud, and murder, fraught with more than all the horrors of open war," which permitted the new regime to triumph. It openly challenged the legality of the new regime: ". . . consequently the present legislature of Mississippi is not a legal body, and . . . its acts are not entitled to recognition by the political department of the Government of the United States. . . ." The report even projected federal action but, after having made the case for it, added that "the President may, in his discretion, recognize it as a government *de facto* for his preservation of the public peace."[2]

Thus even the Boutwell Report legitimized turning over the maintenance of the "public peace" to murderers and criminals. Nor did anything to the contrary result from the report; no steps were taken by any federal body. In fact, many Republican newspapers and journals dismissed the report's findings as irrelevant or opposed its conclusions. *The Nation* observed, "Senator Boutwell's report seems to meet with universal condemnation from the Republican press. . . ."[3]

With the final overthrow of all the Radical regimes, the

Commercial and Financial Chronicle of New York wrote that the South "now presents a more hopeful condition than any other portion of the country. She is virtually out of debt; her people have learned to economize . . . labor is under control for the first time since the war, and next year will be more entirely so, permitting of further economies. . . ."[4]

Under the growing pressure of the demands for civil service reform and an end to Radical Reconstruction, the Stalwart Republican machine began to try to adapt to the changing views of the ruling class. By making concessions it hoped to deflect the mounting attack against its privileges.

As early as 1874 Grant considered throwing his support to the Conservatives in South Carolina. That he was dissuaded from doing so was probably due in part to the choice of moderate "reformer" Chamberlain as the gubernatorial candidate of South Carolina's regular Republicans. In the tortuous political strategy of Washington such considerations were not in contradiction to waving the bloody shirt at election time or promoting the Civil Rights Bill of 1875, which the Republicans had no intention of implementing.

By 1876 some Republicans—especially, of course, the Halfbreeds, but also some among the Stalwarts—were seriously considering a fundamental change in their Southern policy. They thought it might be judicious to become white supremacists themselves. If they could only find a way to establish Republican governments in the Southern states that would be anti-Radical and anti-Black but loyal to the national party machine, they could then continue to control the federal patronage but without conflict with the Northern ruling class.

Such concepts were consistent with the mentality of machine politicians. They suffered from the illusion that mass moods established through great historical events could simply be manipulated at will.

The machine Republicans began a new series of oscillations between two different policies. In the North they continued to wave the bloody shirt for votes, while in the South they began intermittently to champion white supremacy, seeking to remold their political apparatus on a new anti-Black premise.

The policy followed by Rutherford B. Hayes toward the South in 1876 and 1877 exhibits this new oscillation. But before tracing the attempted transformation of the Republican Party into a "white man's party" in the South, we must take a look at the so-called Compromise of 1877.

The Myth of the 1877 Compromise

The end of Radical Reconstruction is most often explained as part of a compromise made to settle the disputed presidential election of 1876. This compromise is referred to as one between the North and South or the Republicans and Democrats. The explanation of it is presented along the following lines.

In 1876 the presidential election was very close and the count was contested. It was resolved in 1877 through a compromise between the North and South, Democrats and Republicans. The Republicans were given the presidency and in return they withdrew the federal troops from the South, ending Radical Reconstruction and returning the South to Democratic Party "home rule."

This so-called compromise is a myth. It is neither the reason why Radical Reconstruction ended nor why the Republicans were able to retain the presidency after losing both the popular and electoral college votes. This myth is so widespread and pervasive that it is necessary to review the detailed but enlightening information provided by C. Vann Woodward in his investigation of the events in *Reunion and Reaction*.

Bourgeois elections can never be fair. Although each citizen may have one vote (of course in 1876 only males over twenty-one years of age could vote), control over the means of influencing public opinion lies overwhelmingly in the hands of a small minority. The power to print propaganda, to hire campaign workers, and to influence by financial means all the institutions, from school to church, lies disproportionately in the hands of the rich. But for an election to be effective for the bourgeoisie, it must at least have the appearance of being fair and legal. That is, there must be some correspondence between the votes cast and the people elected.

In capitalist society there is always a thin line between legal and illegal manipulation of elections. Ballot-box stuffing and other election irregularities were and are a frequent occurrence throughout the country. Further, we have seen that terrorism to prevent Blacks from voting Radical had become a feature of post-Civil War elections in the South.

In the presidential election of 1876, after all the cheating on the count, buying of votes, intimidation of Black voters, etc., the final tally gave the Democrats a majority. Nationally, Samuel J. Tilden, the Democratic candidate, received 4,287,670 votes to Republican Hayes's 4,035,924. In the electoral college the margin was even wider. Tilden received 203 to Hayes's 166. Although everyone knew that the Democrats had stolen votes throughout the South, the Republicans were known to have done the same elsewhere so that, all in all, it was accepted immediately after the election that Tilden had won.

But at the very moment the Republican press was accepting defeat, the Republican machine had the electoral boards it controlled in Louisiana, South Carolina, and Florida challenge the count and declare those states for Hayes. This would shift exactly 19 electoral votes. Hayes would then have 185 to Tilden's 184. Upon hearing of this move, the Democrats challenged one electoral college vote for Hayes in Oregon to place them in a better position for maneuvering. Thus, excluding the 20 challenged electoral college votes, Tilden had 184 and Hayes 165. For Hayes to win he needed every electoral vote under challenge.

As we shall see, Hayes did carry the day with the votes of many Democrats when the disputed election was finally resolved by Congress. Why didn't these Democrats stick by Tilden? If unable to block Hayes otherwise, they at least had it within their reach to force a new election under quite favorable circumstances for Tilden. The popularly accepted answer to this key question—that Hayes offered to end Radical Reconstruction in return for Democratic votes—is not a sufficient explanation for at least one obvious reason: Tilden was completely committed to end Radical Reconstruction, and that goal could more easily have been attained by placing *him* in the White House.

We must also note that Radical Reconstruction had already ended in most states and was being contested only in Louisiana and South Carolina. In both places Grant, the Republican president, had permitted the consolidation of the counterrevolutionary forces and had practically limited the role of federal troops to guarding the buildings occupied by the Republican "state governments."

General Christopher C. Augur, in command of the federal troops protecting the Radical government in New Orleans, delineated his role during the time the illegal White Leagues were consolidating their power as follows: "I have declined to interfere on either side until there was a violent breach of the peace. . . . My orders simply authorize me to prevent bloodshed."[5] It was clear to any observer that the Republicans were not going to block the consolidation of the Conservative gains for long. Hayes was known to be even more appeasement-minded than Grant.

Although Hayes waved the bloody shirt during the campaign to gather votes throughout the North, he was a Half-breed reformer and, in his private letters, expressed his sympathy for ending Radical Reconstruction. Writing in 1875 to a Conservative friend in the South, Guy M. Bryan, Hayes expressed his attitude towards labor, complaining of strikers who "make war on property." "As to Southern affairs," Hayes wrote, "'the let alone policy' seems now to be the true course." The "let alone policy" clearly meant permitting the counterrevolution to triumph.[6]

Watching as the Conservative-Democrats triumphed step by step, state by state, in the South, the politicos in command of the Conservative or Democratic Party in that region could see that the Republican Party, "Despite its professed radicalism . . . had obviously become the conservative party, spokesman of vested interests and big business, defender of an elaborate system of tariffs, subsidies, currency laws, privileged banks, railroads, and corporations, a system entrenched in the law by Republicans while the voters were diverted by oratory about Reconstruction, civil rights, and Southern atrocities."[7]

They were, moreover, fully aware that the ascendancy of either Hayes or Tilden would in all probability mean the completion of the counterrevolution in the South. Consequently, something else must have induced the Southern Conservative politicians to cross national party lines and put Hayes in the White House. This involved such barefaced acts as accepting as valid a majority vote for the Republican presidential candidate in the very states where they maintained that Conservative candidates had won all the other contests in the election. It was dangerous because it so flagrantly negated the propaganda line on which these Southern politicians had campaigned and been elected and because of possible reactions from their constituents.

It is also significant that the Democrats nationally never agreed to giving Hayes the presidency; only the Southern supporters of Tilden defected and went over to Hayes. The Northern Democrats fought to the bitter end for Tilden's claim to the presidency. Clearly this was not a compromise between Democrats and Republicans.

In seeking support for Hayes's candidacy among Southern Conservatives in Congress, the offer to remove federal troops from Louisiana and South Carolina, already almost totally in the hands of the Conservatives, although important, could not alone have produced the necessary support for Hayes.

There is no question that a great deal of bargaining took place over the electoral crisis. The negotiations were accompanied by public denunciations and threats of violence while behind closed doors the bargainers were getting down to serious business. Bribes as high as $200,000 were reportedly discussed. Interestingly, C. Vann Woodward discovered that the real agreement of 1877 that brought Hayes to the White House was spelled out quite explicitly in the public press at the time. But most historians seem to have preferred a myth which, as we shall see, played a role in the very course of these negotiations.

What Hayes and the Republican Party wanted seems clear: the presidency. But more complex is what the Southern Conservatives wanted in return for backing Hayes. They, of course, demanded assurances that they would control Louisiana, Florida, and South Carolina. But they had other things in mind as well.

As a region the South was poverty-stricken compared with the East or West. After a brief bargain-hunting spurt there just after the Civil War, capital flowed mainly westward, not southward. What trickle did flow south dried up after the panic of 1873. Federal subsidies to business followed the main geographical pattern of investments. Capitalists with investments in the South and their political representatives were disappointed in the federal government's bypassing of the South as it gave away both money and natural resources. Between 1867 and 1873, the federal giveaways amounted to $103 million, of which the entire South received only $9.5 million—less than what went to New York alone. The same pattern held for railroad subsidies. Up to 1873, the railroads had received $104 million of federal largesse, of which the South got but $4.4 million.

The Southern politicians, both Radicals and Conservatives—but now almost entirely Conservatives—sought to develop the infrastructure of the South's economy. They wanted all kinds of federally financed internal improvements, for example, better harbors and the repair of harbors damaged during the war. The lower Mississippi River area was desperate for flood control, especially after a devastating flood in 1874. Moreover, the crisis of 1873 caused the abandonment of many unfinished projects, including the clearing of canals, repairing of fallen bridges, dredging of rivers, and the repairing of existing railroads or the building of new lines. There was no railroad from New Orleans to Texas, and the long-dreamed-of Southern line to the West Coast was still in its planning stage.

The problem faced by the Southern politicians and interested capitalist promoters was the sharp turn in national public opinion against any further federal giveaways. Two separate processes had contributed to the development of this public feeling against further big subsidies to railroads or appropriations for internal improvements.

One of these was the anger of the small farmers at the ruthless gouging the railroads subjected them to for carrying their crops to market. Originally farmers had welcomed the extension of the rail network, enabling them to ship their products, but they had quickly learned that all their profits would be drained away in freight charges unless the rail barons were brought under control.

The second was the movement for reforming the government and the political parties. This took the form of demands for civil service reform and an end to the "excesses" of the second American revolution. This movement, as we have seen, was rapidly winning the support of the ruling class itself. But it was difficult to draw a line between opposing the Republican Party machine's abuses and the giveaways to the railroads. In the public mind they were one and the same. And in the depression conditions following the panic of 1873, the reform campaign gathered powerful momentum.

The Democratic Party had rebuilt its influence on a national scale precisely by championing these reform measures. The struggle against Radical Reconstruction itself was tied to the reform against railroad giveaways, "corruption," etc. Tilden—although once an attorney for major railroad lines—was associated with those opposing further giveaways. Hayes was also opposed but to a lesser extent; and, as a Republican, he was in a more flexible position.

In bourgeois democracies it often happens that there is no direct correlation between economic power and its parliamentary representation. For example, the United States has gone through a long period of overrepresentation of rural versus urban areas. Capitalists have frequently had disproportionate political and economic weights in whole regions. In the case of the period under discussion, this worked to the advantage of the Southern Conservatives. Although relatively less industrialized, the South had a high percentage of the votes in Congress. Thus, in determining federal policies, those capitalists controlling the Southern political delegation held an especially favored position.

The electoral crisis of 1876 made possible maneuvers otherwise

180 Racism, Revolution, Reaction

out of reach. One capitalist who quickly saw this was Thomas A. Scott of Pennsylvania. As assistant secretary of war he had had responsibility for rail transport during the Civil War. Afterwards he made a fortune in the industry, winning control of the Pennsylvania Railroad, the biggest freight carrier in the world.

Scott, however, had been hit hard financially by the 1873 depression. When the electoral crisis came in 1876, he was busy promoting the idea of a Southern line to the West Coast through a new company, the Texas and Pacific Railroad. Scott was easily able to line up Southern politicians in support of his plan. At first these had included many Radicals, but with the political shifts taking place in the South, Conservatives became predominant among the supporters.

One of Scott's difficulties was the project's audacity. He was seeking a government subsidy double the total of all federal expenditures for wagon roads, canals and railroads from 1789 to 1873. His moves were being hampered and checkmated by rival robber barons, especially by Collis P. Huntington, who controlled the Central Pacific. But Scott's plan was so attractive and the political opportunity so propitious that during the electoral crisis Huntington made an agreement with him and they threw their combined influence behind the Texas and Pacific plan.

What then began to take shape in the course of a series of complicated private meetings and secret agreements, often discovered and reported in the newspapers—and sometimes deliberately leaked out—was a deal between the Southern Conservatives and the Republican Party under the control of the Half-breeds around Hayes. The gist of it was that the Southern Conservatives would turn their backs on Democratic candidate Tilden and deliver enough votes in Congress to give Republican Hayes the presidency as well as control of the House of Representatives in the next Congress, in which the Democrats had won a narrow majority. In return Hayes would deliver enough Republican votes in Congress to give the South federal funds for the desired internal improvements, including the Texas and Pacific Railroad. Furthermore Hayes would give them one or two cabinet posts and the federal patronage in the South that they would have got if they had stuck with the Democratic Party and made Tilden president.

The Southern Conservatives obviously could not present such an agreement to their constituents in its true colors. For after all their heated campaign rhetoric against Northern Republican rule and the railroads, and in support of the "South"—meaning to most poor whites the agricultural South—they were going to vote not only for a Republican president but for an immense new giveaway to Northern rail interests.

Instead they found it more expedient to stress to the public their desire to end the electoral crisis to avert possible civil strife and bloodshed and their success in ensuring the complete end of Radical Reconstruction with the promised removal of federal troops from South Carolina and Louisiana.

Hayes also found this explanation to his liking. It was better for his image as a leader of the more moderate Half-breed reform wing of his party to be portrayed as achieving stability and conciliation by resolving a dangerous crisis and ending the troublesome Radical Reconstruction experiment. This was certainly preferable to defending the more complicated economic and political arrangements in their crass details. What Hayes needed to complete the picture was elaborate public pledges from the South that Blacks would be fairly treated under the new regimes. This would protect his left flank from attack by the Stalwarts. Such pledges were promptly forthcoming, for the Southern Conservatives had no scruples about making them. Beginning with Wade Hampton in South Carolina, declarations promising protection of the rights of all, especially Blacks, were made by the leaders of the new Red Shirt and White League regimes.

Last minute maneuvering and secret discussions, quickly and deliberately revealed to the press, helped reinforce this version of the agreement. Thus a myth serving most of those involved was launched. Later this myth would play a role in a broader campaign justifying the triumph of the counterrevolution in the South.

The actual mechanics of the agreement to give the presidency to Hayes took a complicated form. Congress set up an electoral commission to rule on the disputed election returns. It consisted of representatives, senators, and Supreme Court justices—seven Democrats, seven Republicans, and one independent. The independent turned out to be a Republican, and to the outrage of the Democrats all disputed votes were awarded to Hayes by an 8-7 vote. The Democrats thereupon began a filibuster to prevent the recording of the vote and the Southern Conservatives delivered their support to Hayes by breaking the filibuster.

Hayes met opposition from within his own party. The

remaining Southern Radicals, of course, opposed the agreement, since it spelled an end to any hopes of their returning to power. Even more threatening were the mixed feelings some of the powerful Stalwart leaders, such as Conkling, had about Hayes. They feared Hayes would use the presidency to strengthen his position within the Republican Party against the Stalwarts. Conkling and others actually considered whether Tilden in the White House might not be better for them. In any case they showed little enthusiasm for Hayes's efforts.

One of the more ticklish problems for the engineers of the deal to give Hayes the presidency was how to present the "count" of the Louisiana vote to the public. The problem was how to count in both the Republican Hayes and the Conservative-Democratic candidate for governor, Francis T. Nicholls. This was especially difficult because Hayes's vote had run behind that of the Republican candidate for governor, Stephen B. Packard. A solution was finally achieved by bribing members of Packard's government, including Blacks, to support Nicholls's claim to the governorship.

Interestingly, the Louisiana matter exposed the "honesty" of many respected reformers. Half-breed leaders such as Garfield and Sherman took one position in public and the opposite in private meetings. Carl Schurz, the firebrand reformer, was deeply involved in the general agreement and did not protest the Hayes-Nicholls arrangement.

These negotiations also indicate how the evolution of events had altered the position ex-Radicals were taking. Overseeing the count in Louisiana for the Democratic Party were no other than two ex-Republicans, the once super-Radical George W. Julian and his collaborator in the Liberal Republican Party of 1872, Lyman Trumbull.

Inaugurated in March, Hayes withdrew the federal troops that were guarding the Radical-occupied statehouses in South Carolina and Louisiana the following month. Those Radical regimes immediately capitulated, leaving the rival counterrevolutionary state governments in unchallenged control. In a move to force Hayes to call the new Congress into a special early session, and for its effect on public opinion, the outgoing House of Representatives had adjourned without voting any appropriation for the army. Hayes supporters adduced this as one of the reasons why he had to remove the troops in the South. But lack of funds didn't prevent him from sending troops to fight the Indians in the West and to put down strikers in the North a few months later.

The actual agreement made in 1877 was spelled out publicly in the *Cincinnati Enquirer* of February 14, 1877. The *Enquirer* explained: "As an inducement to secure these votes [of the Southern Conservatives for Hayes], the guarantees to the South are: First, one or two cabinet places; second, the control of their own State Governments; third, a guaranteed policy on the part of the Republicans of liberal appropriations for Southern internal improvements; fourth, the passage of the Texas Pacific Railroad Bill. The plot even extends farther and contemplates the capture of the House of Representatives after the 4th of March next. If Hayes is counted in there will be no extra session of the House. During the recess enough Southern Democrats will be favored with patronage to induce them to stand in with the conspirators and enable the Republicans to secure its organization."[8]

The above quote proves that the actual basis of Hayes's election was public knowledge at the time. But the simpler, essentially false version of the agreement was the one widely circulated because, as Woodward points out, it "was much easier to explain to puzzled constituents than were complicated arrangements regarding the election of speakers, the organization of the House, the control of patronage, cabinet appointments, railroad finance, branch roads, and numerous 'internal improvements of a national character.'"[9]

When Hayes withdrew the troops in South Carolina and Louisiana he withdrew them from protecting the remaining Radical governments, not from those states. This was quite satisfactory to the Southern Conservative leaders and all that had been demanded. This is an important distinction because historians generally refer to the federal troops, being removed from the South, which is inaccurate. Significant numbers of troops remained.

In fact in 1876 federal troops were not only in South Carolina and Louisiana but were also stationed in all the states dominated by the triumphant counterrevolution: Alabama, Arkansas, Georgia, Mississippi, North Carolina, Tennessee, Texas, and Virginia. But in South Carolina and Louisiana their official mission still was to defend the Radical regimes from physical attack. Hayes's action did not remove them but simply ended their role in defending the constitutional rights of Blacks. This policy continued for eighty years until, in 1957, federal troops were used to enforce school desegregation in Little Rock, Arkansas.

American history books, even recent ones, in their treatment of this period, have also conveyed the false impression that a vast army was occupying the Southern states. When the war ended in 1865 there were 200,000 federal troops in the South. This figure was reduced to 17,000 in 1866. In 1867, with the beginning of Radical Reconstruction, the number was increased to 20,000, tapering off to 9,000 in 1870 and 6,000 in 1876. Of this 6,000, more than half were stationed in Texas for frontier duty. In the three states where the presidential vote was contested the troop figures were: Florida, 300; Louisiana, 529; South Carolina, 683. Thus the troops had become more of a token force than an "army of occupation."[10]

Besides delivering on his promise to turn power over to the Conservatives in South Carolina and Louisiana, Hayes appointed David M. Key, a Southern Democrat, to the important patronage-dispensing position of postmaster general in his cabinet. And Louisiana received more federal aid in 1877 than any other state. But some of the big items in the agreement failed to materialize.

For one thing, railroad tycoon Huntington double-crossed Scott and secretly began extending the Southern Pacific Railroad eastward into Arizona. He did this without subsidies and in defiance of the War Department, for the line crossed Indian reservations. But Huntington laid tracks "while the soldiers slept," and then presented Hayes with a fait accompli and told him he could complete the South-to-Pacific rail link without subsidies and without Scott. Hayes was pleased with the prospect because it would spare him the public outcry against a huge giveaway to Scott. The latter, who had been busy buying up congressmen, finding himself outmaneuvered, sold his Texas and Pacific interests to Jay Gould of the Union Pacific, who had been in with him on the original arrangement. Gould came to terms with Huntington and laid track westward. The lines made a junction in 1882 near El Paso, Texas, finally giving the South its rail link with the Pacific.

Hayes was no sooner in the White House than Southern representatives pressed forward with a veritable avalanche of requests for internal improvements. It was too much, given the temper of the country as a whole, and most were denied. The Southern congressmen in turn did not give the Republicans control of the new House of Representatives. This failure to take control of the House away from the Democrats was used by the Stalwarts to begin a campaign against Hayes within the Republican Party for his failed bargain.

Leaving the so-called Compromise of 1877 at this point, let us return to an examination of the Republican Party's evolution.

When Hayes first saw the election returns in 1876 and thought he had been defeated and Tilden elected, he issued a "bloody shirt"-type statement which included the following:

"I don't care for myself; and the party, yes, and the country, too, can stand it, but I do care for the poor colored men of the South. . . . The result will be that the Southern people will practically treat the constitutional amendments as nullities and then the colored man's fate will be worse than when he was in slavery, with a humane master to look after his interests. That is the only reason I regret the news as it is."[11]

A few months later, after the electoral commission had awarded him the presidency, Hayes changed his tune and opined that Blacks would be best off under those very forces who he said would bring about a situation "worse" than slavery.

Hayes was laboring under the illusion that he could win over to the Republican Party many of the Southern Conservatives who had supported his presidency. His turn from "bloody shirt" rhetoric to praise of racist leaders was to further that end. In addition, along with Carl Schurz, Postmaster General David Key, and Secretary of State William M. Evarts, Hayes toured the South, trying to build a new image for the Republican Party.

Inside the Republican Party an argument now raged over whether the new turn would succeed in getting the Southern Conservatives to switch over from being Democrats to being Republicans. But such a switch was impossible. The smashing of Radical Reconstruction had required the building of a mass movement based on the traditions from slavery times—the racist oppression and ideology associated with the Democratic Party. The mobilization of the poorer whites had been based precisely on these traditions, including anti-Republican, anti-industrialist demagogy. Southern politicians could not now easily turn around and break with the Democratic Party. Only in a few isolated cases did this occur.

On the contrary, Southern politics was now going through the process of consolidating the counterrevolution. This took place over a prolonged period. The association with the Democratic

Party and its tradition grew steadily stronger until the South became a "solid" one-party region of reaction.

With the approach of new elections in 1878 and recognition of their failure to win Southern Conservatives, the Republicans returned to the "bloody shirt." Making this turn were Hayes and Evarts. Schurz was more consistent. He would go on in 1884 to walk out of the Republican Party, as he had in 1872, and help elect the Democratic presidential candidate, Grover Cleveland.

With the rise in 1880 of Garfield and then, a year later, Chester Arthur to the presidency, new efforts by the Republicans to break into the South as an anti-Black party would again be made, only once more to end with a retreat to the "bloody shirt" stance.

By 1888, with the triumph of Benjamin Harrison as the Republican Party presidential candidate after four years of Democratic Party occupancy of the White House, an even greater effort was made toward converting the Republican Party in the South into an all-white party. In that year every Republican Party candidate in North Carolina, for example, was an ex-Confederate. But most Southerners who now aligned themselves with the Republican Party did so only to obtain federal patronage posts which were available when the Republican Party was in power in Washington.

Within the party apparatus in the South a concerted campaign to drive Blacks out of such positions and turn them over to whites met with general success until, by the turn of the century, the Republican Party was becoming as much a "white man's" party as the Democratic.

There was one last "bloody shirt" flare-up, occasioned by the electoral victory of 1888, which gave the Republicans not only control of the White House but majorities in both Houses of Congress. Massachusetts Congressman Henry Cabot Lodge demanded that the Constitution be upheld in the South and introduced a bill with teeth in it to that effect. His own party voted down his "force bill," and the "bloody shirt" was finally buried. By 1893 no major Republican politician, Lodge included, was proposing federal protection for Blacks.

Under Harrison the last pretenses were being dropped. While declaring that he would punish lynchers if he could, he pleaded that "as President, the Constitution and the laws limit my power." But with the power he did possess he made the first appointment of an ex-Confederate, Howell E. Jackson, to the U.S. Supreme Court, although just the day before another terrible lynching—the burning alive of a Black—had occurred in the South. Without blinking an eye the Senate unanimously approved Jackson's nomination.

The Supreme Court Joins the Counterrevolution

Even before the final overthrow of the Radical regimes, the all-Republican Supreme Court had begun a series of rulings giving legal cover to the growing counterrevolution. Essentially the court sought to claim that protection of the legal rights of Blacks was not in the jurisdiction of the federal government.

The court threw out an indictment of a group of whites in Louisiana who had broken up a meeting of Blacks. It ruled, in 1875, that the right to assemble and to bear arms pertained to citizens of a state, not of the United States, and that therefore only state courts had jurisdiction. During the same year two sections of the 1870 act providing for federal supervision of elections and enforcement of rights guaranteed by the Fourteenth and Fifteenth amendments were declared unconstitutional.

In 1882 the entire Ku Klux Act was, in effect, declared unconstitutional. That case revolved around a band of counterrevolutionaries who had taken a Black out of the hands of the police and maltreated him. The Supreme Court ruled that the Thirteenth, Fourteenth, and Fifteenth amendments to the Constitution authorized Congress to protect the civil rights of individuals who suffered violations at the hands of a state but not at the hands of private citizens. Thus assaults or murders by bands of private individuals could not be interfered with by federal officials.

In 1883 the Supreme Court declared the Civil Rights Act of 1875 unconstitutional. The high court's rulings against Blacks kept pace with the reactionary developments in the South. When in the 1890s the full spectrum of anti-Black state laws began to be codified, the Supreme Court kept finding legal bases for these new laws. In 1896 it made its notorious "separate but equal" ruling that school segregation was constitutional. Even direct violations of the Fifteenth Amendment, which guaranteed the franchise to Black males, were sanctioned.

The triumph of the counterrevolution and its consolidation can be traced to decisions and support provided at the national level. No other explanation can be justified on the basis of the then existing relationship of forces. The power to decide was in the ruling class of the North.

10

Industrial Capitalism and Conservative Rule

The process of Reconstruction did not end in 1877 but was carried forward by different means in the subsequent period.

We use the term Reconstruction here to mean the molding of Southern society in the ex-Confederate states to the requirements and dominance of industrial capitalism. These states had to be "reconstructed" to fit into the new order. Radical Reconstruction was the manner chosen in 1867 to carry out this change. The Radical regimes achieved the goal of reconstruction in the above sense. The smashing of those regimes and the accompanying loss by Blacks of their democratic rights did not alter that accomplished fact. There was no returning to the pre-Reconstruction era.

A look at the new, Conservative regimes that came to power can help prove this. They are often called the "redemption" governments and their leaders, the "redeemers." Frequently these leaders are also referred to as the "Bourbons." The term is usually meant to be derisive and to imply an obdurate aristocratic nature, while "redemption" and "redeemer" were and are used in a complimentary way to imply a return to the past. None of these terms is really accurate. Most historians have chosen to accept the term "redeemer" and for that reason we will adopt it as well.

Our thesis so far has insisted that the pro-industrial capitalist forces came to dominate the economy and politics of the South. We have pointed out that this current had already existed to some extent in the pre-Civil War South. Its political expression at that time was to be found in the Whig Party.

At the end of the war this current was strengthened politically because in the popular mind the defeat was associated with the Democratic Party. At least this is indicated by the preponderance of ex-Whigs influencing the new state governments that came out of the first postwar elections in the South. Radical Reconstruction carried the process of bourgeois mastery to a rapid conclusion. Economically the decisive power shifted from land ownership to banks and railroads. A new political apparatus was established which was responsive to industrial capitalist needs. Land ownership itself evolved; there arose many new, often large, absentee owners.

The plantations of the South and the big farms of the Midwest were now essentially similar in political-economic terms. This is in contrast to pre-Civil War days when the Southern plantation system, because of slavery, had a different sociopolitical dynamic. The major difference between the South and the Midwest came from the former's labor supply, or more accurately, labor shortage and low productivity. Here the baneful heritage from slavery could not easily be eliminated. The general backwardness of the region made it unable to attract European immigrants to solve the labor shortage. In this situation the new industrial rulers found some elements of the traditions of slavery that worked to their advantage.

The ending of Radical Reconstruction was associated with "solving" the labor problem. This involved no change of those who socially dominated and economically controlled the New South. What was undertaken was a drive to beat Black labor down to a caste status, thus permitting its superexploitation. This was made feasible because of deep-rooted traditions of racial oppression left over from slavery.

To accomplish this partial reshackling of Black labor, a mass reactionary movement had to be built. The triumph of that movement altered the form of Reconstruction from Radical to Conservative without touching its basic pro-industrial capitalist line.

If this is so, then those individuals who became the prime promoters of the new Conservative regimes should have manifested an underlying continuity of industrial business interests and policies with the Radical regimes.

Who Were the Redeemers?[1]

Joseph E. Brown was one of the leading redeemers in Georgia. He had been for industrial interests prior to the Civil War. During the war he played a prominent role in his state as the Confederate governor. After the war he tried to work with the

Johnson Conservatives, but when Radical Reconstruction triumphed he switched over to the Radicals. After the Radicals were overthrown, he changed once again to become a Democratic redeemer. During that entire time he was promoting railroad and other business interests.

Brown ruled in "redeemed" Georgia along with two other men, General John B. Gordon and Alfred H. Colquitt. These three dominated Georgia's redemption politics for twenty years, pretty much rotating the governorship and U.S. Senate seats among themselves.

While the Radicals were in power Brown was appointed chief justice of the state supreme court and arranged for the leasing of a state-owned railroad, the Western and Atlantic, to a company of which he was president. After the Radicals were removed from office, Brown continued his rise in the capitalist ranks, becoming president of the Southern Railway and Steamship Company, the Walker Coal and Iron Company, and the Dade Coal Company.

The second member of the triumvirate, General Gordon, had been a well-known Confederate general. In the 1880s he became commander in chief of the United Confederate Veterans and was idolized by many as an incarnation of the Old South. More important were his economic loyalties. His investments included insurance, publishing, mining, manufactures, and real estate, in addition to railroads. He was on retainer to the Louisville and Nashville Railroad at an annual salary of $14,000. What exactly he did to justify this income has apparently not been recorded for posterity.

The third member, Colquitt, at first sight appears to be even more of a throwback to the Old South than Gordon. He came from an old planter family. But he also was involved in large-scale speculations in railroads and had interests in a New England textile mill, a Tennessee fertilizer factory, and coal mines.

The Radical governor, Rufus B. Bullock, had to flee Georgia at the time of the Conservative takeover. But he soon returned to join with the others in promoting business. Bullock became president of the Atlanta Chamber of Commerce. H.I. Kimball, another Radical, followed in Bullock's footsteps as the president of a textile mill in Atlanta. Conservative and Radical Georgians were essentially one and the same when it came to business. The leading politicians of both groups represented the same interests and often worked together closely.

According to historian Howard K. Beale, not all Georgians went along with the pro-industrial capitalist orientation of the redeemers. "In Georgia 'white supremacy,'" he writes, "meant the supremacy of the business interests of Brown, Gordon, and Colquitt over the interests of thousands of small farmers who later revolted. . . . Toombs and Stephens, who really represented the Old South, saw, unlike later historians, the significance of the political situation and, along with Watson, who subsequently led the Populists, opposed these 'restorers of white supremacy.'"[2]

Beale concludes, "Indeed there seems to have been a striking similarity between waving the banner of 'white supremacy' and waving the 'bloody shirt' in the North. Both were waved simultaneously by a dominant party to avoid being turned out of office by a majority of farmers who objected to the use of government for furthering the interests of business groups."[3]

Often the Northern interests had to affix a "Southern" face to their operations after the Conservative regimes took power. One must recall that the overthrow took place under the slogan of "home rule," aimed against the Northern "carpetbaggers." This cover was usually acquired by hiring ex-Confederate officers of fame who, for a fee, would serve as the public spokesmen for the Northern corporations.

One of the most powerful corporations in the South was the Louisville and Nashville Railroad (hereafter referred to as the L&N). Its controlling stockholders were top rank Northern capitalists such as Jay Gould, Thomas Fortune Ryan, Jacob Schiff, and August Belmont. The group included influential Republicans and Democrats. As their chief lobbyist they hired ex-General Basil W. Duke of the Confederate army. Duke had the standard mustache, goatee, and Old South reputation.

In Alabama the L&N linked itself through investments with mining companies in the northern part of the state. Albert Fink, superintendent of the L&N and its leading entrepreneur, joined hands with James W. Sloss to exploit northern Alabama's mineral resources with guarantees of appropriate treatment from the state government.

Sloss was a power in Alabama's Conservative-Democratic Party. The L&N backed the Conservatives in Alabama during Radical Reconstruction. In competition with the L&N was another railroad line, the Alabama and Chattanooga Railroad. Investing heavily in the Alabama and Chattanooga line were powerful northern capitalists Henry Clews, Russell Sage, and

William D. Kelley. This group worked through the Radicals to promote its interests.

Both groups of capitalists squeezed the state for funds. In 1874 when the Radical regime was replaced by the Conservatives, the two railroads and their allies were deeply involved in the struggle for domination over the state government. Substantial funds poured in from the North to support the local Conservative-Democratic campaign for "home rule."

The Conservative victory brought George S. Houston to the governorship of Alabama. Houston had headed those in the state who remained loyal to the Union during the war and now, while governor, was also a director of one of the branches of the L&N.

Houston had his friend Rufus W. Cobb, an attorney for the L&N, prepare legislation for a settlement between the state's bondholders and the railroads which was particularly favorable to the L&N. Cobb, who also was the president of the Central Iron Works, which was subsidized by the L&N, succeeded Houston as governor of Alabama. Houston went on to the U.S. Senate. When he died he was replaced by Luke Pryor, who was also identified with the general business interests around the L&N.

Similar interests, often directly tied to Northern capital, dominated all the "redemption" governments. In Florida the first Conservative governor, George F. Drew, was originally from New Hampshire, where he had heavily invested in lumber and industry.

Like many of the leading Conservatives, Drew was an ex-Whig. In North Carolina all four of the first "Democratic" candidates for governor had been Whigs before the war. All the members of that state's supreme court were likewise ex-Whigs.

In Tennessee the first redemption governor, John C. Brown, also an ex-Whig, was tied to the Pennsylvania Railroad magnate Thomas A. Scott, serving as vice-president of Scott's Texas and Pacific Company. He was also involved in coal and iron. The next governor, James D. Porter, was later elected president of the Nashville, Chattanooga, and St. Louis Railroad. He was also a director of the Tennessee Coal, Iron and Railroad Company.

In South Carolina the leadership of men like Wade Hampton and the Hamburg murderer, now U.S. senator, Matthew C. Butler gave the regime the appearance of being associated with the Old South. Both men came from low country plantation families of aristocratic traditions. But even South Carolina's redeemers consistently backed the policies of the industrial capitalists and opposed agricultural interests whenever the two conflicted.

An excellent example of how Northern interests actually controlled the Conservative opposition is revealed in the case of South Carolina. During Radical rule the Conservatives organized a taxpayers' conference to mobilize opposition against the Republicans. But Northern capitalists who had purchased state bonds did not want the irregular doings of the Radical Reconstruction government exposed. They feared that such an exposure would cause a sudden drop in the value of the bonds. Instead they wanted it to appear that South Carolina's financial condition under the Radicals was sound.

In order to control the taxpayers' convention they hired two leading Conservatives—none other than Matthew C. Butler and Martin W. Gary. Gary, it will be recalled, led the overthrow in 1876 as commander of the Red Shirts. These two succeeded in having the convention put its stamp of approval on the Radical regime's finances.

Gary was also involved in railroad interests associated with John J. Patterson, a Northern Republican, who purchased a United States Senate seat for $40,000 and was an associate of railroad promoter Thomas Scott. Gary and Patterson organized a railroad ring engaging in corrupt practices. Also involved were James L. Orr, who had been the Conservative governor of the first government in South Carolina (1865), and another redeemer, General B. H. Harrison.

When the final victory of the counterrevolution came in South Carolina, investigations were begun into the corruption of the Radical regime. But the investigators had themselves participated in the corruption since the very same interests were behind both regimes.

The investigations were therefore carefully selective. For example, there was no probe of the notorious bond ring, which printed more state bonds than officially authorized and secretly sold them through New York financial circles, nor of the immensely profitable phosphate ring, which had obtained a monopoly of the state-owned mineral rights to the chemical used in fertilizers. Both of these corrupt rings continued under redemption. Even the few trials of allegedly corrupt Radicals that took place were carefully stage-managed to prevent disclosures of the misdoings of the redeemers themselves.

A revealing example of how Northern interests manipulated the Conservative regimes in the South was furnished by

Louisiana. There a state lottery company controlled by Northern capitalists wielded powerful influence over the politics of the state during and after Radical Reconstruction. Some historians believe the lottery played an important role in bribing Republican legislators to go over to the Conservatives in the election crisis of 1876. In any case, a paper called the *Democrat* became the outspoken opponent of the lottery after redemption, considering it part of the corruption of the Radical past.

The *Democrat* was the organ of the Conservatives in New Orleans. When its exposés became embarrassing to the lottery owners, a spectacular series of events followed. First, by a federal court ruling, the *Democrat* lost its contract for government printing, a crucial source of income. The paper was then bought by interests connected with the lottery. After the change in owners, not only did the *Democrat* reverse itself but so did the federal court, restoring the paper's government contracts.

But the power of the lottery did not end there. When the first Conservative governor turned against it, the lottery company used its power to get its charter written into the state's constitution through a new constitutional convention and saw to it that the governor was removed.

To assure itself of a "Southern" image, the lottery arranged after the overthrow of the Radical regime for two of the most famous Confederate generals, P.G.T. Beauregard and Jubal A. Early, to act as supervisors at the drawings.

Another indication of who controlled Southern politics in this period is that in Mississippi the first two redemption governors, John M. Stone and Robert Lowry, were railroad attorneys. And of Mississippi's seventeen Democratic congressmen elected between 1876 and 1890 only seven were found to be sympathetic to the interests of farmers.

The redeemers stood for the same policies as the Northern industrialists. "The reconstructed South came to be regarded in the eighties as a bulwark of, instead of a menace to, the new economic order," concludes C. Vann Woodward.[4]

One of the reforms instituted by the new regimes was a general lowering of property taxes at the expense of social programs such as schooling. Under the redeemers, the taxes, especially the poll tax, tended to be regressive, that is, the tax levied relative to income was higher for the poor than the rich.

The lowered taxes on land helped plantation owners and undoubtedly some smaller farmers. But the general pro-industrial orientation of the tax structure was maintained. Especially favored were railroads, utilities, and insurance companies.

Many of the smaller white farmers who joined in the campaigns to smash the Radical regimes believed they would be replaced by anti-big business regimes favoring the small farmer. Because of this illusion the "Democratic" counterrevolution had succeeded in blocking the spread of Greenback-type political formations in the South. In 1878, for example, the leading paper of the Mississippi Democratic Party argued: "There is no reason for any . . . member of the Democratic Conservative party to abandon it and join the new fangled combination calling itself National or Greenback party. . . ."[5] But with the triumph of redemption and the quick realization on the part of the small farmers that the same basic economic policies of the Radicals were to be continued, a rebellion developed in their ranks.

This took two forms: an internal struggle within the Democratic Party and, in some areas, the formation of new third parties. In Texas, a Greenback-Labor party was formed. In Alabama, a relatively strong third party under the name "People's Anti-Bourbon" entered the elections. It "denounced the new Democratic-Conservative party for its favoritism to railroads, banks, insurance companies, and other corporate interests, its inhumane convict labor system, its inefficient and unfair common-school system, and for its 'ring rule.'"[6]

The *New Orleans Times* referred to this mood among the poorer whites as the "communistic spirit." The prosperity of the 1880s deterred the new current for a period. But it experienced a stronger resurgence with the Populist rebellion in the 1890s.

From this evidence we can see that the myth that the old agriculture-oriented ex-slaveowning class of planters rose up to reclaim the South in a compromise agreement with Northern interests in 1877 does not hold water. This myth not only was accepted among most historians until recent times, but still is heard in leftist circles.

An attendant falsehood to be found in the history books is that, in contrast to the Radical regimes which had been corrupt, the new Conservative regimes were impeccably honest or, at least, relatively incorruptible. The truth is that the corrupt practices endemic to a capitalist society not only continued in the South but, if anything, were unusually high in the period after the

Radical regimes. By the mid-1880s, though the Republican machine's self-financing was ended, political corruption as such continued North and South among both Democrats and Republicans.

Virginia's Conservative state treasurer was among the first of the redeemers to be caught. He was charged with embezzlement but escaped prosecution by pleading insanity. Georgia's state treasurer was impeached, the general controller convicted, and the commissioner of agriculture made to resign when scandals of various kinds, including the stealing of funds, were revealed. Tennessee's state treasurer, who was associated with the L&N, decamped in 1883 with $400,000 of the state's funds. Alabama's Conservative treasurer, possibly taking his cue from Tennessee, absconded three weeks later with $232,000. In Arkansas an unexplained shortage of $294,000 was discovered but who was responsible was never revealed. The state treasurer, Thomas J. Churchill, became the governor in 1880 and was replaced by Major William E. Woodruff, who after ten years in office left only $138,789 unaccounted for. Kentucky's treasurer took off in 1888 with $229,009.

Mississippi's embezzlers deserve special mention. Contrary to history book claims of corruption under Radical auspices, that regime had been almost comly honest. The only loss of state funds was $7,251 taken by the treasurer of the Natchez hospital. But under redemption, state treasurer William L. Hemingway stole no less than $315,612.[7]

John R. Lynch, a moderate Black congressman from Mississippi during Radical Reconstruction, made an interesting observation about Hemingway and the missing $315,612 in his book *The Facts of Reconstruction,* written in 1913. Lynch held that Hemingway, whom he knew personally, would never have stolen money for personal gain. Instead, Lynch argued, the money was sent North to pay off the people who had financed the counterrevolution. Lynch admits he cannot back up his suspicion with proofs but notes the absolute silence of Hemingway during his trial as an indication that he could under no conditions reveal where the funds had gone. What happened to the $315,612 is not known to this day.

The grand prize for embezzlement goes to Louisiana's treasurer, Major E.A. Burke. He is believed to have been a Northerner originally, although he claimed to be a Kentuckian by birth. He became the "campaign manager" of the Democratic overthrow of

Radical Reconstruction in 1876. He worked with or for the lottery company and became the owner of the *Democrat* when it was taken over to stop its antilottery campaign. Burke also played an active part in arranging the deal of 1877 which made Hayes president and ended the federal troops' protection of the Radicals in Louisiana. After redemption he became the state's treasurer and later was found to have stolen $1,777,000.[8]

Disfranchisement

The disfranchisement of Blacks coincided with the rise of the new Conservative regimes. This was done in fact before it was codified in law. Fear of possible negative reactions in the North made subterfuge necessary for a period. Conservatives taxed their imaginations to find ways to deny Blacks the right to vote without directly disfranchising them by law.

Gerrymandering of districts was one method. Shoestring districts as long as 300 miles but only 20 miles wide were created. In this way all Black-majority areas could be put into one district, thus limiting the number of representatives who could be influenced by the Black electorate.

More effective was the eight-ballot-box system devised in South Carolina. Instead of one ballot box, eight boxes were set up for the various political posts being contested. Voters had to drop ballots in each box accordingly. Ballots in the wrong box were void. Since very large numbers of Blacks were still illiterate, their votes could be invalidated by occasionally altering the order of the boxes.

Another method used where large numbers of Blacks still voted was to move the polling place at the last minute. This would be done without notifying the Black voters of the change, resulting in a sharp drop in the size of their vote.

The usual devices of bribery and ballot-box stuffing were, of course, also in vogue. The stuffing of ballot boxes developed into an art. The law required that a blindfolded person should remove excess ballots one at a time if more appeared in the ballot box than there were registered voters in the district. This rule made it quite simple to alter the electoral results. At that time, any size ballot could be used. The Conservatives would have some of their supporters conceal tiny tissue ballots within the folded ballots they cast. After the ballots were counted it would be discovered that there were too many votes. The blindfolded election official would then proceed to remove ballots, being careful to leave a large portion of the tissue ballots.[9]

Consequently, although large numbers of Blacks remained registered, the number voting rapidly dropped off. For instance, in the presidential election of 1884 the vote in South Carolina plummeted to 91,000 compared with 182,000 in 1876. Mississippi shows a drop from 164,000 to 120,000, and Louisiana from 160,000 to 108,000.

The Democrats, including the "distinguished Mississippian" L.Q.C. Lamar, the future Supreme Court justice, argued that the vote was dropping because Blacks were intelligent enough to see that their real interests lay with the Democratic Party, and since there was now little opposition to the Democrats—in many states the Republicans did not even run slates—Blacks were no longer bothering to vote.

Only later, in the 1890s, did the campaign to disfranchise Blacks come aboveground through open legislation. New legal measures were then devised by the Southern legislators to get around the Fifteenth Amendment, which they were uncertain the Supreme Court would allow to be completely invalidated. In this they underestimated the court's willingness to join in disfranchising Blacks. For when the new laws came up for review, the justices continued their tortured reasoning to approve these violations of the Constitution.

One of the first methods of "legal" disfranchisement used was a literacy test requiring that prospective voters give a "reasonable interpretation" of the state constitution. Registration officials were empowered to judge whether an applicant had passed the test. The result was that whites could and Blacks couldn't. What's more, the advocates of the new law did not at all hide their intent: "But it would not be frank in me, Mr. Chairman, if I did not say that I do not expect [it] to be administered with any degree of friendship by the white man to the suffrage of the black man. I expect the examination with which the black man will be confronted, to be inspired with the same spirit that inspires every man in this convention. . . ." So argued one of the delegates at Virginia's constitutional convention.[10] Yet the Supreme Court ruled that the law in itself did not violate the Fifteenth Amendment.

Southern legislators found the literacy test by itself to be insufficient because it left large numbers of literate Blacks the right to vote. As United States Senator James K. Vardaman of

Mississippi explained, he was "opposed to Negro voting; it matters not what his advertised mental and moral qualifications may be. I am just as much opposed to Booker Washington as a voter, with all his Anglo-Saxon reënforcements, as I am to the cocoanot-headed, chocolate-colored, typical little coon. . . ."[11]

Louisiana Democrats came up with a novel idea to shield illiterate whites from disfranchisement by these laws. They voted to give the right to vote to anyone whose father or grandfather possessed the right to vote on January 1, 1867—before Blacks had gained the franchise. The one flaw found in this was that many Blacks might be able to prove they had white fathers! Nevertheless, several states adopted this "grandfather clause."

The Supreme Court kept swallowing each new circumvention of the Fifteenth Amendment until some states passed laws declaring the Democratic primary an all-white affair. The Supreme Court rejected the initial legislation as being too crude. After several attempts to improve the wording, a solution was finally found. Instead of the state legislature passing a law, the Democratic Party declared itself a whites-only organization and accordingly held whites-only primaries. This, the Supreme Court ruled in 1935, was perfectly fine and not in violation of the Fifteenth Amendment.[12]

Most of these laws were adopted at constitutional conventions in the late 1890s or at the turn of the century when new state constitutions were written. But the authors of the new laws felt the mass of voters might not ratify the new proposals. Poor whites feared the new laws would result in disfranchising them as well as Blacks. To ensure that there would be no defeat at the polls, the state conventions simply declared the new constitutions in force without the customary referendums. In Alabama, the only state in which a referendum was held, the poor white upcountry districts voted against it.

The results of the various new laws were an almost total elimination of Black registered voters and a substantial drop in white registration. In Mississippi, of a potential 257,305 voters in 1890, the number registered was only 76,742. In place of the state's potential Black majority vote of 37,105, a white majority of 58,512 was created. The actual vote in 1892 was 52,809, or only 20 percent of the potential electorate.

By 1940 only 2 percent of the potential Black electorate voted in twelve Southern states.

The 1879 Exodus

One of the early consequences of the defeat of the Radical regimes was the desire of Blacks to leave the South and go North. After the crop failure of 1878 many Blacks decided to emigrate to Kansas.

The reaction of the Southern regimes and the business community of the North revealed much about the aims of the new denial of rights to Blacks. Direct physical violence was used to prevent the departure of Black labor from the South. Under the developing caste system, the simple right to move freely would also be denied Blacks.

Senator John J. Ingalls of Kansas stated that twenty Blacks had been murdered for their efforts to participate in or organize the exodus. The Mississippi River was blockaded by forces under the command of ex-Confederate officer James R. Chalmers, who threatened to sink any boat carrying Blacks. The result was that some 1,500 Blacks were left stranded on the river bank.[13]

Deputy sheriffs sent by plantation owners used force to kidnap escaping Blacks and compel them to remain in the South. Thomas W. Conway, who along with other Northern whites tried to help the emigration, wrote President Hayes, "Every river landing is blockaded by white enemies of the colored exodus, some of whom are mounted and armed, as if we were at war, their object being to force the negroes back to the places they left."[14]

The Republican Party politicians tried to take advantage of the exodus to make propaganda against the Democrats, but did little to aid the refugees. A few, like Conway, were genuinely concerned and made concrete efforts to help.

The Northern capitalists went out of their way to show disapproval of any help to the exodus. The New York *Commercial Bulletin* argued, "Can the South or the North be benefited by encouraging the migration of that labor upon which our chief commercial crop is dependent? Can we afford to undermine the prosperity, nay the very existence of Southern trade by diverting from that section the population on which its industry is dependent?"[15]

The *Railway Age* and *Commercial and Financial Chronicle* joined in deploring any thought of Blacks leaving the South. A study of twelve major Northern dailies shows that eleven opposed the migration.[16] To a plea for support from Mississippi planters, the New York *Journal of Commerce* responded: "We can assure the Southerners, once and for all, that excepting a few incurable fanatics who have little money or influence, the people of the North feel no desire to break up the present Southern labor system, and will contribute a hundred dollars to transport the refugees back to their homes from Kansas, to every dollar given by any rabid hater of the South toward depriving the capitalists of the only labor available for them."[17]

As late as the First World War, physical coercion, arrests, and terrorist methods were used to prevent Blacks from leaving the South for jobs elsewhere.

The exodus of 1879 came to an end quickly because of the pressure against it, combined with the growing realization among Blacks that their reception in the North was far from friendly. The federal government and state governments refused to take steps to provide land, jobs, or loans to permit the refugees to begin a new life.

Sharecropping and Peonage

Behind the drive to deny Blacks democratic rights was the aim of forcing them into a semipeonage status. The traditions of racial oppression left over from slavery were now used to force Blacks to work for lower pay than they would have been able to get in an open labor market.

This drive took various forms and developed at different tempos in different parts of the South. It was strongest in the cotton producing areas. New laws were passed placing heavy penalties on Black laborers for failing to live up to the terms of labor contracts. By making failure to work a criminal offense, the repressive apparatus of the state or county was brought into play to force Blacks to work at low pay.

In 1884, Mississippi passed a law that any laborer or tenant who broke his or her contract forfeited all wages or crops due to, or belonging to, the laborer. Laws were also passed setting fines for anyone who tried to hire a laborer or apprentice under contract to another employer.

These laws were then reinforced by interpreting a worker's failure to fulfill the contract as equivalent to receiving goods or money under false pretenses, that is, robbery or extortion. This interpretation had the advantage of permitting the imprisonment of Black sharecroppers for defaulting on labor contracts. Another piece of legislation, called the "pig law," was added to classify any robbery of ten dollars or of a pig as grand larceny, punishable by a possible sentence of five years. Such new laws led to an immediate increase in the number of Black prisoners.

After redemption, the chance of a Black accused of "stealing" a pig or of breach of contract getting a fair trial was nonexistent. The local judge, often a landowner himself, was part of the Democratic Party machine, i.e., the Jim Crow repressive apparatus.

Now every Black worker had the immediate threat hanging over his or her head of direct state repression in any conflict with the employer. Both employers and Blacks were well aware of the interconnection between labor conditions and democratic rights. It was the defeat of the Radical regimes that led directly to the loss of democratic rights and to the imposition of a caste labor system of semipeonage.

A candid explanation of the interconnection between democratic rights and labor conditions from a capitalist point of view was expressed by a Mississippian in the following words: "It is a question of political economy which the people of the North cannot realize nor understand *and which they have no right to discuss as they have no power to determine.* If the Negro is permitted to engage in politics his usefulness as a laborer is at an end. *He can no longer be controlled or utilized.* The South has to deal with him as an industrial and economic factor *and is forced to assert its control over him in sheer self-defense.*"[18]

In 1888 a group of Black clergymen protested against the continuing terror campaign against Blacks. In their written statement they make clear the direct connection between the denial of democratic rights, terrorism, and the exploitation of labor: "These [terrorist] acts are done in deliberate defiance of the Constitution and the laws of the United States, which are so thoroughly nullified that the Negroes who bore arms in defense of the Union have no protection or shelter from them within the borders of Louisiana. During the past twelve months our people have suffered from the lawless regulators as never before since the carnival of bloodshed conducted by the Democratic party in 1868. . . . Fully aware of their utter helplessness, unarmed and unable to offer resistance to an overpowering force which varies from a 'band of whites' to a 'sheriff's posse' or the 'militia,' but which in reality is simply the Democratic party assembled with military precision and armed with rifles of the latest improved patents, toilers forbidden to follow occupations of their choice, compelled to desist from the discussing of labor questions, and being whipped and butchered when in a defenseless condition."[19]

The percentage of Blacks forced into sharecropping contracts with landowners continued to increase well into the twentieth century. Alongside sharecropping, acting as an ever-present threat to Black labor, was the convict lease labor system.

The practice of using convicts as a labor supply was begun after the Civil War. Convicts were leased out to private individuals as slave labor. Radical Reconstruction regimes either stopped the practice or sharply curtailed it with the intention of ending it. But the rise to power of the Conservatives spurred a rapid expansion of the system.

The convicts were both Black and white. But naturally the racist character of the redemption regimes led to a much different treatment for Blacks. The convicts were leased not only for plantation work, but often to industrial capitalists for work on railroads and in coal mines. One of Georgia's triumvirate, Joseph E. Brown, rented slave labor at the rate of eight cents per day per individual for his coal mines. He was granted a twenty-year contract by the state government for 300 long-term prisoners throughout this period.

The horrors of the convict slave labor camps evoked protests even within the South's redemption forces. The report of a Hinds County, Mississippi, grand jury gave this account of conditions at the state prison in 1887: "We found [in the hospital section] twenty-six inmates, all of whom have been lately brought there off the farms and railroads, many of them with consumption and other incurable diseases, and all bearing on their persons marks of the most inhuman and brutal treatment. Most of them have their backs cut in great wales, scars and blisters, some with the skin pealing [sic] off in pieces as the result of severe beatings. . . . They are lying there dying, some of them on bare boards, so poor and emaciated that their bones almost come through their skin many complaining for the want of food."[20]

The annual death rate reached astronomical figures in these camps. In Mississippi one out of nine died each year according to a report made in 1886. In Arkansas the rate went as high as one in four.

Pressure for reforms of the system grew in the 1890s, partially because of the Populist movement. Often Black convicts were used to break strikes. In Tennessee such strikebreaking in the 1890s led to the white miners arming themselves and freeing the Black convicts to win strikes, and this helped put an end to the system in that state.[21]

In some states the practice of leasing convict labor was restricted in the 1890s to state projects. In others, it lasted up until about 1920.

The convict lease system acted as a direct threat to any Blacks who tried to fight back against their employers, since once arrested for any charge they could end up in one of the camps. Finally, if fear of the convict system was not enough to keep Black labor under control, the direct use of lynch law added its own horror to the daily life of Blacks. Lynching was not just some wild excess, but an institutionalized part of the Jim Crow system. In the 1890s known lynchings reached a rate of more than one every other day.

More often than not, lynchings were carried out by the property-owning whites. The myth has it that lynching was an excess of the "poor white trash." That this is a falsification can be verified by reading Ralph Ginzburg's book *100 Years of Lynchings*.

Many lynchings were announced beforehand in the mass media; railroads in several instances provided special excursion trips to the scene, and large crowds gathered. These mobs were often addressed by elected Democratic Party officials. After the speeches a Black person would be hanged, burned alive, or tortured to death.

Efforts to pass a federal antilynching law never succeeded. The hopes of the antilynching-law advocates reached a high point during the 1930s. But President Franklin D. Roosevelt sabotaged the effort by refusing to utter a single public statement favoring such a law.

Combined with the forcing of Blacks into a cheap labor pool for Southern agriculture was a limitation of employment in other fields. The new industries which gradually developed in the South usually were based strictly on all-white labor. The first major industrial expansion was in textile mills. The mills were quite profitable in the 1880s, bringing on the average 22 percent profit. Black labor was excluded from them except as janitors and on the loading platforms.

Many Blacks had been skilled workers during Radical Reconstruction. There had also been a tendency for Blacks to migrate to urban centers and seek jobs as wage workers instead of accepting sharecropping arrangements on the land. After the Conservative regimes began the structuring of the Jim Crow caste system, Blacks were driven out of many skilled trades.

The trade union bureaucracy of the American Federation of Labor backed the all-white policies. Samuel Gompers, the head of the AFL, stated that Blacks should be excluded because they could not "understand the philosophy of human rights."[22]

In the South there were many strikes by whites to prevent the hiring of Black workers. Charles H. Wesley in *Negro Labor in the United States* lists fifty such strikes just in the period 1882 to 1900. At times violent attacks on Blacks were used to drive them from their jobs. This occurred on the railroads. The only countertendencies in the labor movement were the Industrial Workers of the World (IWW) and left-wing Debs socialists, who fought for integrated unions and against Jim Crow early in the present century.

Among the first casualties of the Conservative triumph were the schools which taught Blacks. The counterrevolution made the schools a prime target of racist hate. To many of the redeemers, schools symbolized the concept that Blacks were equals. Some of the schools were burned down. Most simply had their funds slashed.

In South Carolina, for instance, between 1880 and 1895 the annual appropriation for Black schools fell from $2.51 to $1.05 per pupil. Throughout the Southeast the average per capita expenditure on Black schools dropped from 80 cents in 1875 to 63 cents in 1879.

Through enormous sacrifices, Black teachers managed to keep the schools for Black children operating. Often these schools did not open in the fall, as did the schools for whites, because the cotton-picking season was still on. Black children had to labor along with both parents in the fields during that period of peak labor demand.

The development of schools of higher learning was also blocked by the redeemers. As late as 1933 there were only 367 accredited high schools for Blacks in the entire South and border states. At the turn of the century Southern institutions for Blacks claiming college status were principally agricultural and mechanical schools, which received federal funds, and private schools dependent on Northern philanthropy; they had woefully limited curriculums. A Federal Bureau of Education study in 1916, cosponsored by the Phelps-Stokes Fund, said of those offering courses of college grade that only three—Howard University, Fisk University, and Meharry Medical College—"had a student body, teaching force, equipment and income sufficient to warrant the characterization of 'college.' "[23] W.E.B. Du Bois in his book *The Souls of Black Folk* describes in detail the heroic struggle of Blacks in the period of Jim Crow to maintain their schools and provide education for their children.

Education for white children also suffered under the Conservatives. In Tennessee, for example, white illiteracy climbed 50 percent in the period after 1877. It was not until the end of the century, under pressure from the Populist movement, that schools for whites recovered from the general onslaught against education which followed the triumph of the counterrevolution.

The Populists of the 1890s in some areas adopted pro-Black attitudes, and many Blacks joined the movement. The defeat of the Populists in and after the elections of 1896, and the rise of imperialist ambitions in the ruling class, played important roles in a further development of racism. It was around this time that the full juridical codification of the Jim Crow caste system took shape. Blacks were segregated, made to sit in the back of streetcars, to enter public buildings through the back door, etc. But the full Jim Crow system, both in fact and in law, was not consolidated until the twentieth century. Anti-Black legislation continued to be passed in the Southern states (and, on a much smaller scale, spread northward) until the 1940s.

11

Racism and Historical Mythology

The triumph of the Conservative counterrevolution in the South had a deep impact on the nation as a whole. The propaganda campaign which began in the early 1870s around the slogans of "amnesty" and "reform" expanded into a call for "reconciliation" in the North and "home rule" in the South. With the completed overthrow of the Radical regimes in 1877 the campaign did not end but deepened. Its themes now revolved around bringing the nation back together, promoting a new American nationalism, and accepting racism. The Jim Crow system had to be rationalized ideologically just as slavery had been. The Conservative victory gave a new national impulse to racism, which grew until it had virtually stamped out the egalitarian antiracist legacy of the second American revolution.

When this process reached its culmination, not only was the Jim Crow system accepted as just on a national scale but along with it came a whole body of laws and legislation in direct conflict with the Fourteenth and Fifteenth Amendments and some even infringing on the Thirteenth Amendment. But Jim Crow should not be taken as simply a synonym for racism or racial oppression. Racial oppression existed even where the Jim Crow system was never fully, or even only minimally, instituted, as in New England. Jim Crow was but one form of racial oppression, a form which arose under specific historical-economic conditions in the South. In the North and West racial oppression against Chicanos, Native Americans, and Chinese, as well as Blacks, took various forms. The triumph of Jim Crow in the South strengthened racial prejudice and racial oppression throughout the country and against all nonwhites.*

The second American revolution had been a major challenge to racism, as had—less directly—the first American revolution. Radical Reconstruction directly challenged racism. The betrayal of the Radical regimes and the installation of Jim Crow marked industrial capitalism's turn towards taking full advantage of racism as a weapon for its class domination and oppression.

The campaign to revive racism went into full swing in the 1880s. Starting with *Scribner's Magazine* (called *Century Magazine* after 1881) all the major literary periodicals joined the effort. *Lippincott's Magazine, North American Review, Youth's Companion, Cosmopolitan, Atlantic Monthly, Munsey's,* and *McClure's* concentrated during the 1880s and 1890s on themes approving the Conservative take-over in the South.

To justify the new regimes it was necessary to convince the public that Blacks were by nature inferior and that their natural role was one of subordination to whites. In order to reach this goal novels of this period concentrated on explaining, primarily for the consumption of Northern audiences, how the "South"— meaning Southern whites—had always best understood Blacks. The Confederates, readers would be told, had been wrong but heroic in secession, but about Blacks they had always been essentially correct.

To facilitate getting this point across, the myth of the Old Planter South, the paternal slaveholder and the faithful slave, was created. The gallant, chivalrous, kindly slaveowner with his loving slaves was now pictured in book after book. To develop the political point fully the novels of the period particularly favored one plot in which a white Union soldier would meet a lily white Southern woman. Disliking each other at first because of sectional and wartime prejudices, they soon come to realize that they are part of one great nation and have been victims of a terrible misunderstanding. The Northern soldier turns out to have been right in his determination to maintain the Union, and the Southern woman right about maintaining the South's way of life, mainly the treatment of Blacks, i.e., racism. The couple

---

* Prejudice against Chinese was particularly strong; even defenders of rights for Blacks often opposed similar rights for Chinese. During this period a campaign was begun that eventually succeeded in prohibiting Chinese immigration into the United States.

embrace, marry, and live happily ever after. Some authors, striving for originality, would reverse the roles by having a Northern woman teacher, nurse, or daughter of a Union officer embrace and marry an ex-Confederate officer.

Plays, again mainly in the North, centered on the same theme. In one famous play, *Shenandoah* (1889, revived as a musical on Broadway in 1975), no fewer than five such couples embrace and marry.

By 1888 two-thirds of all stories furnished the newspapers by syndicates were "Southern" stories. A whole new school of Southern writers now appeared. Such popular stories as Joel Chandler Harris's *Uncle Remus* and *Br'er Rabbit* were direct products of this campaign. Few Southern writers had become famous in earlier periods of American history. Now the Northern publishers decided to promote them if they wrote on the required theme. An aspiring writer would soon find his or her material rejected unless it fitted the North-South conciliation, Blacks-in-their-place line. Letters were sent to the writers explaining the theme they should promote. One such letter warns that "stories are not used . . . that would tend to revive sectional feeling between the North and South."[1]

Many well-known abolitionists of years gone by joined in the campaign, adding their testimony as examples of Northerners who had gone wrong on the question of Blacks and race relations. None other than Harriet Beecher Stowe, author of *Uncle Tom's Cabin*, joined in support of the redeemers. Living in Florida since the end of the war, she gave her full support to the first Conservative regime under Governor Drew and wrote the Northern press in 1877 that the prospects of Blacks in the South were "all they ought to desire."[2] Maude Howe, daughter of the author of the "Battle Hymn of the Republic," declared in her novel *Atlanta in the South* (1886) that Blacks were happier and better off in slavery than in freedom.

Thomas Wentworth Higginson, who had been a secret backer of John Brown and commanded the all-Black First South Carolina Volunteers regiment during the war, now disgraced his past by condoning the racist campaign.

The most talented political editors of the period took the same road. Edwin L. Godkin of the *Nation* was one of the first to evolve in this manner, making his break with pro-Black radicalism in 1871. By 1890 the *Nation* could piously announce: "There is a rapidly growing sympathy at the North with Southern perplexity over the negro problem. . . . Even those who were not shocked by the carpet-bag experiment . . . are beginning to 'view with alarm' the political prospect created by the increase of the negro population, and by the continued inability of southern society to absorb or assimilate them in any sense, physical, social, or political. . . . The sudden admission to the suffrage of a million of the recently emancipated slaves belonging to the least civilized race in the world . . . was a great leap in the dark. . . ."[3]

With some delay *Harper's Weekly* followed the *Nation*. By 1882 the once Radical-abolitionist magazine caught up with the transformation of its editor, George William Curtis, who beginning with the 1872 Liberal Republican movement had entered into opposition to Radical Reconstruction. Thomas Nast, the most famous cartoonist of his generation, followed in Curtis's footsteps. There is hardly an illustrated book on this period of history that does not include one of Nast's powerful drawings supporting Radical Reconstruction by depicting the mistreatment of Blacks. Yet he too switched in 1884.

Standing almost alone against the mainstream in the literary world were Anna E. Dickinson and Judge Albion W. Tourgee. Tourgee's book *A Fool's Errand*, written in 1879, was the last, if not the only, novel written against the Ku Klux Klan. Following Tourgee's book, which sold 200,000 copies, an astronomical figure for that period, not one book on the subject was published which did not glorify the earlier KKK.

In the 1880s Robert E. Lee, who had died in 1870, was canonized as an American hero. Even the less popular Jefferson Davis was hailed in the press both North and South. In 1889 the United Confederate Veterans was organized and unanimously elected General Gordon of Georgia—the same Gordon of the railroad redeemers—as commander in chief. In 1895 the United Daughters of the Confederacy came into existence. The Confederate flag regained popularity throughout the South and was treated as nothing extraordinary in the North.

Historians fell in step. A whole school, led by William A. Dunning, developed and poured forth racist histories of the Radical Reconstruction period favoring the counterrevolution. As president of both the American Historical Association and the American Political Science Association, Dunning was an influential academic figure.

His theme was simple: Blacks were inferior; attempts to give them equal political and social rights with whites had caused all the turmoil; the new Jim Crow system corresponded to the natural relationship between Blacks and whites and had brought stability to the South. Dunning, a Northerner and son of a manufacturer, directed the high-level propaganda campaign from Columbia University, which took the lead in publishing his and his students' racist contributions to the study of history. In his *Essays on the Civil War and Reconstruction* Dunning concluded with the judgment that Jim Crow would last forever. Seeing confirmation of this in America's imperialist policies, Dunning wrote in 1901, "In view of the questions which have been raised by our lately established relations with other races, it seems most improbable that the historian will soon, or ever, have to record a reversal of the conditions which this process has established."[4]

Not lagging too far behind were the sciences. Soon sociologists, anthropologists, and psychologists were adding their "proofs" of Black inferiority. The all-embracing campaign, which merged with the growth of American nationalism—that is, imperialist chauvinism—dredged up every conceivable argument to justify racism.

The claim by Marxists that under capitalism scientists, as well as historians, are affected by the views and needs of the ruling class is substantiated quite clearly by the racist campaign which began in the late 1870s and continued through the early part of the twentieth century. One example of the use of "science" to justify the ruling class's political line is the following passage written in 1916 by anthropologist Madison Grant: "Race consciousness . . . in the United States, down to and including the Mexican War, seems to have been very strongly developed among native Americans, and it still remains in full vigor today in the South, where the presence of a large negro population forces this question upon the daily attention of the whites. . . . In New England, however . . . there appeared early in the last century a wave of sentimentalism, which at that time took up the cause of the negro, and in so doing apparently destroyed, to a large extent, pride and consciousness of race in the North. The agitation over slavery was inimical to the Nordic race, because it thrust aside all national opposition to the intrusion of hordes of immigrants of inferior racial value, and prevented the fixing of a definite American type. . . ."[5]

The connection between racism, U.S. nationalism, and imperialism is important. As American capitalism began its expansion into the world's colonial areas in the 1890s it had to justify its domination over the peoples there. Since almost all were nonwhites, racist ideology became an integral part of America's imperialist expansion. In 1898, the year of the Spanish-American war, the *Nation*, commenting on a Supreme Court decision upholding the disfranchisement of Blacks in the South, called it "an interesting coincidence that this important decision is rendered at a time when we are considering the idea of taking in a varied assortment of inferior races in different parts of the world which, of course, could not be allowed to vote."[6]

Even though the broad question of historiography cannot be dealt with adequately here, some comments are in order. After the Second World War there was a rise of revolutionary struggles in the colonial world. These struggles not only compelled the imperialist powers to switch to a policy of neocolonialism as opposed to direct colonial domination but also resulted in important anticapitalist revolutionary victories, especially in Asia.

At the same time, the Second World War and its aftermath brought changes in the economy of the South and consequently in the lives of Blacks. The South became urbanized and industrialized; its agriculture was mechanized. Blacks were driven off the land, ending their role as sharecroppers; as proletarianized and urbanized workers, they were turned into a cheap labor supply of a different type. These national and international changes forced American imperialism to adjust the *form* of its racial oppression. Jim Crow, the specific caste system of the South, fell—not automatically, but under the blows of a massive social movement against racial oppression.*

Influenced by these economic, political, and social changes, a new historical school came into existence. Just as the earlier historical interpretation of Dunning had arisen to meet the existing requirements of the ruling class, the new current began to reinterpret the Civil War and the era of Radical Reconstruction in accord with the newly developing needs of American imperialism.

Calling themselves the "revisionists" and dating their origin at the beginning of the Second World War, they have produced an

---

* For an analysis of how Jim Crow ended, see the author's pamphlet *Who Killed Jim Crow? The Story of the Civil Rights Movement and Its Lessons for Today* (New York: Pathfinder Press, 1975).

enormous body of historical material, most of it in the last two decades. The revisionists reject the Dunning school's pro-Jim Crow interpretation. They favor equal legal rights for all and reject theories of a biological inferiority of Blacks as the cause and explanation of the rise of Jim Crow. Nevertheless many works of the white revisionists, especially those written before the civil rights movement of the 1950s and 1960s, still expressed openly racist views. In the period after the civil rights movement, such flagrantly racist statements disappeared.

The revisionists have no explicit, coherent explanation for either the appearance of Radical Reconstruction or its end. Historian David Montgomery, after referring to the contributions of many of the best-known revisionists—McKitrick, Cox, Sharkey, Unger, Franklin, Stampp, and McPherson—admits that "None has offered today's readers a new interpretation of Radical Republicanism to take the place of Beale's."[7]

The revisionists are pragmatists who pride themselves on disproving previous historical interpretations. In their efforts to disprove others they attack not only the Dunning school, which is considered totally discredited (though admired for its research), but especially the economic determinists of the Progressive-liberal school such as Charles and Mary Beard and Howard K. Beale.

The fact is that the history produced by the revisionists is a confused mixture of ideas borrowed from the Dunning school, the economic determinists, and even earlier interpretations. In one important respect the revisionists represent a backward step from the viewpoint of the Beards and Beale. With all its limitations and one-sidedness, the economic determinist school, which arose as an offshoot of the middle-class Progressive movement in the early years of this century, correctly began to give material factors priority over ideas as the motor force of history. It saw the struggle between social classes and conflicting methods of production as the root source of the ideas and theories projected by reformers, politicians, and reactionaries of the Civil War era.

The revisionists tend to reverse this relationship, raising ideas to predominance in the historical process. In doing so they revert to the bourgeois interpretation of the previous century which regarded the Civil War and its aftermath as an idealistic crusade.

One difficulty that the revisionists have is to explain their own origin and nature. Kenneth Stampp attempts an answer to this problem in the opening chapter of *The Era of Reconstruction*. His argument boils down to the claim that the revisionists emerged because they became more sophisticated historians than their predecessors. He also states that racial views within American society have changed and so, in turn, historians have changed their outlook on the era. This is his superficial and inadequate formulation on this crucial point: "As ideas about race have changed, historians have become increasingly critical of the Dunning interpretation of Reconstruction."[8]

Instead of probing further to find out why "ideas about race changed" and trying to see the connection between events and the development of the revisionist school, Stampp stops short. He concentrates rather on boasting of the more "enlightened" method of the revisionists. In rejecting the interpretation of the economic determinists Stampp argues, "We are not suggesting the absence of either political or economic motives, but only the insufficiency of an interpretation that excludes humanitarianism, ideas and ideology. The appreciation of the complexity of motivation and a more sophisticated approach to problems of human behavior are the very essence of Reconstruction revisionism."[9]

The question for historians is not, however, merely to include consideration of all factors but to ascertain their interrelationship, showing what is primary and what is secondary, and how they interact. The charge that the economic determinists were one-sided is valid. They failed to understand correctly the interrelationship between society's superstructure and its economic substructure. But simply to mix economics, politics, ideology, and whatever in a historical smorgasbord does not advance our understanding beyond that of the economic determinists. In fact the revisionists really make a worse error in the opposite direction. Insofar as Stampp takes a stand, he credits Radical "idealism" for the major gains of Radical Reconstruction. While crediting "idealism," Stampp is careful to quickly add a qualifying "in part." Almost all statements made by revisionists are quickly followed by "in part" or an equivalent, reducing them to historical agnosticism. To the revisionists nothing is certain and definitive.

The revisionists would be the last to recognize that their special method and eclectic views reflect the social pressures around them. Their views developed under two major pressures. These were, first, the economic and social changes undergone by American capitalism with the resulting shifts in ruling class policy, and second, the mass struggles of the Afro-American people and the worldwide colonial revolution.

The rise of the civil rights movement pushed the revisionist historians leftward. But the civil rights movement declined with the concessions granted in 1963-65; this eased the pressures felt within the walls of academia. When more radical demands going beyond simple juridical equality, i.e., the ending of Jim Crow, were raised by Blacks, they did not receive the same enthusiastic support from the revisionist historians. And Black nationalist activism underwent a downturn in the early 1970s too.

As American imperialism needed to drop the crudities of the Southern Jim Crow system, the revisionist school rapidly made headway in academic circles. But in disproving the Dunning school, the revisionists opened up a Pandora's box of unanswered historical questions which all point toward the condemnation of the present order. Fearing where their own facts might lead them, they stopped short of conclusions which would directly relate to present-day America. Instead they have sought refuge behind an agnosticism which doesn't endanger the privileges accorded them by the present system.

The revisionists not only fail to clarify the reasons for the rise and fall of Radical Reconstruction but they cannot completely rid themselves of the racism still so pervasive in American society. Even Kenneth Stampp, an extremely capable historian and unquestionably a conscious supporter of racial equality, nevertheless makes statements that reveal a failure to comprehend the depth of racist traditions in our society. Consider Stampp's comment: "One need not be disturbed about the romantic nonsense that still fills the minds of many Americans about their Civil War. This folklore is essentially harmless. But the legend of Reconstruction is another matter. It has had serious consequences, because it has exerted a powerful influence upon the political behavior of many white men, North and South."[10]

Stampp is wrong. The glorification of slave society and the Confederacy is not "harmless" but harmful. It is part of America's racist traditions and education. Such "romantic nonsense" remains as a reinforcement to the general racism in present day America. The widespread tolerance given to the flag of the Confederacy falls in with this pernicious folklore.

Another example of the mystification of the Confederacy is the song made popular a few years ago by Joan Baez, "The Night They Drove Old Dixie Down." Would a comparable song lamenting the collapse of the Nazis be acceptable to Americans? Would Joan Baez be willing to record such a song? Why then is the regime of chattel slavery with its traditions of human bondage treated in such a light-minded manner unless it is a reflection of the racism still prevalent in this country?

The revisionists generally limit their criticisms of racism to Jim Crow laws and their proposals to enforcement of equal rights legislation. They take no position on the question of self-determination. The rise of Black nationalist sentiments is passed off as irrelevant or worse. This is typical of almost the entire present generation of academic historians. Even C. Vann Woodward, a leading exponent of the Beards' basic views (though he veers towards revisionism in *The Strange Career of Jim Crow*), refers to early currents of Black nationalism as "lunatic-fringe movements."[11]

The Strange Career of Jim Crow, a compilation of very informative lectures given by Woodward in 1954 in the South, is a popular book today. The aim of his lectures and book was to break the myth that the Jim Crow system had always existed in the South.

Woodward's book remains weak on, if it is not an outright misunderstanding of, the actual roots of the development of Jim Crow. In establishing the decisive turning point in the development of the Jim Crow system, he gives equal weight to the appearance of Jim Crow laws in the 1890s and the violent overthrow of Radical Reconstruction in the 1870s. Indeed, the former seems to weigh heavier in his scales. He thereby fails to see that the Jim Crow caste system was molded in the violent campaigns that overthrew Radical Reconstruction, even though some of its forms were fully developed only at a later date.

This error leads Woodward to argue that relations between Blacks and whites were *qualitatively* more just and peaceful in the 1880s than the 1890s. His lack of a materialist approach on this question so misleads him that he fails to appreciate the reality of the economic, political, and social conditions of Blacks in the 1880s as opposed to their formal legal status and to superficial appearances.[12]

The illusions Woodward expresses regarding the Democratic Party in 1957—"the outspoken champion of Negro rights"—and his support for gradualism in ending Jim Crow, indicate how closely such views were tied to and reflected the policies of the most farsighted and astute representatives of American imperialism of the same period.

To be fully understood, the paternalism of Woodward's gradualist advice must be placed in its historical setting. In the post–World War II period, America's ruling class sought to shift from the Jim Crow system to racial oppression without the use of a legal caste system. They were pushed to do this for the sake of appearances internationally, to conciliate rising civil rights sentiment domestically, and to remove hindrances to the full use of Black labor in the newly industrialized South. But they wanted to minimize the changes, carry them out gradually over a period of decades, and avoid any disturbances or participation by the masses themselves. Despite such calculations and advice like that of Woodward, the changes came only through massive struggles and violent shocks. The struggles carried the tempo and depth of changes beyond the plans of the ruling class. And yet these changes did not end racial oppression but only legal, or *de jure*, segregation, leaving actual, or *de facto*, segregation. As some have suggested, this constituted a phenomenon within the United States parallel to the passing from colonialism to neocolonialism internationally.

It is ironic that, at the time Woodward was delivering these lectures on the "New Reconstruction," giving historical arguments for ending Jim Crow, one of the politicians who would play a role in ending Jim Crow—under mass pressure from the civil rights struggles of the spring and summer of 1963—was publishing a traditional, racist, Dunning school interpretation of Radical Reconstruction. *Profiles in Courage* by John F. Kennedy, written in 1955, describes Radical Reconstruction as "a black nightmare the South never could forget." The president-to-be applauded those "who sought to bind up the wounds of the nation and treat the South with mercy and fairness—men like President Andrew Johnson. . . ." While portraying Johnson's "mercy and fairness," he painted Thaddeus Stevens as "the crippled, fanatical personification of the extremes of the Radical Republican movement." In these statements it is obvious that Kennedy equated the word "South" with racist whites.[13]

In his glorification of Mississippi's wealthy redeemer and hypocrite, Lucius Quintus Cincinnatus Lamar, Kennedy gave an analysis of what had been wrong with Radical Reconstruction in Mississippi. "No state suffered more from carpetbag rule than Mississippi," he wrote. "Adelbert Ames, first Senator and then Governor, was a native of Maine, a son-in-law of the notorious 'butcher of New Orleans,' Ben Butler. . . . He was chosen Governor by a majority composed of freed slaves and Radical

Republicans, sustained and nourished by Federal bayonets. One Cardoza [a Black—P.C.], under indictment for larceny in New York, was placed at the head of the public schools and two former slaves held the offices of Lieutenant Governor and Secretary of State." (Note the implication that if people had been slaves, that automatically ruled out any wisdom in voting or ability in public office.)[14]

Openly racist interpretations such as Kennedy's are no longer in vogue—at least at the university level. The revisionist school is now completely dominant. Today the more popular text on the history of the Afro-American people being used on campuses is revisionist John Hope Franklin's *From Slavery to Freedom*. Franklin, a Black historian, first wrote this work, subtitled A History of Negro Americans, in 1947. He has revised it three times since then, the last time in 1973.

The chapters on the rise and fall of Radical Reconstruction are a good summary of the revisionist outlook. Interspersed in the text, however, are leftovers from the Dunning-school interpretation. Franklin's book serves as a specimen of the strength and persistence of the academic carry-over of some racist myths, all the more because the thrust of Franklin's text is to refute racism. Yet the lack of a materialist approach leaves such revisionist works marred by racist innuendos traceable to Dunning's school.

One racist tradition that seems to be pervasive is the use of the word "South" to mean only the racist whites of the South. No one can object to the use of shorthand terms as in, for example, "the North fought the South" in the Civil War. But when the term "South" is used specifically to describe the opinion or attitudes of the people of the region and it clearly excludes Blacks as a people, this is a vestige of racism.

Just as in recent years the women's liberation movement has pointed out how widespread the deep-rooted sexist terminology is in common expressions, so Black writers have pointed to the same prevalence of racist terms. The revisionists, with hardly any exceptions, fall into the same use of "South" with its racist assumptions.

This is true of Franklin's text. He writes, for example, "The South universally hailed the disfranchisement of the Negro as a constructive act of statesmanship."[15] As we have noted, and as all revisionists know, not only did the Blacks oppose their disfranchisement but in most states the constitutional conventions which passed such acts refused to put them to the customary vote. They feared poor whites would reject this "act of statesmanship" as a threat to their own right to vote. How can Franklin write "universally hailed" by the "South," unless "South" here means only racist whites, in this case ruling class whites?

Another example is the following statement by Franklin: "The Reconstruction Act of 1867 imposed on the South a regime more difficult to bear than defeat."[16] For whom were the new Radical regimes so difficult to bear? Not the 44 percent of the South who had black skins, nor the substantial sector of whites who voted for the Radical regimes, together a majority of the people of the South. Certainly for Mississippi, South Carolina, and Louisiana the above statement is not valid throughout the Reconstruction period. Once again the "South" is assumed to mean only racist whites.

Franklin's book repeats the hoary racist charge that "many freedmen would not work because they were exhilarated by their new liberty."[17] He compounds this error with the racist use of "Southern" when he comes to the defense of the Afro-American people by saying, "There can be no question that the majority of Negroes worked, despite Southern doubts of their efficiency as free laborers."[18] The truth is *all* Black families, men, women, and children, worked—of necessity they had to. The same cannot be said of whites, since rich whites lived off the labor of others. As to the "efficiency" of Blacks as "free laborers," 44 percent of the population of the South, as well as quite a substantial sector of the whites, had no doubts about it. The "Southern doubts" are understandable only if the meaning of "South" is limited to racist whites.

A further example of the confusion resulting from the revisionist interpretation is Franklin's use of the word "free labor." As we have pointed out, the key to understanding the failure of Radical Reconstruction is the contradiction between free labor and the need of a *cheap* labor supply amidst a general shortage of labor. This is never mentioned by Franklin.

The specific Jim Crow caste system arose precisely because the capitalists involved in exploiting the resources of the South, especially cotton, became aware that Blacks as free laborers—free to move, to organize, to vote, etc.—were incompatible with a profitable agricultural system in the South. Yet Franklin writes the opposite: "By 1870 the cotton kingdom had retrieved much of its losses, and by 1875 the white South had come to realize that cheap free labor could be the basis for a profitable agricultural system."

If we take the word "free" simply to mean not chattel slavery, then Franklin's statement is certainly true. But failure to note the differences between the form of Black labor developing in the South as Radical Reconstruction was defeated and that of Northern white labor blurs the entire dynamic of the period.

Franklin does not leave out economic factors. On the contrary he refers to many of the economic and political developments which point in the direction of a correct analysis. As with the case of Kenneth Stampp's *The Era of Reconstruction*, the best-known revisionist history of the period, Franklin's presentation of the facts is better than his conclusions—whether made in passing or implied.

One of the most persistent myths handed down from the Dunning school is the idea that the overthrow of Radical Reconstruction was a return to "home rule" in the South. Franklin echoes this idea, even though it is clearly disproven by the revisionists themselves. He correctly points out that the Northern industrial capitalists "helped" end Radical Reconstruction, but refers to their intention to "restore home rule to the South" as the North grew "weary of the crusade for the Negro."[19] At another point he says, "At last the South could rule itself without Northern interference or Negro influence."[20]

Because of its continuing influence even among those who consider themselves Marxists, the Dunning myth deserves somewhat closer examination so that its traces can be identified. In broad outline, it goes as follows:

After the Civil War there was a division among Northerners. Some, like Lincoln and Johnson, wanted to carry out a policy of reconciliation, to bring the country back together by showing magnanimity to the conquered South. However, some vindictive people led by such Radicals as Thaddeus Stevens wanted revenge. Out of hate, and in search of graft, these Radicals established carpetbag governments which ruled the South by manipulating the ignorant, inferior Blacks. These governments were maintained by the use of Federal bayonets.

The Radical regimes led to terrible conditions in the South. The economy was disrupted, Blacks refused to work, innocent people were persecuted while graft and other crimes reached all-time highs. To provide funds for patronage and graft, unbearable property taxes were imposed. Efforts by intelligent white Southerners to protect their society gave rise to organizations such as the Ku Klux Klan which committed some unfortunate acts, reports of which have been unduly emphasized and greatly exaggerated.

But fortunately the North soon realized its error. Tiring of the Blacks' never-ending "grievances," and the flagrant corruption and chaos created by the Black-supported carpetbag governments, the North changed its mind. The South was permitted to return to "home rule"; the ex-slaveowning planters reestablished their rightful influence in society, natural white-Black relations reasserted themselves, and the carpetbaggers were sent to prison or back North. The poor misguided Blacks were back in their place and America, with North and South reconciled, took a major step towards becoming a truly unified and peaceful nation. This myth, which many have seen fleshed out in the notorious movie *Birth of a Nation,* became "history."

Radicals who rejected racism recognized that Radical Reconstruction must have had a positive side because under it Blacks had democratic rights. They correctly rejected the racist content of Dunning's historical interpretation but did so by standing it upside down. Where the racist interpretation put a plus, the left put a minus, and vice versa. Radical Reconstruction was essentially good and the return to "home rule" bad, but the basic analysis remained. It was accepted that the ex-slaveowning planters were restored to power and ruled the South after 1877; and heavy emphasis was placed on the agreement of 1877 to explain how that restoration was achieved. This view has remained unchallenged on the left up to present times.

"Marxist" Analysis

In the 1930s the first "Marxist" interpretation of Radical Reconstruction and its overthrow, written by James Allen, codified this error. Allen wrote two books; the first, titled *The Negro Question,* was published in 1936, though it appears to have been prepared a few years earlier; the second, *Reconstruction: The Battle for Democracy,* printed in 1937, is of more interest for the present discussion.

Allen completely accepts the traditional concept of the return to power of the ex-slavocracy. He argues that the slaveowners lost the Civil War but were able to "revive" and "regather" their forces. As the Northern industrial bourgeoisie became conservatized it acquiesced in the resurgence of the ex-slaveowners. An agreement to this effect was reached in 1877 by which the old exslaveowning cotton planter class returned to power.

Insofar as Allen rejects the concept of Black inferiority and sees Radical Reconstruction as a progressive period, his book was more accurate than almost all of the histories on the subject available at the time. The important exception was the monumental work of W. E. B. Du Bois, *Black Reconstruction*.

Black Reconstruction remains unsurpassed for a descriptive, informational history of Radical Reconstruction. It is far more accurate in its factual content than any history of Radical Reconstruction written prior to its publication in 1935. In this sense, Allen's book added nothing fundamentally new except its faulty analysis.

Du Bois employed Marxist categories in a number of places in his book, in some cases in an inaccurate and anachronistic manner. For instance, he referred to the Radical Reconstruction governments as being, in effect, workers' regimes. Scientifically, that would mean the triumph of a socialist revolution. Because of Du Bois's use of certain Marxist categories, many bourgeois historians mistakenly refer to *Black Reconstruction* as a Marxist analysis.

Du Bois's analysis of the fall of Radical Reconstruction is superior to Allen's because he places it more in the context of the general triumph of industrial capitalism and less as the result of a settlement between two specific ruling class sectors, Northern industrial-banking capitalists and Southern planters. In any case, Du Bois did not explicitly refute the thesis that the old ex-slaveowning planter ruling class had returned to power.

Allen made this mistake explicit. Referring to the policies of Andrew Johnson and the danger of a restoration of the ex-slaveowners, Allen writes, "No other class was present to seize the reins of state power in the South. It was equivalent, *as later events showed,* to restoring the former ruling class to the seat of government." Regarding the federal treatment of the Confederate leaders and ex-slaveowning planters he comments, "As a class defeated in civil war and, *for a time at least,* deposed from power, the former slavemasters enjoyed unprecedented leniency."[21]

Continuing his analysis, Allen adds that this leniency "gave this class a breathing spell in which to revive and regather its forces." This class of planters "came to an understanding with the industrial bourgeoisie." The industrial capitalists bargained away the gains of the second American revolution, finally making a pledge to leave the South in the ex-slaveowners' hands, so, according to Allen, "The bourgeoisie had bargained away the revolution in step after step. . . . It has kept its pledge, as given to the Bourbons of 1876, to the present day."

Finally, the refusal of the Northern industrial bourgeoisie to defend democratic rights in the South led to the growth of the counterrevolution. "Such were the consequences of a whole series of fatal retreats which culminated in the peace agreement of 1876 and in the resulting victory of the *coup d'etat* governments of the planters."[22]

Allen's error could possibly be explained by the fact that the histories on the period then available contained the same conclusion. But this is only partial mitigation. Historians who dealt with the Populist period, which had come right after redemption, had clearly established that the new Southern governments represented the interests of Eastern money and railroads rather than agricultural interests. Allen could not have been unaware of this. Other writers contemporary with Allen, such as Louis M. Hacker, Paul Lewinson, and Du Bois, had a more accurate view of the class nature of the counterrevolutionary overthrow of Reconstruction and of the redemption regimes. In the late 1930s Hacker wrote that the redemption regimes "represented a combination of landlordism and the new capitalism allied with northern financial, railway and mineral interests."[23] Another historian writing in 1922 and quoted by Lewinson wrote, "The new Bourbon regime in Georgia was essentially a business man's regime. To a greater or less extent this was doubtless true of other Southern States."[24]

But there is another, more important observation that must be raised. Marxists define classes by their relationship to forms of property. What primarily characterized the ruling class of the Confederacy? Was it landownership or the ownership of slaves? It is fundamental for a correct analysis to recognize that the ownership of slaves is what gave the slavocracy its specific class character as compared with the capitalist class proper. But even if we were to base ourselves on landownership as the criterion, we would have to pose another question. If the industrial bourgeoisie triumphed militarily, politically, and economically, why did it have to "negotiate" or make a deal with any other sector of the bourgeoisie over the control of one-third of its territory?

Negotiations and deals stem from power relations. Allen, and the Communist Party (CP), whose views he represented, agree that the Civil War made the industrial bourgeoisie dominant throughout the United States. Allen even implies in a footnote that the landowners were replaced by other capitalists as the dominant force in the South.[25]

So according to the CP's theoretician, the slavocracy was overthrown and expropriated, the industrial capitalists extended their domination economically and politically, but once having consolidated their power they opened up negotiations with a defeated and expropriated class which in spite of its weakness was now leading a powerful counterrevolution. The industrial bourgeoisie, we are asked to believe, offered these ex-slaveowners control of one-third of the nation in return for placing Rutherford Hayes, instead of Samuel Tilden, in the presidency!

Since World War II the evidence presented by historians that the ex-slaveowners were not returned to power has been rather conclusive. But the CP, in William Z. Foster's book, *The Negro People*, first published in 1954, continues to cling to the thesis of the return of the ex-slaveowning planters to power. He writes, "Southern reaction, based upon the big cotton planters, waged a long, complex, and bitter struggle to capture the state governments in the South from the people's forces. This process the reactionaries called the 'redemption' or the 'restoration.'" Foster continues, "During the eight years of the Grant Administration, there was an increasing tendency in Northern capitalist ranks to conciliate the ex-slaveholders. . . . this new attitude was to come to fruition in an agreement with the Southern reactionaries, among whom the cotton planters were dominant, that put an end to the revolution in the South."[26]

After repeating Allen's basic analysis, Foster takes up the challenge presented by recent historians to Allen's views. He quotes C. Vann Woodward to the effect that the redemption regimes were dominated by industrial capitalist interests having little to do with the old planter regimes. Foster accepts this conclusion only for recent times, but reasserts his support for Allen's conclusions.

Regarding the penetration of Northern capital he writes, "This general trend, which became marked after the Civil War, was to continue until, in our times, not the planters but the financial-industrial capitalist interests control the South." He rejects the conclusion that the industrial capitalists conquered the South in the period of Radical Reconstruction by recalling Allen's arguments: "Allen correctly remarks, however, that, 'Industry in the South developed very slowly during the Reconstruction period.'" From this Foster concludes that "the Northern bourgeoisie in the 1877 Hayes agreement, chose a different, reactionary route, betraying the Negro people and coming to a settlement with its erstwhile cotton-planter enemy and the budding Southern middle class. After this betrayal, as we shall see later on, some industrialization of the South was pushed vigorously by the Northern capitalists."[27]

Foster correctly notes that the Northern capitalists opposed a land reform and instead "chose a different, reactionary route." But he interprets the failure to industrialize the South to the same degree as the North to mean that the industrial-finance capitalists were not dominant in that region. This is faulty thinking, to say the least. When the United States extended its control to the Caribbean area it failed to industrialize any of the countries it conquered. This in no way meant that industrial-finance capital did not control them or dominate their economies. Likewise, for the South after the Civil War and Radical Reconstruction the dominant class was the triumphant industrial bourgeoisie, not the planters.

In the last analysis the cause of this theoretical error is to be found in the peculiar political end Allen's and Foster's books served. They were not aimed at presenting an accurate interpretation of the class struggle as it unfolded during and after the Civil War. Instead they used "Marxist" categories and rhetoric to defend the then current "theories" and policies being advocated from Moscow.

With each new turn of Moscow's foreign policy, the policy of the CP toward Blacks in America has shifted, and with it the CP's historical analysis. At the time Allen wrote his first book, he was trying to justify a line handed down by the Kremlin which was best supported by having the "slaveowners return to power." It was based on a thesis that a special separate majority-Black nation actually existed in the cotton-growing black belt, that this nation was a remnant of slavery, and that only a revolution could alter the peculiar sharecropping form of labor existing within it. To maintain this thesis it was necessary to reject any evidence that Blacks might ever become a minority in the indicated area or that the black belt could be industrialized or mechanized under capitalism.

Thus Allen "proves" in *The Negro Question* that no significant number of Blacks will migrate North or to the cities, that the South will not be industrialized, and that Southern agriculture will not be mechanized. Yet all three of these changes were already occurring and would sweep the South in the two decades following Allen's prediction of their impossibility.

This "black belt nation" theory was fostered during what the Communist International called the "third period." This was the period of Stalin's ultraleft thesis that capitalism was breathing its last and would soon expire. Accordingly for Communists to struggle for almost any reforms would be illusory because they could no longer be granted under capitalism. All studies that backed up Stalin's line, such as Allen's first book, were hailed as brilliant applications of Marxism, while any views questioning or contradicting them were declared counterrevolutionary and their advocates expelled from the CP.

But the third-period policy, which lasted from 1928 to 1935, was suddenly altered after the Seventh World Congress of the Communist International and a new line advanced. Stalin now "discovered" that reforms could be won under capitalism. He further declared that in every country some sections of the capitalists were progressive and should therefore be supported by the workers. Thus began the "popular front" period. Allen's second book is tailored to the popular-front line.

The new premium was on proving that there were different and conflicting wings of the ruling class—progressive and reactionary. The thesis that the slaveowners had returned to power in the South now was useful to justify the new instead of the old line. According to the new policy American capitalists included liberal-progressive, as opposed to reactionary—especially the "Southern ruling-class"—elements. The task of the workers and their leadership was to support the liberal-progressive wing. The thesis about the ex-slaveowners' return to power was retained. But the projection of a separate majority-Black nation in the black belt could only get in the way of a bloc with the "progressive" imperialists and it was therefore quietly filed away.

Then one day in 1939 the Kremlin announced it had concluded a non-aggression pact with Hitler and that the progressive capitalists in the United States weren't progressive after all, but reactionary imperialists, in particular Franklin Delano Roosevelt. Once again the CP made a 180-degree turn. The Black nation theory was dusted off, as well as the superheated third-period rhetoric. Then, lo and behold, the Soviet Union was invaded by Hitler and yet another 180-degree shift was effected. Out went the Black nation theory, back came the progressive capitalists opposed to the Southern and other reactionaries. Roosevelt became the leader of a struggle for "national liberation." The CP insisted that everyone, including Blacks, subordinate their demands to the needs of American imperialism under Roosevelt.

The Communist Party went so far with the new procapitalist capitulation during the war that it supported the imprisonment of Japanese-Americans, opposed the Black March on Washington movement for equality in 1942, tried to break the miners' strike of 1943, and demanded more sacrifice by workers than capitalists.

After the war the CP tried to clean up its image a bit. It blamed the policies it had followed during the war period on its own erstwhile commander in chief, Earl Browder, expelled him, and made some adjustments in its theory regarding the Afro-American people. But up to the present the CP has stuck to the return-of-the-slaveowners line to help justify its search for the progressive bourgeoisie. After Roosevelt, the leading progressive was Henry Wallace, then Adlai Stevenson, and after him John F. Kennedy. Lyndon Baines Johnson, being the leader of the "Southern ruling class" in the early fifties, was opposed by the CP right up to his nomination for vice-president in 1960. By 1964 the CP had discovered that Johnson was actually a progressive capitalist politician after all and had apparently handed over his stewardship of the reactionary capitalists to Barry Goldwater.

Though the Black nation theory was put on the shelf and later openly repudiated, the CP still clings to the thesis of the return of the planter-slaveowners in Foster's book, last reprinted in 1973. Unfortunately, the predominance of the Communist Party in the American left during the 1930s, 40s, and 50s caused Allen's works to be accepted as Marxism. To this day his book on Radical Reconstruction is regarded as an authentic Marxist interpretation of that period. His interpretation has enjoyed general acceptance within the American left even after C. Vann Woodward's documentation, in his book *Origins of the New South,* refuted the return-of-the-slaveowners myth.

12

Thermidor

How should the final defeat of the Radical Reconstruction period be defined? C. Vann Woodward observed that the overthrow of Radical Reconstruction was not carried out by the former slaveholding class, nor was it a "restoration" of their influence or their pro-agricultural socioeconomic policies. He concludes therefore that "only in a limited sense can it be properly called a 'counterrevolution.'"[1]

Woodward's judgment that the prewar regime was in no way reestablished is well founded. But that does not mean that the crushing of the Radical state governments was not a counterrevolution. To make this point clear, the nature of the redemption overthrows has to be analyzed in more precise terms. The starting point and basis for such an appraisal must be the Beards' characterization of the Civil War period as the second American revolution. It was in fact the second and culminating stage of the bourgeois-democratic revolutionary process on American soil.

With this conception as the key, we can turn to the comparative development of previous revolutions of the same kind in order to comprehend the significance of the ending of Radical Reconstruction. Historians of the major bourgeois revolutions have noted certain common features in the sequence of their phases from start to finish. These spring from the diverse interests and shifting alignments of the components of the revolutionary camp.

Every bourgeois-democratic revolution has involved the collaboration of different class forces in a united front of armed struggle aimed at the overthrow of the old regime. George Novack writes in *Democracy and Revolution*, "All the bourgeois revolutions were made by broad coalitions of class forces which entered the fray with very different motives and ends in view. . . . As the struggle intensified, the original partners in the coalition often pulled apart and, at critical junctures, even moved in opposite directions and clashed head-on."[2] The official leadership in the opening phases of the movement usually comes from the upper social strata of the nation. However, the commercial and industrial capitalists are too few in number and too weak a social force to confront and overcome the institutional powers blocking their advancement. They are obliged to enter into collaboration with the small property owners—shopkeepers, artisans, and farmers or peasants—and call upon these plebian elements in order to mobilize a sufficiently powerful force of fighters against the feudal or other nonbourgeois adversaries that block their path to power.

Once the struggle for supremacy between the revolutionaries and the old regime is unleashed, its further course is determined by two major interacting factors. One comes from the necessities of defeating the counterrevolution; the other from the changing relationships among the elements on the revolutionary side. The wealthy and moderate upholders of the newly emergent order would like to triumph and consolidate their power with the least possible social convulsion and a minimum of political reforms. They find this difficult and sometimes impossible to achieve.

On the one hand they run up against determined resistance from the receding classes, who object to being dispossessed of their positions of privilege and relegated to the scrapheap. On the other hand they must give heed to the insistent demands of the more democratic elements among the populace. Tenacious and prolonged tests of strength between the revolutionary and counterrevolutionary camps tend to thrust aside the more timid and conciliatory leaders and factions and bring to the fore bolder figures, leaning upon the insurgent masses or drawn from their midst, who are ready for more decisive and irreconcilable means and courses of action. As the plebian layers and their representatives shoulder aside the more hesitant and well-to-do elements, groupings connected with the common people, or exceptional individuals from the upper strata of merchants and manufacturers but under popular influence, push aside the moderates and take over the leadership of the revolutionary cause. These new leaders lifted up from below give expression to the needs and demands of the broader masses participating in the revolutionary movement and carry the changes far beyond what the upper bourgeoisie was initially disposed to grant.

The more difficult and desperate the struggle to combat the precapitalist forces becomes, the more concessions the upper crust must make to its lower-class collaborators in the coalition and the more power is placed in the hands of the radical petty bourgeois elements. This shift in the relationship of forces is embodied in some instrument of revolutionary change and acquires specific organizational form.

However, as soon as victory looms on the horizon, the upper layers become more and more reluctant to accept or promote further social reforms sought by the plebian masses. Their executives quickly come into conflict with the aims and aspirations of those below them in the revolutionary hierarchy. The organizational instrument created by the revolution is no longer needed and inevitably becomes an obstacle to the stabilization of the new order.

In the case of the Civil War the petty bourgeois leaders had been pushed to the fore by pressures emanating from two different sources which temporarily moved in the same direction: the need felt by the Republican bourgeoisie for more decisive actions against the enemy, and the specific needs of the lower layers. But the leadership became torn by conflicting pressures once these forces began to move in opposite directions.

As leaders of the revolution and administrators of the Union government, the Radicals were in constant, close contact with the upper bourgeoisie—the bankers, manufacturers, new-rich military contractors, land speculators—and they became vulnerable to their corrupting influence and the privileges of office. At the same time the demands of the masses whence they came and by whom they were elected continued to exert a strong pull on them and in some cases impelled them to extend the social changes called for by the tasks of the revolution.

This tug-of-war produced differentiations among the Republican tops. Some proceeded to push ahead for further changes while others hung back, trying to halt them and even to retract steps already taken. This sifting out process separated the thoroughgoing Radicals from the half-hearted ones.

Once the slaveholding power was shattered, the plebian strata in the revolutionary camp did not remain quiescent. They pressed forward in struggle, no longer against the vanquished prewar power setup, but rather against the new rulership of the conquering industrial bourgeoisie.

During such a phase of more advanced class struggle the upper layers, for purposes of self-defense, turn to their own use all those elements of backwardness left over from the overthrown order, including its traditions, ideology, and forms of organization. However, since the impact of the revolutionary events has transformed the consciousness of the people so much, these relics of the past cannot be set into motion by partisans identified with the old order—at least not in the beginning of the effort to slow down and contain further radicalization.

At this juncture the most effective source of leadership in diverting the revolution usually comes from individuals closely connected with the formerly progressive forces, and even their left wing. These ex-revolutionary petty bourgeois figures now attached to the cause of the upper bourgeoisie change into propagandists and organizers of the counterthrust to beat back and hold down the forward movement of the popular masses.

This antidemocratic reaction which sets back the revolution without destroying its fundamental socioeconomic transformation has been designated as the Thermidor. The term is derived from the decisive turn of events in the development of the French revolution that occurred on July 27, 1794, when Robespierre's government was overthrown and the Directorate was installed in its place. (Thermidor was the name given to that month in the calendar adopted by the French revolution.) This event marked the beginning of the downward plunge in plebian power and the end of the revolutionary democracy.

In his work *Reunion and Reaction,* C. Vann Woodward characterized the events around 1877 as a Thermidorean reaction of the same type as occurred in the France of 1794. He stated: "I merely attempt to add a description of the final phase of the revolution, the phase that the French speak of as *Thermidor* in writing of their great revolution."[3] Further on he writes, "But if the Men of 1787 made the *Thermidor* of the First American Revolution, the Men of 1877 fulfilled a corresponding part in the Second American Revolution. They were the men who come at the end of periods of revolutionary upheaval, when the great hopes and soaring ideals have lagged and failed, and the fervors have burned themselves out. They come to say that disorder has gone too far and the extremists must be got in hand, that order and peace must be established at any price. And in their deliberations they generally have been more concerned with preserving the pragmatic and practical gains and ends of revolutions than the more idealistic aims. In this respect the Men of 1877 were not unlike those who had been cast in the same historical role before them."[4]

Unfortunately Woodward did not further develop this perfectly valid analogy, which is so pertinent to grasping the essential nature of the deathblow to Radical Reconstruction. Moreover, he omits any reference to the classes involved and his remarks therefore remain much too abstract and lack concrete social content.

More basically, he gives no clue to the special character of a Thermidorean reaction in contrast to a full-blown victory of the counterrevolutionary forces. For this it is necessary to distinguish between what happens in and to the political superstructure of the country and the economic base upon which it rests. While Thermidor represents a sharp swing to the right in the political regime on the basis of a decisive defeat for the plebian masses, it does not involve a restoration of the prerevolutionary socioeconomic order. The old ruling class, its mode of production and specific property forms, do not come back to life; they have been permanently abolished. That much of the revolutionary conquests remains intact.

The Thermidorean turn in the bourgeois-democratic revolutionary process is essentially limited to a reversal in the political setup through which the agents of the propertied bourgeoisie dislodge the representatives of the more democratic tendencies from the seats of power and take over sovereignty in the country.

The history of the French revolution from 1789 on provides the classical model for the study of the internal workings of a bourgeois upheaval. During its course the shifts in the relationships of the diverse social layers in action were most clearly expressed in conflicting political groupings and tendencies and most dramatically evidenced in distinct changes of the political regime.

In the period of revolutionary ascent, as the mass movement kept swinging more and more to the left, the Girondists, who represented the original leaders of the revolution, were themselves replaced during 1793-94 by the more intransigent petty bourgeois radicals, the Jacobins. Robespierre's regime had to put down the uprisings of the even more radically inclined urban poor led by the Enragés in 1793. This prepared the way for his own removal from power by the Directorate in the coup d'etat of Thermidor (July 27, 1794). Robespierre's downfall ended the deepening of the revolution and ushered in its period of decline.

Thereafter, on the descending curve of the revolution following the Directorate, came the Consulate and the Empire under Napoleon, and then in 1814 the Bourbon monarchy was called back from exile to govern France again.

Since this sequence of political regimes begins and ends with monarchical rule, it might seem that counterrevolution had triumphed all along the line and all the gains of the revolution had been erased. That would be a superficial and erroneous historical judgment. The restored monarchy, which marked the culmination of the recoil from the peak of the revolution, did not do away with the basic socioeconomic changes effected by the bourgeois forces. Socially speaking, the capitalist class had been elevated into the ruling class while the monarchy had been converted from the master of the bourgeoisie into its servant, as in England.

Thus, even the end product of the reactionary tide did not return France to its prerevolutionary status. Although after 1814 the bourgeoisie did not rule in its own right but through the monarchy, in social reality it had clinched its power as the new ruling class in place of the old nobility. As Novack explains, "Louis XVIII governed over a fundamentally different social order than his beheaded namesake. His charter did not recognize the principle of popular sovereignty that even Napoleon tipped his tricorne to through his plebiscites; it restricted participation in the government to a very few large landowners. Nonetheless the restoration left intact the essential social conquests of the revolution: the abolition of feudalism and its privileges, manorialism and its tithes, the principle of equality before the law and, above all, the redistribution of landed property effected by the revolution. The Bourbon king kept his hands off the rights of private ownership and did not interfere with the operations of capitalist enterprise. The regimes of both the revolution and the restoration held sacred and inviolate the public debt held by the men of money and private property. France had become definitively bourgeoisified; power and prestige went with wealth and no longer with birth."[5]

The first American revolution came to the close of its cycle with the adoption of the Constitution in 1789, the very year in which the French revolution erupted. There was a schism between the right and the left wings of the revolutionary coalition, between the upper classes and the lower orders, after the War of Independence had been won. No sooner had the American patriots settled the question of home rule with Britain than they found themselves faced with two further questions: who was going to rule at home and how?

Between 1781 and 1786 a series of contests took place between the democratic agrarian masses and the conservative propertied classes both North and South to determine these critical matters. These domestic conflicts came to a head with Shays's Rebellion in western Massachusetts in the fall and winter of 1785-86. This self-defensive uprising of the agrarian democracy, headed by veterans of the Revolutionary War, against the economic squeezing and oppressions of the urban plutocrats and aristocrats was quickly crushed. This victory for the reaction set the stage for those Woodward calls the Men of 1787, the members of the closed convention which in that year framed the U.S. Constitution. This was the capstone of the Thermidor in the first American revolution.

In the next century the industrial capitalists engaged in a showdown with the popular masses comparable to that faced by the merchant-planter coalition in the culminating stage of the earlier revolution. However, there were distinct differences in the parallel episodes which worked greatly to the advantage of the monied men in the conclusive consolidation of their supremacy in the republic.

The industrial bourgeoisie entered the fray under the leadership of their own party after having taken possession of the national government in Washington in 1861. Although there were profound shifts among the factions comprising the Republican Party as the revolution progressed and regressed, the same parliamentary regime was still functioning at the end of the whole process under the same political organization. At no time was the Republican administration overthrown and displaced by a rival party and regime, representing different class forces, as happened in France.

One factor that has prevented many historians from recognizing that the Civil War was both a social and a political revolution was its regional aspect. The fact that the conflict between the slaveholders and the free forces of the North took place in separate territories between different systems of production, governments, and armies, has obscured many of the parallels between the last bourgeois revolution in America and its predecessor.

The second American revolution had still another peculiarity.

The merchant capitalists had been the dominant wing of the bourgeoisie in the revolutions in Holland, England, France, and North America from the sixteenth up to the nineteenth centuries. The plebian forces were largely made up of small proprietors and no significant industrial proletariats had yet come on the scene.

After the industrial revolution did get into full swing and the final wave of bourgeois-democratic movements came to the fore from 1848 to 1871, the only one that awarded complete supremacy to the industrial capitalists was that in the United States. Elsewhere, during this midcentury period of wars and revolutions, the native bourgeoisies were too frightened by the revolutionary forces they set in motion and failed to pursue their class objectives to the end. Instead, they turned against their revolutions and came to terms with their precapitalist rivals. After the uprising of the workers in the Paris Commune of 1871, none of the European bourgeoisies dared risk embarking upon a decisive settlement of accounts with the forces of the old order but preferred to conclude a compromise sharing of power with them. On the other hand, the capitalist class of the U.S. made a clean sweep of the slavocracy, the last of the precapitalist formations that contested its claim to power.

In Europe, as early as 1850, on the basis of the experience of the 1848 revolutions, Karl Marx explicitly drew the conclusion that the big bourgeoisie could no longer lead even its own revolution to a successful outcome. He emphasized this lesson in an address to the central committee of the Communist League in which he counseled the workers not to subordinate the fight for their own class interests to either the big or the little bourgeoisie since neither of them could be counted upon to combat the counterrevolution with the necessary vigor. He rounded off his analysis by advising the workers that their "battle cry [should be] the Revolution in Permanence."[6]

Fifty years later, after witnessing the actions and reactions of the class forces in the Russian revolution of 1905, Leon Trotsky expanded on this observation of Marx to explain the reasons why the bourgeoisie had become transformed into an utterly conservative and counterrevolutionary force since the advent of world imperialism.

In the twentieth century that meant that those peoples which aspired to emulate the democratic revolutions of the more advanced nations could achieve their aims only under the leadership and through the triumph of the working class. The unfinished historical tasks of the bourgeois revolution would have to be fulfilled by a socialist revolution. This was the gist of his celebrated theory of permanent revolution which he first applied to the problems of the Russian revolution and later extended on a worldwide basis.

The industrial capitalists of the United States were able to succeed where their counterparts in Europe and Japan failed because of the position of strength they held from the very beginning of the Civil War. They did not have to wrest governmental power from another class or social layer but had only to defend its possession. They entered the struggle with state power in their hands in almost two-thirds of the nation. The Northern working class was poorly organized and extremely undeveloped politically. This can be seen in the low level of political consciousness among the workers of New York City who rose up in the antidraft demonstrations of the summer of 1863 compared with the Parisian workers of 1871.

The cohesiveness of the Northern bourgeoisie and its allies stands out in contrast with the situation below the Mason-Dixon line during the same period. There the slavocracy, in a desperate gamble to reverse the political ascendancy of the industrial bourgeoisie, carried through a secessionist movement which, in some cases through coup d'etats, brought eleven state governments into the Confederacy. It failed to carry along four border slave states—Missouri, Kentucky, Maryland, and Delaware—and lost part of Virginia through a split between pro-Confederate and pro-Northern forces.

As the Confederacy lost territory to the advancing federal armies, its state regimes were replaced by Union military dictatorships. Although a few steps were taken to reestablish civilian governments prior to the Confederate surrender in April 1865, most of the areas conquered by the Northern troops were directly governed by the military as the war ended.

In 1865 this provisional military rule was replaced by officials who had served in the old governmental apparatus and politicians trained in the pre–Civil War South. These were mainly men who had opposed secession and were generally favorable to industrial development.

In less than two years these interim regimes were once again superseded by military rule, which had a different orientation and rested upon a different alignment of class forces. These new military dictatorships extended bourgeois-democratic reforms beyond the limited parliamentary regimes they had replaced and in turn gave way to far more radical and democratic regimes. In the end these progressive governments were overthrown by retrogressive regimes that severely curtailed the democratic rights of the masses, especially those of Black labor.

These complex developments in the South were part of broader political processes within the nation as a whole that must be viewed in the context of the problems confronting the Northern bourgeoisie as it mounted to power. To assure their political ascendancy, the industrialists first had to weld together a coalition of forces, starting with the small farmers of the Midwest and reaching into the artisans, shopkeepers, and wage-workers of the North and ultimately bringing in the Afro-Americans. Spurred forward by the abolitionist current emanating from the urban and rural petty bourgeoisie, the Radicals in Congress and the Union states put heavy pressure on Lincoln to abandon his moderate policies. Such figures as George W. Julian, Carl Schurz, and others like them came forward at this juncture with a program of action that went beyond what the more hesitant members of the industrial bourgeoisie preferred.

However, as the slaveholders' counterrevolution appeared intransigent and unconquerable, the possibility of defeat in warfare caused the upper bourgeoisie to cast off its conservatism and make greater concessions to the plebian masses to ensure their support in winning the war. Under the circumstances, they grew more willing to countenance the policies of the more determined wing of the revolutionary leaders. As the war unfolded, the Jacobins of the second American revolution, headed by Thaddeus Stevens and Charles Sumner, gained more and more influence. In 1863 the emancipation of the slaves was proclaimed, at least in the occupied territories, the ex-slaves were armed, and talk of dividing up the land of the plantation owners began to be heard. In some limited areas the land was actually seized and distributed to its ex-slave cultivators.

This shift to the left was accompanied and implemented by the increased power of Congress in relation to the presidency. But as soon as victory came into view, the upper bourgeoisie reverted to its conservative stance and resisted further social reforms.

Consequently, the ending of the Civil War unleashed a series of conflicts among the forces of the original revolutionary combination throughout the country, in the East, the Midwest, and the

South. Farmers sought inflationary money and credit policies and, later, regulation of the piratical railroad companies. Workers demanded higher pay, an eight-hour day, and the right to organize. The knottiest of all these struggles was the thrust of the Southern ex-slaves for civil rights and a land reform.

These difficult problems broke up the unity of the Republican high command as some among them endorsed the demands of the masses and others opposed them. As Howard K. Beale states in *The Critical Year,* many of the Radicals who promoted the interests of the industrial bourgeoisie were also responsive to certain of the demands of the farmers and workers, even on issues directed against the immediate desires of the capitalist rulers. This contradiction has puzzled certain revisionist historians. It simply reflected the fact that these Radicals were subjected to pressures from both sources.

Once they climbed to the top, these leaders in the councils of the Republican administration came into daily contact with the richest of the rich. The sweet taste of the spoils of office and other forms of corruption tainted almost all of them. They were either bought or brought over to the industrialists and bankers. Few among them had so staunch an ideological commitment to the goals of the revolution as Thaddeus Stevens of Pennsylvania, even though he himself was an industrialist. He wanted to carry the reconstruction of the South through to a sweeping democratization of its structure by means of an extensive land reform and the guarantee of democratic rights for both Blacks and poor whites.

Following Lee's surrender it appeared that the hopes of the Radicals would come to naught. But the way was cleared for the prosecution of their plans by the difficulties experienced by the industrial capitalists in clinching their political domination after their military and economic successes. This gave one last impetus to the revolution as the Radicals moved to the fore once again in 1866-67.

However, their full program, which had been partially put into effect during 1864-65, even before the war ended, was destined to be defeated. By 1868, when the Senate failed to remove Andrew Johnson from the presidency by impeachment, Thaddeus Stevens could see the writing on the wall. Disconsolately, as his death neared, while he was battling against the overwhelming opposition in Congress to land reform in the South and desperately striving to secure what rights he could for the ex-slaves, he complained that the country was "going to hell."

As soon as the men of money felt that their political hegemony had been solidly entrenched, they began to view all the commotions in the country that were stirred up by revolutionary expectations as dangerous turmoil. The independent power of the Republican machine over Congress, which had enacted and executed the crucial measures required for the attainment of the industrial magnates' supremacy, became a millstone around their neck. The watchword was no longer "war to the death" but "binding up the wounds of fratricidal strife."

Only after the extreme Radicals were put in their place did the new masters of the house set about bridling the runaway corruption of the Republican administration, stabilizing labor relations in the South, curbing the rising trade union movement, and putting down the resistance of the small farmers to the exactions of the railroads and grain merchants.

Early in the seventies this coalescence of tasks led to the emergence of a new ideological current that was labeled "Liberal Republicanism" in contrast to the radicalism of the late sixties. This tendency continued the program of the industrial capitalists under the aegis of a Republican leadership which sought an end to the "excesses" of revolutionary action in order to consolidate the reconstructed bourgeois order and permit it to operate more efficiently.

This accorded with the historical function of nineteenth century liberalism. "Historically," explains Novack, "liberalism emerged from the bourgeois reaction against the 'excesses' of the French Revolution during the rise of industrial capitalism, when the industrial and commercial bourgeoisie was consolidating its supremacy. It was a reformist and gradualist tendency whose spokesmen exalted evolution as the antithesis to disruptive revolution. Chateaubriand caught the essence of its temper when he said: 'We must preserve the political work which is the fruit of the Revolution. . . . but we must eradicate the Revolution from this work.'"[7]

The new liberal reformism advocated by former left wing Radicals served as the ideological cover for the Thermidorean reaction. The capitalist class gained invaluable support from the association of such figures as Carl Schurz, George Julian, and Charles Sumner with its search for stabilization on its terms. As the capitalists tightened their control after 1873, reaction proceeded apace across the country.

In the West, proposals for halting assaults upon the Native Americans were shelved and their genocidal extermination became an official and even openly avowed policy. In the East, strikes were broken and unions destroyed in an antilabor offensive culminating in the massacre of workers in 1877.

It was in the South, however, where the work of the revolution had made its deepest impact and caused the greatest dislocation, that the severest measures to turn around the gains made by the lowest strata of the people were imposed. Here a veritable political counterrevolution was unleashed. The state governments which defended and extended democratic rights and social reforms for Black labor were violently overthrown and repressive regimes established in their stead.

Although the scene of the struggle was the South, its real leaders, organizers, and beneficiaries were located in the North among the Eastern bankers, railroad barons, and industrial magnates. The mouthpieces for the designs of this top layer of the big bourgeoisie were ex-revolutionaries such as Schurz and Julian, who now enlisted behind them thousands of their former foes from the ranks of the Confederacy.

Thermidorean reaction invariably selects from the past many of the instruments and practices it directs against the masses. In this case the living legacy of racism was used to the hilt. That is not all. Once the reaction gets well under way, it starts rewriting and falsifying the true record of the revolution in order to justify its acts and aims. This revision of the history of the second American revolution started in the 1880s when the myth of the paternalistic "Old South" plantation life came into vogue. Soon the genuine heroes and heroines of the revolutionary surge, Thaddeus Stevens, Black Radicals, Northern women volunteer teachers of Black children in the new schools, were transformed into villains, while the promoters of reaction from Andrew Johnson to Confederate generals were hailed as men of vision and courage under adversity. The real revolutionary traditions were obscured and the memory of revolutionary achievements eclipsed.

First the upward, then the downward, course of the revolution was mirrored in the factional shifts within the Republican Party. When the revolution displayed its maximum energy, the consistent, most uncompromising bourgeois revolutionaries headed the procession. Afterwards these Radicals were shoved aside by the Stalwart wheelhorses of the Republican machine. Some of the original revolutionaries capitulated and joined the liberal reformers who succeeded in ousting the Stalwarts. This "Half-breed" faction within the Republican ranks competed in demagogy with the resurrected and rehabilitated Democratic Party, still tarnished with its service as the tool of the slavocracy.

The redemption regimes in the South were often characterized as "the Bourbons," a term derived from the consummated counterrevolution in France which brought back the Bourbon monarchy and its retinue. The new Southern governments did retain a likeness in one important respect to those of pre-Civil War times.

The slavocracy had ruled dictatorially behind the facade of an all-white parliamentary regime. The redemption regimes were eventually no less lily-white than those prior to the Civil War and, as in the slave South, the poor whites were partially disenfranchised. Some of the old social and political relations were reconstituted—but under the new economic order.

Despite the setbacks suffered by the progressive plebian forces, Black and white, during the climactic phase of Radical Reconstruction, the results of their activities had not counted for nothing. They left permanent marks upon the postwar South. If the Black Codes of 1865 had not been discarded, the exploitation and oppression of millions of Blacks would have been much more severe. Those codes, for example, sought to deny to Blacks even the juridical right to own land. Some Blacks were able to set themselves up and remain as small independent farmers in certain areas around the cotton plantations. If Radical Reconstruction had not been instituted, schools for Black children, with all their limitations, would probably not have been available until a much later date.

No less significant was the tradition of struggle for the rights of the Afro-American people bequeathed by Radical Reconstruction. This made itself felt in many unexpected ways from then on. The Thirteenth, Fourteenth, and Fifteenth amendments to the Constitution, passed at the height of radical fervor, remained "the law of the land" and as such stood in flagrant contradiction to the pall of reaction that descended on the South. Faint as it might be, the residual memory that Blacks had once voted, sent congressmen and senators to Washington, elected senators and representatives who did outstanding work in state legislatures, served on juries, and participated in the state militias hung over the Jim Crow system. It was a condemnation of what existed and a silent reminder that things had once been different, and could again be different, for the Black masses.

This was to be a source of inspiration for the massive civil rights actions three generations later. Even though they were not always consciously viewed in that light, the struggles of the 1950s and 1960s objectively took off from the achievements and the unfinished tasks of the days of Radical Reconstruction. The partisans of the civil rights crusade could see that the reality of their condition was in stark contradiction with their constitutional liberties and they aspired to close the gap between the ideals enunciated during the second American revolution and the intolerable consequences of their degradation after the 1870s. This was one of the ideological mainsprings of the struggles that succeeded in eliminating the specific Jim Crow disabilities in the South.

Radical Reconstruction was undercut and fatally weakened from the start because its upswing did not bring about the confiscation of the plantations and redistribution of the land for the benefit of the ex-slaves, its direct cultivators. Partially begun in the later months of the war, an extensive land reform program was not ruled out in advance. Such a redivision of property would have greatly altered the subsequent development of the South and the role of the Blacks in it.

The post-Civil War South could have arrived at social stability along two opposite lines: either through the progressive path of land reform or else through the reactionary denial of civil rights to Blacks. The democratic rights that the Afro-Americans acquired for a while could not survive without an adequate economic basis—and that meant "forty acres and a mule" as well as the necessary credit between crops. Thus the struggle for possession of the soil became the pivotal issue of Radical Reconstruction.

Its crucial importance can be made clear if the steps that would have been needed to preserve the gains of Radical Reconstruction are envisaged. The terror invoked by the minority of white property-owners would have had to be met by the stern countermeasures of the majority. The Black-based militias would have had to be seriously organized and made ready for action. Whenever a band of racist terrorists or nightriders lynched, whipped, or otherwise maltreated Blacks, they would have had to be punished in an exemplary manner.

Hanging a few dozen of the racists on the rampage and expropriating their property would have resulted in a rapid collapse of their aggressions. To assure that they would not ride again, the militias, the apparatus of resistance against their attacks, would have had to be permanently institutionalized. The Afro-Americans would have had to feel safe in the exercise of their constitutional rights to the full extent. Under the protection of the Black-based militias, their class struggle would have taken new and more advanced forms in defending their lives and welfare.

What would landowners have done when Black tenants refused to turn over the crop to them at the end of the farming season? What would have happened when Black cultivators took over abandoned lands and began farming on their own account? What measures would Black majority governments in South Carolina and Mississippi have eventually undertaken in response to that majority's cry for land? Decisive defense of Radical Reconstruction under Black leadership would inescapably have intensified the class struggle along these lines.

Furthermore, a mass movement with the redistribution of the land as its central axis would have attracted to its side huge numbers of land-hungry poor whites and created an extremely formidable force. The argument that whites could not be won over because of their deep-seated racism is disproved by the support they gave to Radical Reconstruction in its early stages. In states such as Texas and Tennessee where whites decisively outnumbered the Blacks, the Radicals triumphed because of white support. When the Radicals took over the state government in the border state of Missouri, for example, only whites could vote.

A victorious land reform in the South would have inspired the small farmers of the Midwest and the wage workers of the North to press forward their demands more vigorously. The economic as well as political consequences of a consistent defense of democratic rights for Black labor in the South was not lost on the newly installed Northern rulers. They were not disposed to encourage any such drastic agrarian upheaval as a land reform, which would in principle have challenged not only the property rights of the remaining defeated Southern planters but the private property basis of the whole bourgeois system.

Many historians have attached considerable weight to the handicaps of a people who had been held in ignorance through servitude as an explanation for the defeat of Radical Reconstruction. Although the burdens of the slave past undoubtedly held back the Blacks, this factor was not so decisive as others. The rural dispersion and isolation of the Black population and their lack of allies on the national level proved more important in their defeat than illiteracy and other negative legacies of enslavement.

The industrial workers were still in their organizational and political infancy and were situated in another region, mainly in the Northeast. Even their best leaders paid little heed to the needs of landless Black labor, although the National Labor Union did open its ranks to Black wage workers. The bulk of the white workers were infected to one degree or another with the virus of racism.

Most of the population in the rural districts was made up of small property owners, who, as a body, had no impelling incentive to care for the interests of Black labor. The rural petty bourgeoisie was highly susceptible to racist demagogy and by and large its Southern contingent served as foot-soldiers in the ranks of the counterrevolution. The other oppressed nationalities—Chicanos, Native Americans, and Chinese—were poorly organized and defenseless, far removed from the South, and themselves hounded by the powers that be.

Under these circumstances the struggles carried on for their rights by the Afro-Americans and their sympathizers were rendered extremely difficult and finally went down to defeat. Such was the tragic outcome of Radical Reconstruction.

Today, a century later, the major factors that produced this tragic result have all undergone change. The nation is thoroughly urbanized, industrialized, and proletarianized. The traditional regional differences are fast fading. The South itself has been transformed by these processes. Black labor is no longer dispersed through the countryside but concentrated in the cities, North and South.

The participation of Blacks in the industrial work force, which was minimal until the rise of the CIO and the advent of the Second World War, has objectively altered the relation of the working class as a whole to the Afro-American people. Their integration into the ranks of organized labor forbids any repetition of what happened to them in 1877. The monopolists' attempts to beat back gains by Afro-Americans and keep them down economically are no longer a question isolated from the rights of all working people. Such anti-Black attacks can be and often are recognized as a menace to themselves by large numbers of white workers, despite lingering racist attitudes. Resistance from them would go hand in hand with the solidarity forthcoming from Chicanos, Puerto Ricans, Native Americans, Asians, and members of other oppressed nationalities.

The American working class as a whole has never suffered a decisive and crushing defeat at the hands of its class enemies. It has not lost any of the fundamental social gains and democratic liberties it has won through arduous struggle. Apart from the genocide against the Native Americans and oppression of the conquered Chicano people of the Southwest, there has been only one great exception to this record. That is the historical defeat inflicted upon the Afro-Americans in the South culminating in 1877.

The responsibility for this defeat and continued racial oppression rests with the industrial and finance capitalists who still dominate the United States. That is the foremost lesson of the defeat of Radical Reconstruction.

The revolutions of the bourgeois era had a contradictory, two-sided nature corresponding to the social heterogeneity of its participants and the diversity of their objective historical tasks. On the one side were the economic and political objectives of the upper crust of large property owners, and on the other the goals pursued by the plebian forces, which had a more popular and democratic character. As has been explained, these disparate aims did not necessarily coincide throughout the revolutionary process.

Although the Northern merchants and manufacturers acquired considerable power out of the War of Independence, they failed to attain undivided supremacy in the new republic. For seventy years they had to share rulership with the representatives of the Southern slavocracy and yield to them on many issues of domestic and foreign policy.

By destroying chattel slavery, reorganizing the federal government according to their designs, and wiping out the remaining resistance of the Native Americans, the victorious industrial and financial moguls removed all the precapitalist barriers to their further progress and power. This completed the strictly bourgeois side of the second American revolution.

However, the democratic side of the revolution fell far short of its goals and defaulted most grievously in highly important respects. The Afro-Americans, and in their wake the other oppressed nationalities, were denied their democratic rights and equal status even on bourgeois terms. They remained subordinated nationalities which, instead of being assimilated like sundry ethnic groups from Europe into the body of the American population, were depressed and repressed so harshly that they became second-class citizens.

By the same token the conditions flowing from the restoration of white supremacy in the South set a seal on the process of molding the Afro-American masses into a distinctive national entity oppressed by the rulership of industrial and financial capital. Thus they have yet to achieve the self-determination, the control over their destiny, that peoples elsewhere won through the bourgeois and later the socialist revolutions.

Contemporary America thereby harbors two diametrically different kinds of nationalisms. One is the utterly reactionary chauvinism fostered by the masters of America; the other is the progressive striving for self-determination by the oppressed nationalities.

These opposed nationalisms which are present within the structure of the United States likewise confront each other on a world scale. Since the rise of imperialism the entire globe has been divided between the imperialist oppressor powers and the nations and peoples subjugated and exploited by them. The patriotism of the imperialist countries like the United States, Britain, France, Canada, Portugal, and Japan is a cloak for their predatory ambitions. On the other hand, the patriotism of the oppressed peoples of Africa, Asia, and Latin America has a progressive content since it is attached to their struggles for national liberation and social advancement.

The bourgeois revolutions sought to do away with particularism and unite the separate segments of the people into one single sovereign state, such as the American federal republic. The Civil War was fought, among other things, to preserve and protect that union.

Nonetheless, while these experiences cemented a specific American nationality, neither of the two successive American bourgeois revolutions carried the process of assimilation to the end by welding all parts of the population into a single homogeneous entity. Large layers embracing millions of inhabitants have been excluded from full participation in the affairs of the dominant nationality. These were left unassimilated by "the melting pot."

While this phenomenon of an uncompleted consolidation of all the population into a single nationality is by no means peculiar to the United States, in no other major industrial country of the capitalist world has so numerous and central a layer of the population been subjected to second class status and grossly unequal treatment. The members of the oppressed nationalities within the borders of the United States today total some 40 million people—a gigantic force that is twice as large as the population of Canada.

The specific land question that the bourgeois revolution failed to settle in the South has since that time been solved by and large in other ways by the subsequent evolution of the U.S. economy, which has transformed the basis of agricultural production from the small family farm to enormous and heavily capitalized "factories in the field." All the same, this development has not disposed of the national question posed by the conditions of existence of the Blacks. This problem has been incorporated into the tasks to be tackled by the coming American revolution.

By virtue of the peculiar path of American history, this next revolution will necessarily have a combined character. It will primarily and predominantly consist of a new and higher "irrepressible conflict" between the monopoly capitalists and the working masses. This proletarian revolution will be integrally linked with the struggle of the oppressed nationalities for their democratic right of self-determination.

The socialist objectives of the working class will go hand in hand with the ending of racial oppression. The second American revolution, the crusade against the slaveholders, first raised the banner of emancipation for the Afro-Americans. The third American revolution, aiming at the abolition of capitalism along socialist lines, can and will realize the demand for their full liberation.

Notes

Chapter 1
Between Two Revolutions

1. *Black Reconstruction,* p. 716.
2. Cited in ibid., p. 100.
3. Cited in Benjamin Quarles, *The Negro in the Civil War,* pp. 224-25.

Chapter 2
Wage Workers and the Civil War

1. Issues of November 1, 1832, and August 15, 1833. Cited in Bernard Mandel, *Labor: Free and Slave,* p. 83.
2. Cited in Mandel, p. 89.
3. Cited in Herman Schlüter, *Lincoln, Labor and Slavery,* pp. 50-51.
4. Cited in Mandel, p. 87.
5. Cited in Mandel, p. 94.
6. *Works,* vol. I, pp. 453-54. Cited in David Herreshoff, *The Origins of American Marxism,* p. 19.
7. Benjamin A. Gould, "Investigations in the Military and Anthropological Statistics of American Soldiers." Cited in David Montgomery, *Beyond Equality: Labor and the Radical Republicans, 1862-1872,* p. 94.
8. Mandel, pp. 188-89.
9. *Fincher's Trades' Review,* June 6 and 18, 1863. Cited in Mandel, p. 190.
10. Montgomery, p. 95.

Chapter 3
Class Alignments in the South After Appomattox

1. *The Rise of American Civilization,* vol. II, p. 170.
2. Ibid., p. 263.
3. Pp. 21-22, 96, 115-16.
4. Oscar Handlin, *America: A History,* pp. 579-80.
5. Cited in Roger W. Shugg, *Origins of the Class Struggle in Louisiana,* p. 242.
6. John Hope Franklin, *From Slavery to Freedom,* p. 248.

7. Thomas B. Alexander, "Persistent Whiggery in the Confederate South, 1860-1877," in *Reconstruction: An Anthology of Revisionist Writings*, edited by Kenneth Stampp and Leon F. Litwack, pp. 281-82.

Chapter 4
The Rise of Radical Reconstruction

1. The book was *Manual for the Instruction of "Rings," Railroad and Political* by James Parton. See Howard K. Beale, *The Critical Year: A Study of Andrew Johnson and Reconstruction*, pp. 262-63.
2. Cited in Beale, pp. 296-97.
3. Beale, p. 294.
4. Cited in Beale, pp. 168-69.
5. Cited in Beale, pp. 203-4.
6. Cited in Matthew Josephson, *The Politicos*, p. 48.

Chapter 5
Class Struggle Under the Radical Regimes

1. The figures on registration and convention representation are taken from Du Bois, *Black Reconstruction*, pp. 371-72. Except in the cases of Mississippi and Arkansas, the figures on registration are confirmed by William A. Russ, Jr., in his article "Registration and Disenfranchisement Under Radical Reconstruction," *Mississippi Valley Historical Review*, September 1934. For those states, Russ gives figures which would make Blacks 57 percent of the voters in Mississippi and 39 percent in Arkansas. The percentage of Blacks in each state is calculated from 1860 census figures given in Lerone Bennett, Jr., *Black Power U.S.A.: The Human Side of Reconstruction, 1867-1877*, p. 91.
2. *Black Reconstruction*, p. 619.
3. Allen W. Trelease, "Who Were the Scalawags?" in Stampp and Litwack, p. 313.
4. Cited in *Black Reconstruction*, p. 490. Emphasis in original.
5. Gerda Lerner, ed., *Black Women in White America: A Documentary History*, p. 111. Emphasis in original.
6. Cited in *Black Reconstruction*, p. 621.
7. Cited in Paul Lewinson, *Race, Class, and Party: A History of Negro Suffrage and White Politics in the South*, p. 21.
8. Cited in Joel Williamson, *After Slavery: The Negro in South Carolina During Reconstruction, 1861-1877*, p. 116.
9. *Black Reconstruction*, p. 492.
10. Cited in Lewinson, p. 39.
11. Pp. 246-47.
12. Pp. 8-10.
13. Cited in Alexander, "Persistent Whiggery," in Stampp and Litwack, p. 291.
14. Ibid.

15. "The Scalawag in Mississippi Reconstruction," ibid., p. 265.
16. Bennett, p. 273.

Chapter 6
The Industrial Capitalists Consolidate Their Victory

1. Cited in Louis M. Hacker, *Triumph of American Capitalism*, p. 376. Emphasis in original.
2. Josephson, *The Politicos*, p. 197.
3. Cited in ibid., p. 160.
4. Earle Dudley Ross, *The Liberal Republican Movement*, p. 61.
5. Cited in James M. McPherson, *The Struggle for Equality: Abolitionists and the Negro in the Civil War and Reconstruction*, p. 427.
6. P. 379.
7. Ibid. Also C.K. Yearley, *The Money Machine*, p. 21.
8. Cited in Patrick W. Riddleberger, "The Radicals' Abandonment of the Negro During Reconstruction," *Journal of Negro History*, vol. XLV (1960), p. 95.
9. Cited in ibid., p. 97.
10. Cited in Riddleberger, "The Break in the Radical Ranks: Liberal vs. Stalwart in the Elections of 1872," *Journal of Negro History*, vol. XLIV (1959), p. 156.
11. Cited in Riddleberger, "The Radicals' Abandonment of the Negro," ibid., vol. XLV (1960), p. 90.
12. Cited in William B. Hesseltine, "Economic Factors in the Abandonment of Reconstruction," *Mississippi Valley Historical Review*, vol. XXXII (1945), p. 209.
13. P. 208.
14. *Era of Reconstruction*, p. 211.
15. Cited in Paul H. Buck, *The Road to Reunion, 1865-1900*, p. 88.

Chapter 7
Counterrevolution—the Mississippi Model

1. Cited in Vernon Lane Wharton, *The Negro in Mississippi, 1865-1890*, p. 142.
2. *Societas*, Spring 1974, pp. 107-8.
3. Williamson, p. 261.
4. *The Negro in Mississippi*, p. 181.
5. Ibid., p. 182.
6. Cited in Richard N. Current, ed., *Reconstruction, 1865-1877*, p. 144.
7. Cited in Herbert Aptheker, *To Be Free: Studies in American Negro History*, p. 178.
8. Cited in ibid., p. 179.
9. Cited in Otis A. Singletary, *Negro Militia and Reconstruction*, p. 137.
10. Cited in *Era of Reconstruction*, p. 204.
11. Cited in Allen, *Reconstruction: The Battle for Democracy*, p. 199.
12. Singletary, p. 118.
13. C.H. Brough, "The Clinton Riot," in *Publications of the Mississippi*

Historical Society, vol. VI (1902), p. 61. Cited in Aptheker, *To Be Free,* p. 178.
14. Cited in Wharton, pp. 194-95.
15. Cited in ibid., p. 195.
16. Cited in Current, p. 146.
17. Cited in Wharton, p. 206.

Chapter 8
The Final Defeat

1. Cited in Current, pp. 155-57.
2. Cited in Alrutheus A. Taylor, *The Negro in South Carolina During Reconstruction,* p. 248.
3. Cited in Williamson, p. 271.
4. Cited in ibid., p. 257.
5. Cited in ibid., p. 257.
6. Cited in ibid., p. 344.
7. Cited in Lerner, p. 249.
8. P. xvii.
9. Cited in Williamson, pp. 271-72.
10. Singletary, p. 143.
11. Cited in Taylor, pp. 246-47.
12. Taylor, pp. 249-50.
13. *Essays on the Civil War and Reconstruction,* pp. 368-69.

Chapter 9
The Republican Party's Betrayal

1. P. 360.
2. Cited in Current, pp. 146-47.
3. Cited in Aptheker, *To Be Free,* p. 184.
4. Cited in ibid., p. 187.
5. Cited in James E. Sefton, *The United States Army and Reconstruction, 1865-1877,* p. 249.
6. Cited in C. Vann Woodward, *Reunion and Reaction,* p. 25.
7. Ibid., p. 36.
8. Cited in ibid., pp. 225-26.
9. Ibid., p. 224.
10. Sefton, pp. 260-63.
11. Cited in Stanley P. Hirshon, *Farewell to the Bloody Shirt: Northern Republicans and the Southern Negro, 1877-1893,* pp. 24-25.

Chapter 10
Industrial Capitalism and Conservative Rule

1. The factual information in this chapter about the business interests and connections of various political figures and their involvement in corruption is drawn principally from C. Vann Woodward, *Origins of the New South, 1877-1913.*

2. "On Rewriting Reconstruction History," *American Historical Review,* vol. XLV (1940), pp. 817-18.
3. Ibid., p. 818.
4. *Origins of the New South,* p. 50.
5. Cited in ibid., p. 83.
6. Ibid., p. 84.
7. Wharton, p. 179.
8. Woodward, *Origins of the New South,* pp. 71-72.
9. Dunning, pp. 371-72.
10. Cited in Lewinson, p. 85.
11. Cited in ibid., p. 84.
12. Decision in *Grovey* v. *Townsend.* See George Brown Tindall, *The Emergence of the New South, 1913-1945,* p. 558.
13. Hirshon, pp. 66, 68.
14. Cited in ibid., p. 69.
15. Cited in ibid., p. 70.
16. The papers studied were the *Boston Evening Transcript,* the *New Haven Register,* the *New York Times,* the *Philadelphia North American,* the *Washington Star,* the *Cincinnati Enquirer,* the *Pittsburgh Dispatch,* the *Indianapolis Journal,* the *Detroit Tribune,* the *Chicago Tribune,* the *St. Louis Globe-Democrat,* and the *San Francisco Examiner.* See Rayford W. Logan, *The Betrayal of the Negro,* p. 176.
17. Cited in Hirshon, p. 71.
18. Cited in Aptheker, *A Documentary History of the Negro People,* p. 763. Emphasis in original.
19. Cited in ibid., p. 742.
20. Cited in Wharton, p. 241.
21. Woodward, *Origins of the New South,* pp. 233-34.
22. Cited in ibid., p. 361.
23. Thomas J. Jones, *Negro Education: A Study of the Private and Higher Schools for Colored People in the U.S.* (Washington, 1917). Cited in Tindall, p. 269.

Chapter 11
Racism and Historical Mythology

1. Cited in Paul H. Buck, p. 226.
2. Cited in Woodward, *Origins of the New South,* p. 20.
3. Cited in Stampp, *Era of Reconstruction,* pp. 17-18.
4. P. 385.
5. *The Passing of the Great Race,* pp. 77-79. Cited in Stampp, *Era of Reconstruction,* p. 21.
6. Cited in Woodward, *Origins of the New South,* p. 324.
7. *Beyond Equality,* p. viii.
8. Pp. 22-23.
9. *Era of Reconstruction,* p. ix.
10. Ibid., p. 23.
11. *The Strange Career of Jim Crow,* p. 110.
12. C. Vann Woodward comments on this question in his article "The

Strange Career of a Historical Controversy," which is included in his book *American Counterpoint,* pp. 234-60. He acknowledges that his account in *The Strange Career of Jim Crow* of when segregation came into existence was in part inaccurate.
13. *Profiles in Courage,* pp. 134, 107, 115.
14. Ibid., pp. 140-41.
15. *From Slavery to Freedom,* p. 275.
16. Ibid., p. 252.
17. Ibid., p. 247.
18. Ibid., p. 248.
19. Ibid., pp. 258, 266.
20. Ibid., p. 267.
21. *Reconstruction: The Battle for Democracy, 1865-76,* pp. 38, 211. Emphasis added in both citations.
22. Ibid., pp. 212, 13, 206, 209-10.
23. *The Triumph of American Capitalism,* p. 381.
24. Cited in *Race, Class, and Party,* pp. 70-71.
25. *Reconstruction: The Battle for Democracy,* p. 142.
26. Pp. 332, 335.
27. Pp. 338-40.

Chapter 12
Thermidor

1. *Origins of the New South,* p. 22.
2. P. 51.
3. P. v.
4. Pp. 233-34.
5. *Democracy and Revolution,* pp. 88-89.
6. *Selected Works,* vol. I, p. 117.
7. *Democracy and Revolution,* p. 120.

Bibliography

The following is a list of books, pamphlets, and articles which served as sources of facts or ideas in the preparation of this book.

To those interested in further reading I would recommend the following: For a general survey of slavery, see Kenneth Stampp's *The Peculiar Institution*. For a short outline of Radical Reconstruction, see the same author's *The Era of Reconstruction, 1865-1877*. As an exposition of the role of Blacks during this period, no book has surpassed W.E.B. Du Bois's *Black Reconstruction*. For the period after Radical Reconstruction, C. Vann Woodward's *Origins of the New South, 1877-1913* is recommended.

Note: where a later edition is listed, the original publication date is given in parentheses.

Articles and Pamphlets

Alexander, Thomas B. "Persistent Whiggery in the Confederate South, 1860-1877." *Journal of Southern History,* XXVII (1961).*

Aptheker, Herbert. *Negro Slave Revolts in the United States, 1526-1860.* New York: International Publishers, 1939.

Beale, Howard K. "On Rewriting Reconstruction History." American Historical Review, XLV (1940).

———. "What Historians Have Said About the Causes of the Civil War." *Social Science Research Bulletin,* no. 54, 1946.

Bond, Horace Mann. "Social and Economic Forces in Alabama Reconstruction." *Journal of Negro History,* XXIII (1938).*

Braden, Anne. "The Southern Freedom Movement in Perspective." *Monthly Review,* August 1965.

Breitman, George. *How a Minority Can Change Society: The Real Potential of the Afro-American Struggle.* New York: Pathfinder Press, 1965 (1964).

———. *Race Prejudice: How It Began, When It Will End.* New York: Pathfinder Press, 1971.

Coben, Stanley. "Northeastern Business and Radical Reconstruction: A Re-examination." *Mississippi Valley Historical Review,* XLVI (1959).*

Cox, John H., and Cox, LaWanda. "General O.O. Howard and the

'Misrepresented Bureau.'" *Journal of Southern History,* XIX (1953).
―――. "Negro Suffrage and Republican Politics: The Problem of Motivation in Reconstruction Historiography." *Journal of Southern History,* XXXIII (1967).*
Curry, Richard O. "The Abolitionists and Reconstruction: A Critical Appraisal." *Journal of Southern History,* XXXIV (1968).
Donald, David. "The Scalawag in Mississippi Reconstruction." *Journal of Southern History,* X (1944).*
Fels, Rendigs. "American Business Cycles, 1865-1879." *American Economic Review,* XLI (1951).
Genovese, Eugene D., et al. "Legacy of Slavery and Roots of Black Nationalism." *Studies on the Left,* vol. 6 (1966), no. 6.
Graebner, Norman A. "Northern Diplomacy and European Neutrality." In *Why the North Won the Civil War,* ed. by David Donald. Baton Rouge: Louisiana State University Press, 1960.
Graham, Jay Howard. "The 'Conspiracy Theory' of the Fourteenth Amendment." *Yale Law Journal,* XLVII (1938).*
Henry, Robert S. "The Railroad Land Grant Legend in American History Texts." *Mississippi Valley Historical Review,* XXXII (1945).
Hesseltine, William B. "Economic Factors in the Abandonment of Reconstruction." *Mississippi Valley Historical Review,* XXII (1935).
Magdol, Edward. "Local Black Leaders in the South, 1867-75: An Essay Toward the Reconstruction of Reconstruction History." *Societas—A Review of Social History,* Spring 1974.
Riddleberger, Patrick W. "The Break in the Radical Ranks: Liberal vs. Stalwart in the Elections of 1872." *Journal of Negro History,* XLIV (1959).
―――. "The Radicals' Abandonment of the Negro During Reconstruction." *Journal of Negro History,* XLV (1960).
Roberts, Dick. *The Fraud of Black Capitalism.* New York: Pathfinder Press, 1970.
Russ, William, Jr. "Registration and Disenfranchisement Under Radical Reconstruction." *Mississippi Valley Historical Review,* XXII (1935).
Scroggs, Jack B. "Southern Reconstruction: A Radical View." *Journal of Southern History,* XXIV (1958).*
Swinney, Everette. "Enforcing the Fifteenth Amendment, 1870-1877." *Journal of Southern History,* XXVIII (1962).
Thomas, Tony. *In Defense of Black Nationalism.* New York: Pathfinder Press, 1971.
Trelease, Allen W. "Who Were the Scalawags?" *Journal of Southern History,* XXIX (1963).*
Trotsky, Leon. *Leon Trotsky on Black Nationalism and Self-Determination.* New York: Pathfinder Press, 1967.
Weisberger, Bernard A. "The Dark and Bloody Ground of Reconstruction Historiography." *Journal of Southern History,* XXV (1959).

---

* These articles are included in Stampp and Litwack, *Reconstruction: An Anthology of Revisionist Writings.*

Books

Allen, James S. *The Negro Question in the United States.* New York: International Publishers, 1936.
———. *Reconstruction: The Battle for Democracy, 1865-1876.* New York: International Publishers, 1937.
Allen, Robert L., with the collaboration of Pamela P. Allen. *Reluctant Reformers: Racism and Social Reform Movements in the United States.* New York: Doubleday (Anchor), 1975 (1974).
Aptheker, Herbert. *A Documentary History of the Negro People in the United States.* Vol. II. New York: International Publishers, 1964.
———. *To Be Free: Studies in American Negro History.* New York: International Publishers, 1968 (1948).
Beale, Howard K. *The Critical Year: A Study of Andrew Johnson and Reconstruction.* New York: Frederick Ungar, 1958 (1930).
Beard, Charles A., and Beard, Mary R. *The Rise of American Civilization.* Vols. I and II. New York: Macmillan, 1930.
Bennett, Lerone, Jr. *Black Power U.S.A.: The Human Side of Reconstruction, 1867-1877.* Baltimore: Penguin Books, 1969 (1967).
Buck, Paul H. *The Road to Reunion, 1865-1900.* Boston: Little, Brown, 1937.
Buck, Solon Justus. *The Granger Movement.* Lincoln: University of Nebraska Press, 1969 (1913).
Callow, Alexander B., Jr. *The Tweed Ring.* New York: Oxford University Press, 1972 (1966).
Coleman, Charles. *The Election of 1868.* New York: Octagon Books, 1971.
Current, Richard N., ed. *Reconstruction, 1865-1877.* Englewood Cliffs, N.J.: Prentice-Hall, 1965.
Curry, Richard O. *Radicalism, Racism, and Party Realignment: The Border States During Reconstruction.* Baltimore: Johns Hopkins University Press, 1969.
Douglass, Frederick. *The Life and Times of Frederick Douglass.* New York: Collier Books, 1962 (1892).
Du Bois, W.E.B. *The Autobiography of W.E.B. Du Bois.* New York: International Publishers, 1968.
———. *Black Reconstruction: An Essay Toward a History of the Part Which Black Folk Played in the Attempt to Reconstruct Democracy in America, 1860-1880.* Cleveland and New York: World Publishing Co., 1964 (1935).
———. *The Souls of Black Folk.* Greenwich, Conn.: Fawcett, 1961 (1903).
Dumond, Dwight Lowell. *Antislavery Origins of the Civil War in the United States.* Ann Arbor: University of Michigan Press, 1959 (1939).
Dunning, William A. *Essays on the Civil War and Reconstruction.* New York: Harper and Row, 1965 (1897).
Faulkner, Harold Underwood. *American Economic History.* New York: Harper and Brothers, 1954 (1924).
Foster, William Z. *The Negro People in American History.* New York: International Publishers, 1973 (1954).

Franklin, John Hope. *From Slavery to Freedom: A History of Negro Americans.* New York: Knopf, 1974 (1947).
―――. *Reconstruction: After the Civil War.* Chicago: University of Chicago Press, 1961.
Frazier, E. Franklin. *Black Bourgeoisie: The Rise of a New Middle Class in the United States.* New York: Collier Books, 1962 (1957).
Genovese, Eugene D. *Political Economy of Slavery.* New York: Pantheon Books, 1965.
Ginzburg, Ralph. *100 Years of Lynchings.* New York: Lancer Books, 1969.
Hacker, Louis M. *The Triumph of American Capitalism.* New York: Columbia University Press, 1940.
Handlin, Oscar. *America: A History.* New York: Holt, Rinehart and Winston, 1968.
Herreshoff, David. *The Origins of American Marxism.* New York: Monad Press, 1973 (1967).
Hesseltine, William B. *Confederate Leaders in the New South.* Baton Rouge: Louisiana State University Press, 1950.
Hicks, John D. *The Populist Revolt: A History of the Farmers' Alliance and the People's Party.* Lincoln: University of Nebraska Press, 1961 (1931).
Higginson, Thomas Wentworth. *Army Life in a Black Regiment.* Boston: Beacon, 1962 (1869).
Hirshon, Stanley P. *Farewell to the Bloody Shirt: Northern Republicans and the Southern Negro, 1877-1893.* Chicago: Quadrangle Books, 1968 (1962).
Josephson, Matthew. *The Politicos: 1865-1896.* New York: Harcourt, Brace and World, 1938.
―――. *The Robber Barons.* New York: Harcourt, Brace and World, 1962 (1934).
Kennedy, John F. *Profiles in Courage.* New York: Harper and Row, 1964 (1956).
Kipnis, Ira. *The American Socialist Movement, 1897-1912.* New York: Columbia University Press, 1952.
Korngold, Ralph. *Thaddeus Stevens.* New York: Harcourt, Brace and World, 1955.
Lenin, V.I. *New Data on the Laws Governing the Development of Capitalism in Agriculture.* Part 1: "Capitalism and Agriculture in the United States of America." *Collected Works,* vol. 22. Moscow: Progress Publishers, 1964 (1915).
Lerner, Gerda, ed. *Black Women in White America: A Documentary History.* New York: Random House (Vintage), 1973 (1972).
Lewinson, Paul. *Race, Class, and Party: A History of Negro Suffrage and White Politics in the South.* New York: Grosset and Dunlap, 1965 (1932).
Logan, Rayford W. *The Betrayal of the Negro.* New York: Collier Books, 1965 (1954).
Lynch, John R. *The Facts of Reconstruction.* New York: Neal Publishing Co., 1931 (1913).
Lynd, Staughton, ed. *Reconstruction.* New York: Harper and Row, 1967.

McKitrick, Eric L. *Slavery Defended: The Views of the Old South*. Englewood Cliffs, N.J.: Prentice-Hall, 1965 (1963).

McPherson, James M. *The Struggle for Equality: Abolitionists and the Negro in the Civil War and Reconstruction*. Princeton, N.J.: Princeton University Press, 1967 (1964).

———, et al. *Blacks in America: Bibliographical Essays*. Garden City, N.Y.: Doubleday (Anchor), 1972 (1971).

Mandel, Bernard. *Labor: Free and Slave*. New York: Associated Authors, 1955.

Mardock, Robert Wilson. *The Reformers and the American Indian*. Columbia: University of Missouri Press, 1971.

Marx, Karl, and Engels, Frederick. *The Civil War in the United States*. New York: Citadel Press, 1961 (1937).

———. *Selected Works*. Vol. 1. Moscow: Foreign Languages Publishing House, 1962.

Montgomery, David. *Beyond Equality: Labor and the Radical Republicans, 1862-1872*. New York: Random House (Vintage), 1967.

Novack, George. *Democracy and Revolution*. New York: Pathfinder Press, 1971.

———. "Civil War in New York: The Anti-Draft Demonstrations of 1863." Unpublished manuscript. Library for Social History, New York.

———, et al. *America's Revolutionary Heritage*. New York: Pathfinder Press, 1976 (1966).

Parkes, Henry Bamford. *The United States of America: A History*. New York: Knopf, 1953.

Phillips, Ulrich Bonnell. *Life and Labor in the Old South*. Boston: Little, Brown, 1963 (1929).

Pratt, Fletcher. *A Short History of the Civil War*. New York: Pocket Books, 1956.

Quarles, Benjamin. *The Negro in the Civil War*. Boston: Little, Brown, 1969.

———. *The Negro in the Making of America*. New York: Collier Books, 1964.

Randel, William Peirce. *The Ku Klux Klan*. New York: Chilton Books. 1965.

Record, Wilson. *The Negro and the Communist Party*. Chapel Hill: University of North Carolina Press, 1951.

Richardson, Joe M. *The Negro in the Reconstruction of Florida, 1865-1877*. Tallahassee: Florida State University Press, 1965.

Rose, Willie Lee. *Rehearsal for Reconstruction: The Port Royal Experiment*. New York: Random House, 1964.

Ross, Earle Dudley. *The Liberal Republican Movement*. New York: Henry Holt and Co., 1919.

Schlüter, Herman. *Lincoln, Labor and Slavery*. New York: Russell, 1965 (1913).

Sefton, James E. *The United States Army and Reconstruction, 1865-1877*. Baton Rouge: Louisiana State University Press, 1967.

Sharkey, Robert P. *Money, Class, and Party: An Economic Study of Civil*

War and Reconstruction. Baltimore: Johns Hopkins University Press, 1967 (1959).
Shugg, Roger W. *Origins of the Class Struggle in Louisiana: A Social History of White Farmers and Laborers During Slavery and After, 1840-1875.* Baton Rouge: Louisiana State University Press, 1968 (1939).
Simkins, Francis B. *The Tillman Movement in South Carolina.* Gloucester, Mass.: Peter Smith, 1964 (1926).
Singletary, Otis A. *Negro Militia and Reconstruction.* New York: McGraw-Hill, 1963 (1957).
Smith, Frank E. *Congressman from Mississippi.* New York: Random House (Pantheon), 1964.
Stampp, Kenneth M. *And the War Came: The North and the Secession Crisis, 1860-1861.* Chicago: University of Chicago Press, 1964 (1950).
———. *The Causes of the Civil War.* Englewood Cliffs, N.J.: Prentice-Hall, 1959.
———. *The Era of Reconstruction, 1865-1877.* New York: Knopf, 1965.
———. *The Peculiar Institution: Slavery in the Ante-Bellum South.* New York: Random House (Vintage), 1956.
———, and Litwack, Leon F., eds. *Reconstruction: An Anthology of Revisionist Writings.* Baton Rouge: Louisiana State University Press, 1969.
Sternsher, Bernard, ed. *The Negro in Depression and War: Prelude to Revolution, 1930-1945.* Chicago: Quadrangle, 1969.
Taylor, Alrutheus A. *The Negro in South Carolina During Reconstruction.* Washington, D.C.: Association for the Study of Negro Life and History, 1924.
Tebbel, John. *The Compact History of the Indian Wars.* New York: Hawthorne Books, 1966.
Thomas, Tony, ed. *Black Liberation and Socialism.* New York: Pathfinder Press, 1974.
Tindall, George Brown. *The Emergence of the New South, 1913-1945.* Baton Rouge: Louisiana State University Press, 1967.
Tourgee, Albion W. *A Fool's Errand.* New York: Harper and Row, 1966 (1879).
Trelease, Allen W. *Reconstruction: The Great Experiment.* New York: Harper and Row, 1972 (1971).
Ware, Norman J. *The Labor Movement in the United States, 1860-1895.* New York: Random House (Vintage), 1964 (1929).
Wesley, Charles H. *Negro Labor in the United States.* New York: Vanguard Press, 1927.
Wharton, Vernon Lane. *The Negro in Mississippi, 1865-1890.* New York: Harper and Row, 1965 (1947).
Williams, Eric. *Capitalism and Slavery.* New York: Capricorn Books, 1966 (1944).
Williamson, Joel. *After Slavery: The Negro in South Carolina During Reconstruction, 1861-1877.* Chapel Hill: University of North Carolina Press, 1965.
Woodward, C. Vann. *American Counterpoint: Slavery and Racism in the*

North-South Dialogue. Boston: Little, Brown, 1964.
———. *The Burden of Southern History.* Baton Rouge: Louisiana State University Press, 1960.
———. *Origins of the New South, 1877-1913.* Baton Rouge: Louisiana State University Press, 1951.
———. *Reunion and Reaction: The Compromise of 1877 and the End of Reconstruction.* New York: Doubleday (Anchor), 1956.
———. *The Strange Career of Jim Crow.* New York: Oxford University Press, 1957 (1955).
———. *Tom Watson: Agrarian Rebel.* New York: Oxford University Press, 1963 (1938).
Yearly, C.K. *The Money Machine.* Albany: State University of New York Press, 1970.
Yellen, Samuel. *American Labor Struggles, 1877-1934.* New York: Monad Press, 1974 (1936).

Index

Abolitionists, 22, 23, 36-39
Adams, Charles Francis, 113
Adams, Henry, 113, 115
Agriculture, 24. *See also* Cotton economy; Farmers
Alabama, 147, 170, 191-92
Alcorn, James L., 139, 142, 143-44
Allen, James, 221-24, 226
American Anti-Slavery Society, 113-14
American Colonization Society, 22
American Federation of Labor, 205
Ames, Adelbert, 142, 144, 154-56, 217
Andersonville, 59
Andrew, John A., 77, 113
Anti-Monopoly parties, 123
Apaches, 30
Arkansas, 145, 170
Army, 27. *See also* Federal troops; Militias
Arthur, Chester A., 110, 126
Astor, John Jacob, 125
Astor, William, 119
Atlantic Monthly, 208
Augur, Christopher C., 176

Badger, A.S., 171
Baez, Joan, 215
Beale, Howard K., 11, 190-91, 213, 238
Beard, Charles A. and Mary R., 11, 213, 228
Beauregard, P.G.T., 51, 194
Belknap, William Worth, 126
Bell, John, 60
Belmont, August, 72, 191
Bill of Rights, 15
Bird Club, 113
Birth of a Nation, 221
Black belt, 55

"Black belt nation" theory, 225-27
Black Codes, 58, 88, 145, 241
Black conventions, 91
Black nationalism, 215
Black officeholders, 86-87, 88, 89, 143, 144, 159
Black Reconstruction (Du Bois), 222
Blacks: and abolitionist movement, 22, 23; as caste, 57-58, 70, 145, 168, 189, 201-2, 219; in Civil War, 25, 27-28, 84; and Democrats, 166-67; democratic rights of, 91, 144, 157, 168, 187, 202, 242; denied right to leave South, 200-201; disfranchisement of, 152-53, 197-99, 212; and education, 89, 205; enfranchisement of, 63, 77, 78, 82, 85-86, 87, 169; and farmers, 84; and industrialists, 103, 140; and landowners, 91-96; and Liberals, 113, 114, 118, 119; mass sympathy for, 81, 85, 127, 128; in militias, 145, 147-49, 155, 161-62; Northern, 33, 48, 87; and poor Southern whites, 97, 102; as prisoners, 202, 203; and Radical Reconstruction, 139, 241; and Republicans, 167, 169; as sharecroppers, 212; and unions, 205, 244; and white workers, 33-34, 45, 46, 48, 84, 203, 244, 245
Black women, 164-65
Blaine, James G., 105, 126
"Bloody shirt" tactic, 82, 120, 121, 127, 186
Border states, 24, 25, 128, 236
Bourbon monarchy, restoration of, 233
"Bourbons" (in South), 188, 241
Bourgeois democracy, 175, 179
Bourgeoisie. *See* Commercial interests;

264 Index

Industrial capitalists
Bourgeois revolutions, 52-53, 83, 104, 111, 119, 228-31, 235, 246-47
Boutwell, George S., 152
Boutwell Report, 152, 156, 173
Breckinridge, John C., 51, 59, 61
Brisbane, Albert, 37
Britain, 20, 24
Browder, Earl, 227
Brown, B. Gratz, 112-13, 118
Brown, John, 21, 209
Brown, John C., 192
Brown, Joseph E., 143, 189-90, 203
Brownson, Orestes, 37
Bryant, William Cullen, 113
Bullock, Rufus B., 143, 190
Burke, E.A., 196-97
Butler, Ben, 110, 217
Butler, Matthew C., 51, 161, 192, 193

Cain, R.H., 163, 165
Caldwell, Charles, 148, 152, 155, 156
Cameron, Simon, 26, 105, 109
Capitalist class, 14, 116, 117. *See also* Bourgeois revolutions; Commercial interests; Industrial capitalists
Cardoza, 218
Carpenter, Matthew, 105
Carpetbaggers, 141, 142, 220, 221. *See also* Northerners; Radical Reconstruction, and corruption
Central Pacific Railroad, 180
Century Magazine, 208
Chalmers, James R., 200
Chamberlain, Daniel H., 140, 159, 163, 165
Chandler, Zachariah, 105, 109
Chase, George K., 154, 155
Chase, Salmon P., 105, 117
Chattel slavery. *See* Slavery
Cherokees, 29, 88
Cheyennes, 30
Chickasaws, 29
Choctaws, 29
Chrisman (Judge), 157
Churchill, Thomas J., 196
Civil Rights Bill of 1875, 174, 187
Civil rights movement, 7, 215, 242
Civil service reform, 110, 125
Civil War, 9, 234; and abolitionists, 23; Blacks in, 25, 27-28, 84; and Europe, 24; and Indians, 29-30; and industrialists, 25, 26, 27; radicalization caused by, 63, 81, 84-85; and Radicals, 45; and socialists, 42, 48; women in, 63-64; and workers, 26, 39, 40, 43-48
Clayton, Powell, 145
Clews, Henry, 191
Cobb, Rufus W., 192
Colfax, Schuyler, 126
Colonial revolutions, 212, 215
Colquitt, Alfred H., 190, 191
Comanches, 29
Commercial interests, 65, 69, 70-71, 115, 116, 117
Communist International, 226
Communist Party, 224, 225-27
Compromise of 1877, 175-85, 224, 225
Confederacy, 236. *See also* Secessionist movement
Confederate flag, 210, 215
Confederate leaders, former, 49-51, 61-62, 143, 186
Confederate Leaders in the New South (Hesseltine), 50
Conkling, Roscoe, 105, 109, 110, 126, 182
Conservatives, 76, 79-80, 99-100, 124, 139-42, 151, 176-78; and Democrats, 80, 128, 141, 142. *See also* Redeemers
Constitution, 14-15, 21, 233, 234
Constitutional Unionists, 60
Convict labor system, 203-4
Conway, Thomas W., 200
Cooke, Jay, 108, 122
Cooper, Peter, 124
Copperheads, 116-17
Corruption, 78, 109-10, 119; under Radical Reconstruction, 100-107, 195-96
Cosmopolitan, 208
Cotton economy, 17, 19, 20, 21, 24, 25, 54, 55
Credit Mobilier, 125-26
Crews, Joseph, 148
Curtis, George William, 113, 115, 210

Dana, Charles A., 116
Davis, Jefferson, 59, 90, 210
Democracy. *See* Bourgeois democracy; Bourgeois revolutions; Democratic rights
Democrat (New Orleans), 194, 197
Democratic Party: and Blacks, 166-67; and commercial interests, 65, 66, 69, 115, 116, 117; and Conservatives, 80, 128, 141, 142; and Liberals, 120, 122, 182; Northern, 65, 72, 74-75; and Northern capitalists, 61-62, 124, 127;

Index

postwar collapse of, in South, 99-100; and racism, 79, 185; and reform movement, 119; revival of, after 1868, 115-17, 141-42; and slavocracy, 20; and terrorism, 152, 154, 160-61, 202, 204; and workers, 20, 39, 43, 45, 48. *See also* Redeemers

Democratic rights: of Blacks, 58, 91, 144, 157, 168, 187, 202, 242 (*see also* Black Codes; Jim Crow); of workers, 40, 55, 57

Dent, Louis, 143
Depew, Chauncey, 125
Dickinson, Anna E., 210
Directorate (France), 231, 233
Dodge, William E., 119, 125
Doolittle, James R., 117
Douglas, Stephen A., 60
Douglass, Frederick, 23, 34, 82, 105, 114
Draft, 26, 46
Draft uprisings, 46-48
Drew, George F., 192
Drexel, Anthony J., 125
Du Bois, W.E.B., 222, 223
Duke, Basil W., 191
Dunning, William A., 170, 210-11
Dunning school, 212, 213, 215

Early, Jubal A., 51, 194
Economic determinists, 11, 213, 214
Education, 89-90, 205-6
Election of 1800, 17
Election of 1860, 24
Election of 1872, 118-20
Election of 1876, 175-76
Elections, bourgeois, 175
Eliot, Charles W., 113
Emancipation, gradual, 21
Embargo of 1807, 18
Emerson, Ralph Waldo, 43
The Era of Reconstruction (Stampp), 220
Erie Canal, 21
Europe, 24, 32, 52, 53
Evans, George Henry, 38
Evarts, William M., 185
Exodus of 1879, 200-201

Factories, 32
Farmers, 66-68, 179; and Blacks, 84, 244; and capitalists, 20, 23, 24, 53, 66-67, 68-69; political movements of, 122-23; and redemption regimes, 195; and slavocracy, 19, 20, 22, 23, 40, 68, 116-17. *See also* Land reform; Poor whites; Sharecropping

Federal troops, 27, 93, 102, 154, 163, 170, 172, 176, 183, 184-85, 236-37
Feminism, 63-64
Fenian Brotherhood, 64-65
Fessenden, William P., 108
Fifteenth Amendment, 114, 187, 198, 199, 207, 241
Finance capital, 71
Fincher, Jonathan, 46
Fink, Albert, 191
First American revolution, 233-34
Fish, Hamilton, 108, 126
Fitzgerald, William F., 155
Florida, 17
A Fool's Errand (Tourgee), 90, 210
"Force bill," 186
Foster, William Z., 224
Fourteenth Amendment, 77, 80-81, 187, 207, 241
Franklin, John Hope, 218-19
Freedmen's Bureau, 54, 91, 93
Free labor, 39, 55, 219-20
Free Soil Party, 39
French revolution, 231, 232-33, 239
From Slavery to Freedom (Franklin), 218
Fugitive slave laws, 23

Garfield, James A., 105, 126, 127-28
Garrison, William Lloyd, 22, 114
Gary, Martin W., 160, 193
George, James Z., 152-53, 155
Georgia, 145, 189-90
Germans, 33, 42, 43
Girondists, 232
Godkin, Edwin L., 115, 209
Gompers, Samuel, 205
Gordon, John B., 190, 191, 210
Gould, Jay, 125, 184, 191
Grange, 68
"Grandfather clause," 199
Grant, Madison, 211
Grant, Ulysses S., 30, 108-9, 122, 126, 154, 155, 165-66, 170, 171-72, 173, 174, 176
Greeley, Horace, 34, 37, 59, 113, 118, 119, 122
Green, John T., 159
Greenback Party, 68, 124, 195

Hacker, Louis M., 223
Half-breeds, 122, 126, 127, 174, 181, 182

266 Index

Halstead, Murat, 113
Hamburg Massacre, 161-63
Hampton, Wade, 159-60, 168, 181, 192
Hancock, W.S., 30, 173
Hard money, 67, 116, 123
Harper, Frances E.W., 164
Harper's Weekly, 210
Harris, Joel Chandler, 209
Harrison, Benjamin, 186
Harrison, B.H., 193
Hayes, Rutherford B., 105, 168, 175-77, 180, 181-84
Haynes, A.J., 148
Hemingway, William L., 196
Heyward, William, 92
Higginson, Thomas Wentworth, 209
Historians, 10, 11, 210. *See also* Dunning school; Economic determinists; Revisionists
Holden, W.W., 143
"Home rule" for the South, 118, 140, 141, 220, 221
Homestead Act, 23, 39-40, 53, 123
Houston, George S., 192
Howard, Oliver Otis, 54
Howe, Maude, 209
Howe, Timothy O., 121
Huntington, Collis P., 180, 184

Idealism, historical, 213
Immigrant workers, 32-33, 42, 44, 45
Imperialism, 206, 211, 215
Indentured servants, 56
Indians, 29-30, 56
Industrial capitalists: and Blacks, 13, 66, 78, 103, 140; and Civil War, 25, 26, 44; and commercial capitalists, 69-71, 74; control of South by, 224-25; and corruption, 78, 109-11; and Democrats, 124, 127; and farmers, 20, 23, 24, 66-67, 68-69, 73; and land reform, 94, 95; and masses, 237; and Radical Reconstruction, 65-66, 82-83, 99, 100, 102-3, 124-25, 128, 139, 140, 169, 188-89; and Republican Party, 23, 39, 77-78, 106-8; and revolution, 111, 234-37; rule of, 73, 115, 117; and slavocracy, 22
Industrial revolution, 32
Industrial Workers of the World, 205
Industries. *See* Manufacturing
Inflation, 44
Ingalls, John J., 200
Integration, 89-90

Internal improvements, 20, 21, 178, 179
Irish, 33, 34, 42-43, 48, 64-65
Iroquois, 29

Jacobins, 232
Jay, John, 125
Jefferson, Thomas, 17
Jim Crow, 206, 207, 208, 212, 216-17, 219
Johnson, Andrew, 27, 58, 59, 74-75, 79, 81, 90, 108, 112
Johnson, Lyndon Baines, 227
Julian, George W., 105, 109, 119, 122, 127, 182, 237, 239, 240

Kansas, 21, 200
Kelley, William D., 192
Kellogg, William P., 170
Kennedy, John F., 217-18, 227
Key, David M., 184, 185
Kimball, H.I., 190
Kiowas, 29
Know-Nothings (American Party), 43, 60
Ku Klux Act, 121, 149, 169, 187
Ku Klux Klan (KKK), 58, 145, 150, 210, 221

Labor movement, 35-43, 64
Labor parties, 35, 64
Labor system in South, 54-58, 91, 145. *See also* Blacks, as caste
Lamar, L.Q.C., 198, 217
Land grants, 78, 217
Landowners, 57, 58, 95-96, 98-99, 102
Land reform, 52-54, 247; and bourgeois revolutions, 52-53, 233; and Northern capitalists, 51, 54, 58, 94, 95; and poor whites, 93-94, 96-97, 243; and Radical Reconstruction, 76-77, 90-91, 242-43
Lea, Henry C., 125
Lee, Robert E., 51, 59, 210
Lewinson, Paul, 223
Liberalism, 239-40
Liberal Republicans, 113, 114, 118, 119, 120, 122
Lincoln, Abraham, 24, 25-26, 27, 28, 59
Literacy tests, 198
Lodge, Henry Cabot, 186
Logan, John A., 105
Longstreet, James A., 171
Louisiana, 81, 170-72, 182, 194
Louisiana Purchase, 17
Louisville and Nashville Railroad, 190, 191-92
Lowry, Robert, 194

Index 267

Loyal Leagues, 93, 95
Lynch, John R., 196
Lynching, 8, 204. *See also* Terrorism

Manufacturing, 17-18, 20-21, 32, 115
Marx, Karl, 235
Merchants, 13, 16, 20, 21, 98-99, 235. *See also* Commercial interests
Meridian, Mississippi, 146-47
Mexico, 17
Midwest, 20, 22, 23, 115, 123
Militias, 102, 147-49, 155, 161, 162, 168, 243
Mississippi, 142-44, 146-47, 196
Missouri, 112-13
Modocs, 151
Molly Maguires, 59
Moneylenders, 98-99
Montgomery, David, 114, 213
Morgan, J.P., 125
Morton, Levi P., 125
Morton, Oliver, 77, 105, 109
Moses, Franklin J., 143, 158

Napoleon, 233
Nast, Thomas, 210
The Nation, 209-10
Nationalism, 211, 212, 246
National Labor Union, 64, 244
National Union Party, 74
Native Americans, 29-30, 56
Navajos, 30
Navy, 27
The Negro People (Foster), 224
The Negro Question (Allen), 221, 226
New Departure, 116-17, 119
New England Association of Mechanics and Workingmen, 36-37
New Orleans, 81, 170-72
Nez Percé, 30
Nicholls, Francis T., 182
Nonintercourse Acts, 18
Northern capitalists, 51, 61-62. *See also* Commercial interests; Industrial capitalists
Northerners in South, 64, 87, 102
Northern public opinion, 155, 157, 173
Northwest, 19
Novack, George, 11, 14, 228-29, 233, 239

Oppressed nationalities, 244, 245, 246
Origins of the New South (Woodward), 11, 227
Orr, James L., 193

Packard, Stephen B., 182
Panic of 1857, 36
Panic of 1873, 122-23, 178, 179
Paris Commune, 59, 97, 235
Patterson, John J., 110, 193
Pennsylvania Railroad, 180
Peonage, 57, 58, 201. *See also* Sharecropping
People's Club, 151
Petty bourgeoisie, 31, 229, 230, 231, 237
Phillips, Wendell, 23, 82, 105, 114
Planters. *See* Landowners; Slaveowners
Poor whites, 195; and Blacks, 97, 102; and Conservative rule, 140, 141, 185, 199; and Radical Reconstruction, 87, 93, 96-97, 243; and slaveowners, 19, 20, 21, 40
Pope, John, 89
Popular front, 226
Populism, 68, 123, 124, 195, 203, 206
Porter, James D., 192
Price, Daniel, 146
Profiles in Courage (Kennedy), 217
Progressive movement, 213
Pryor, Luke, 192
Pure Radicals, 101

Racism, 7-10; and capitalists, 48, 102-3; and Democrats, 79, 185; eroded by Civil War, 84; and imperialism, 211-12; and Jim Crow, 207-8; and Radical Reconstruction, 102, 208; and Republican Party, 185; and revisionists, 213, 215; and scientists, 211; and slavery, 21, 33, 57, 102; among white farmers, 96-97, 244; among white workers, 48, 244-45. *See also* Jim Crow; Poor whites; Segregation
Radical Reconstruction: and Blacks, 139, 241; class struggle under, 91-96; and corruption, 100-107, 195-96; Dunning version of, 220-21; education under, 89-90; and Federal troops, 93, 154, 163, 170, 172, 176, 183, 184-85, 236-37; and industrial capitalists, 13, 65-66, 82-83, 99, 100, 102-3, 124-25, 128, 139, 140, 169, 188-89; and land reform, 90-91, 96-97; and Liberal reformers, 118, 159; opposition to, 78-80; reforms under, 88-89, 90; and Republican Party, 77, 120-21, 127, 139, 174, 177; and whites, 87, 96-97; and women, 90, 164-65
Radicals (Radical Republicans), 80-81;

268 Index

and capitalists, 230, 238; and Civil War, 26-27, 45; elements among, 76-77, 104; and masses, 230, 238; and workers, 45
Railroads, 18, 21, 78, 99, 100, 123, 128, 178, 179
Reconstruction governments, pre-1867, 58, 59, 61, 72-73, 75, 236-37
Reconstruction Acts of 1867, 85, 219
Reconstruction: The Battle for Democracy (Allen), 221
Redeemers, 142, 188-94. *See also* Conservatives
Red Shirts, 161, 162, 165, 166, 168
Reform Independent parties, 123
Reform movements, 35-36, 159
Regulators, 163
Reid, Whitelaw, 113
Republican Party, 29, 73-74; and Blacks, 29, 167, 169; and Conservatives, 79-80, 185-86; and industrial capitalists, 23, 39, 106-8; and Radical Reconstruction, 77, 120-21, 127, 139, 174, 177; rise of, 23, 25, 27
Republican Party machine, 71-72, 104-5, 107, 109-11, 126, 174. *See also* Stalwarts
Reunion and Reaction (Woodward), 11, 231
Revisionists, 11, 212-16, 218-19, 238
Revolutions of 1848-49, 33, 235
Rivers, Prince, 162
Robespierre, 231, 232
Rockefeller, John D., 125
Rockefeller, William, 125
Rollin, Louisa, 164
Roosevelt, Franklin D., 204, 226-27
Roosevelt, Theodore, Sr., 125
Ross, Edmund, 108
Russian revolution (1905), 235
Ryan, Thomas Fortune, 191

Sage, Russell, 191
Saxton, Rufus B., 105
Schiff, Jacob, 191
Schurz, Carl, 105, 109, 112-13, 118, 119, 124, 127, 182, 185, 237, 239, 240
Scott, Robert K., 158, 159
Scott, Thomas A., 110, 180, 192, 193
Secessionist movement, 24, 236
Second American revolution, 13, 53, 228, 234-35; compared with European revolutions, 49-50, 52-53
Segregation, 89-90, 102, 187, 217. *See also* Jim Crow
Self-determination, 246
Seminoles, 29
Seward, William, 105
Seymour, Horatio, 72, 75, 116
Sharecropping, 94-96, 201-3
Shays's Rebellion, 14, 234
Shenandoah, 209
Sheppard (Colonel), 148
Sheridan, Philip H., 30, 75, 77
Sherman, John, 77, 105, 127-28
Sherman, William T., 28, 29, 30, 76
Shugg, Roger W., 98
Sioux, 30
Slaveowners, 13-14, 20; as capitalists, 14, 68; disappearance of, 49-50, 98; "return" of, 195, 222-25, 228; and small farmers, 16-17, 19, 20, 21
Slavery, 9, 14, 56-57; and Civil War, 25, 26-27; and farmers, 19, 20, 22, 23; and free labor, 39; and racism, 21, 33, 57, 102
Slave trade, 21
Sloss, James W., 191
Socialist revolution, 247
Socialists, 42, 48, 205
Soft money, 14, 67, 116, 123
South: backwardness of, 101, 102, 189; industry in, 20, 60, 101; and Northern capitalists, 51, 224-25; postwar governments in, 58, 59, 61, 72-73, 75. *See also* Confederacy; Cotton economy; Radical Reconstruction
"South," meaning Southern whites, 118, 218-19
South Carolina, 87, 94, 147, 148, 158-63, 165-68, 192-93
Southern Democrat, 59, 60, 61
Southwest, 19
Spanish-American War, 212
Stalin, Joseph, 226
Stalwarts, 120-21, 122, 126, 174, 182, 240-41
Stampp, Kenneth, 213-14, 215
Stephens, Alexander, 82, 191
Stevens, Thaddeus, 45, 82, 105, 107, 109, 237, 238, 239
Stevenson, Adlai, 227
Stewart, John A., 125
The Strange Career of Jim Crow (Woodward), 216
Strikes, 35
Strike wave of 1877, 124, 172
Stone, John M., 194

Stowe, Harriet Beecher, 209
Sumner, Charles, 78, 82, 105, 109, 113, 120, 121, 237, 239
Supreme Court, 15, 20, 187, 198, 199

Tammany Hall, 43, 119
Tariffs, 20, 66, 67, 69, 70, 75, 118
Taylor, Moses, 119
Teachers, 64, 87, 102, 146, 205
Ten-hour day, 35, 36
Tennessee, 81, 192
Terrorism, 58, 93, 144-46, 150-54, 202, 242-43
Texas and Pacific Railroad, 180, 184
Thermidor, 231-32, 234, 239-40
Third period, 226
Thirteenth Amendment, 187, 207, 241
Tilden, Samuel, 72, 119-20, 127, 175, 176, 177, 179
Tilton, Theodore, 114
Toombs, Robert, 51, 191
Tourgee, Albion W., 90, 210
Trotsky, Leon, 235
Trumbull, Lyman, 77, 106, 108, 118, 122, 182
Tubman, Harriet, 22
Tuscaroras, 56
Tweed Ring, 101, 119-20
Two-party system, evolution of, 71-72, 115-20. *See also* Conservatives; Democratic Party; Republican Party; Whigs

Underground Railway, 22
Union army. *See* Federal troops
Union Leagues, 58, 93
Union Pacific Railroad, 125, 184
Unions, 35, 205, 245
United Confederate Veterans, 210
United Daughters of the Confederacy, 210

Vallandigham, Clement L., 116
Vardaman, James K., 198-99

Vermilye, Jacob M., 125
Virginia, 128

Wade, Benjamin, 105, 108, 109, 121
Walker, Gilbert C., 128
Wallace, Henry, 227
Wanamaker, John, 125
War of 1812, 17-18
Warmoth, Henry C., 139
Washington, George, 16
Watson, Tom, 191
Watterson, Henry, 113
West Indies, 56
Weydemeyer, Joseph, 42
Wharton, Vernon Lane, 149-50
Whigs, 60, 61, 70, 87, 100, 104, 105, 106, 188, 192
Whiskey Rebellion, 16
Whiskey Ring, 126
White, Horace, 113
White Leagues, 151, 170, 171
White Line, 151
White primaries, 199
Williams, Jim 148
Williamson, Joel, 148
Wilson, Henry, 113, 126
Winthrop, Robert C., 115
Wirz, Henry, 59
Women: in Civil War, 63-64; in factories, 32, 35; and Radical Reconstruction, 90, 164-65
Woodruff, William E., 196
Woodward, C. Vann, 11, 175, 178, 216-17, 227, 228, 231-32
Workers, 31-35, 42; and Blacks, 33-34, 45, 46, 48, 84, 203, 244, 245; and Civil War, 26, 39, 40, 43-48; and Democratic Party, 20, 39, 45, 48; and democratic rights, 40, 55, 57; and draft, 26, 46; petty-bourgeois ambitions of, 40-41; and Republican Party, 23. *See also* Labor movement
Workingmen's Party, 35
Wounded Knee massacre, 30